Visual Language Guide
French

Barron's

CONTENTS

Grammar Overview 6

6 Sentence Structure
6 Articles
6 Nouns
6 Adverbs
6 Possessive, Indirect Objects
7 Pronouns

7 Adjectives
7 Helping Verbs and Modal Verbs
8 Verbs
8 Negation
8 Pronunciation

Quick Overview 9

9 The 11 Most Important Words
9 The 22 Most Important Expressions
11 The 33 Most Important Verbs
11 Constructing Sentences

12 Everyday Conversation
13 Comparatives
13 Opposites
14 Important Vocabulary
14 Questions About Questions
14 This and That

General Information 15

15 **Numbers**
15 Cardinal Numbers
15 Ordinal Numbers
15 Fractions and Quantities
16 **Weights and Measurements**
16 Weights
16 Fluids
16 Length
16 Area

17 **Date and Time**
18 Days of the Week
18 Months
18 Holidays
18 Times
18 Seasons
19 Telling Time
22 **The Weather**
24 **Pronunciation**

Conversation 25

25 **First Contact**
27 What You Hear
27 Familiar Greetings
27 Set Phrases
28 Excuse Me!
29 Introductions
29 Forms of Address
30 **Origin**
30 Where Are You From?
32 Relatives
32 Occupations
33 Professions
36 **Feelings and Opinions**
36 How Are You?
36 Terms of Endearment
37 Congratulations
37 Enthusiasm
37 Opinion

37 Indignation
38 Problems
38 Insults
38 **Agreement**
38 First Approach
40 Polite but Firm
40 Impolite and Very Firm
40 Things Are Getting Serious!
41 **Using the Telephone**
43 **Writing Letters**
43 A Personal Letter
44 A Business Letter
45 Salutations
45 Greetings
45 Important Vocabulary
46 **What People Talk About**
46 Subjects
46 Politics

On the Move 47

47 **At the Border**
48 Customs Regulations
48 Customs
49 **Traveling by Plane**
49 Booking a Flight
51 Security Check
52 On the Plane
52 Arrival
53 Important Vocabulary
54 **Taxi**
55 **By Car and Motorcycle**
55 Renting a Car
57 The Car
59 The Motorcycle
60 On the Move
60 Directions
61 Notices and Traffic Signs
62 Parking
63 Filling Up
64 Breakdowns
66 In the Repair Shop

68 Traffic Regulations,
   Violations
69 Accidents
70 **Traveling by Bicycle**
70 The Bicycle
71 Renting a Bicycle
73 **Taking the Train**
73 Buying Tickets
74 At the Ticket Window
75 On the Platform / On Board
   the Train
75 What You Hear
76 Important Vocabulary
77 **Taking the Bus**
78 **Traveling by Boat**
80 **In the City**
80 Asking for Directions
81 What You Hear
81 Traveling on Foot
82 Directions
83 Local Traffic

Overnight Accommodations 85

86 **Finding a Room**
85 Where Can One Spend the
   Night?
86 Signs
87 Reserving by Phone
88 **In the Hotel**
88 At the Reception Desk
89 What You Hear
90 Requests and Desires
91 The Hotel Staff
91 Complaints

91 Departure
92 Accessories
95 **Vacation Home**
95 Reserving a Vacation Home
96 Vacation Home: Practical
   Matters
97 Equipment
98 Important Vocabulary
99 **Youth Hostels**
100 **At the Campground**
102 **On the Farm**

Eating and Drinking 105

105 **Cuisine**
105 Where to Turn
106 Meals
107 Meal Times
106 What You Hear
106 What You Often Need
106 Signs and Posters
107 **In the Restaurant**
108 Ordering
109 Making a Reservation
110 Paying

110 Praise
110 Complaints
111 On the Table
111 Is Something Missing?
112 **The Menu**
113 **Breakfast**
114 Drinks
114 Eggs
115 Bread and Rolls
115 Miscellaneous
116 **Appetizers, Soups, and Salads**

116 Appetizers	122 **Vegetables**
116 Soups	126 **Herbs and Spices**
116 Salads	127 **Cheese**
116 Salad Dressings	127 **Fruit**
116 Vinegar and Oil	130 **Nuts**
117 **Fish and Shellfish**	131 **Cakes**
118 **Meat Dishes**	131 **Desserts**
118 Types of Meat	132 **Snacks**
118 Steaks	133 **Drinks**
119 Cuts of Meat	133 What Would You Like?
119 Ways to Prepare	133 Coffee
120 **Poultry**	133 Tea
120 **Wild Game**	134 Refreshments
121 **Side Dishes**	134 Miscellaneous
121 Potatoes	134 Beer
121 Noodles	134 Liquors
121 Rice	135 Wine and Champagne
121 Bread	136 Wine-Producing Regions

Shopping 137

137 **In the Store**	155 **Dry Cleaning, Laundromat**
137 What's Most Important	156 **Shoes**
137 Forget Something?	157 **In the Sporting Goods**
139 What You Often Need	**Shop**
140 What You Hear or Read	159 **Housewares**
140 In a Department Store	164 **Tools**
141 Shops	165 **Camping Equipment**
142 Colors	166 **The Bookshop**
142 Designs	166 **Writing Implements**
143 At the Market	168 **Painting Supplies**
144 **Foods**	168 **In the Photography Shop**
146 Quantities	168 What Is Broken?
146 Sales Conversations	169 Accessories
147 **Drugs and Cosmetics**	169 Films
149 **For Children and Babies**	170 Developing Film
150 **Tobacco Products**	171 **Video**
151 **Clothing**	172 **Electronic Devices**
151 What You Hear	173 **Stereo**
151 Sizes	173 **Computer**
152 Articles of Clothing	174 **At the Optician's**
154 Sewing	176 **At the Watchmaker's**
154 Fabrics	176 **Jeweler**
155 **Leather Goods**	177 **At the Hair Stylist's**

Beach, Sports, and Nature 179

179 **Types of Sports**	182 Creative Vacations
179 What's Happening?	182 **At the Beach**
182 Renting	186 **Indoor and Outdoor**
182 Instruction	**Swimming Pools**

186 **Water Sports**
186 **Wind Surfing**
187 **Diving**
188 **Sailing**
190 **Fishing**
191 **Hiking and Climbing**

192 Equipment
192 Important Vocabulary
193 **Nature**
194 **Winter Sports**
194 **Spectator Sports**

Culture and Entertainment 195

195 **At the Tourist Office**
196 **Sightseeing and Tours**
196 What Is There?
197 **Churches and Monasteries**
198 **In the Museum**
198 Notices and Signs
198 What's It Like?

199 **Performances**
199 What Is There?
199 What You Hear or Read
199 Information
200 Theater and Concerts
200 Buying Tickets
200 Discos and Nightclubs

Offices and Institutions 201

201 **Offices and Institutions**
201 **Post Office**
201 The Right Address
202 At the Post Office Counter
202 Telegrams
202 Picking Up Mail
203 **The Bank**

204 **Police**
204 Help! Thief!
205 At the Police Station
205 What Happened?
206 What Was Stolen?
206 Important Vocabulary
206 **Lost and Found**

Health 207

207 **First Aid**
207 What You Hear
208 **Drugstore**
208 Directions for Taking
     Medications
209 **At the Doctor's**
209 The Human Body
211 Parts of the Body

211 At the Doctor's
212 What the Doctor Says
212 Specialists
213 Illnesses
214 What's the Matter?
214 **At the Gynecologist's**
215 **At the Dentist's**
216 **In the Hospital**

Business Travel 217

217 **At the Reception Desk**
217 **At the Conference Table**
218 Important Vocabulary

219 **Corporate Structure**
220 **Contracts**
220 **Trade Fairs**

Glossary 221

221 **English-French**
239 **French-English**

ℹ️ French may be one of the most difficult Romance languages to learn. Therefore, the following brief introduction will provide only very basic knowledge.

Sentence Structure
Sentence structure follows the general pattern for all Romance languages:

Article	Subject	Adjective	Verb	Adverb	Object
The	policeman	tall	spoke	slowly	with my husband.
Le	policier	de grande taille	parlait	doucement	avec mon mari.

Articles
The definite article changes in the singular and plural, and according to gender. Before a vowel and a mute *h* (as opposed to an aspirate *h*), **le** and **la** change to **l'**:

the window – la fenêtre / the windows – les fenêtres
the dog – le chien / the dogs – les chiens
the school – l'école / the schools – les écoles

As with the definite article, there are two basic forms of the indefinite article: **un** and **une**, which correspond to the definite article.

Nouns
The plural is usually formed by adding **-s**, but there are exceptions:

cheval – chevaux (horse)
château – châteaux (castle)

Adverbs
Adverbs are frequently (but not always) formed by adding the ending **-ment** to the feminine form of an adjective:

actif – activement
aimable – aimablement
suffissant – suffisamment
doux (douce) – doucement

Of course there are also exceptions to this rule:

bon – bien
mauvais – mal

Possessives and Indirect Objects
Possessives are indicated using the preposition **de**; indirect objects are expressed using the preposition **à**:

la maison de M. Rochard – Mr. Rochard's house
une bouteille de vin – a bottle of wine
le rire des jeunes filles – the girls' laughter

The preposition **de** and the reflexive pronoun **se** are shortened to **d'** and **s'** before vowels and mute *h*. The conjunction **si** (if) is abbreviated only before **il** and **ils**.

Pronouns

There are quite a number of pronouns; the following is a simplified summary:

Subject		Object accentuated	non-accentuated	Possessive 1	Possessive 2
I	je	à moi de moi	me mes	mon (ma) mes	le mien/les miens la mienne/les miennes
you (fam.)	tu	à toi, de toi	te	ton (ta), tes	le tien/les tiens
you (formal)	vous	à vous de vous	vous	votre, vos	le vôtre/les vôtres
he	il	à lui de lui	lui	son (sa) ses	le sien/les siens les siens/les siennes
she	elle	à elle	lui	son (sa) ses	le sien/les siens la sienne/les siennes
we	nous	à nous de nous	nous nos	notre	le nôtre/la nôtre la nôtre/les nôtres
you (pl.)	vous	à vous de vous	vous vos	votre	le vôtre/les vôtres la vôtre/les vôtres
they	ils elles	à eux à elles d'eux d'elles	les	leur/leurs	le leur/les leurs la leur/les leurs

Possessive 1 is used as an adjective before nouns (ma voiture); Possessive 2 stands alone and is used as a pronoun (elle est la mienne.)

Adjectives

Adjectives normally follow the nouns they modify and change form according to gender and number:

un homme intéressant – an interesting man
des homes intéressants – interesting men
Comparitives generally are formed using **plus**:
grand – plus grand – le (la) plus grand(e)
Adjectives such as *good* and *bad* are exceptions:
bon – meilleur – le (la) meilleur(e)
mauvais – pire – le (la) pire
As adverbs:
bien – mieux – le mieux
mal – pis – le pis

Helping and Modal Verbs

être to be	avoir to have	faire to make, do
je suis	j'ai	je fais
tu es	tu as	tu fais
il/elle est	il/elle a	il/elle fait
nous sommes	nous avons	nous faisons
vout êtes	vous avez	vous faites
ils/elles sont	ils/elles ont	ils/elles font

Verbs

There are four basic conjugations. There are also a large number of irregular verb forms that are beyond the scope of this brief introduction:

	trouver to find	punir to punish	vendre to sell	recevoir to receive
je	trouve	punis	vends	reçois
tu	trouves	punis	vends	reçois
il/elle	trouve	punit	vend	reçoit
nous	trouvons	punissons	vendons	recevons
vous	trouvez	punissez	vendez	recevez
ils/elles	trouvent	punissent	vendent	reçoivent

Negation

Sentences are made negative using **ne...pas**; e.g., **Je ne fume pas.**

Pronunciation

We have intentionally avoided using phonetic spelling. Experience shows that tiresome stammering with phonetic spelling leads to painful results. Besides, you can simply point to most things in this book. However, these are the most important pronunciation rules:

	Rule	Example	Pronunciation
c	before *e* or *i*, soft *c* like **s**	cidre	sidre
	otherwise hard like **k**	cas	ka
ch	like **sh** in **short**	chaud	show
g	before *e* or *i* like the **g** in **mirage**	géant	jéant
	otherwise like the **g** in **go**	galant	galan
qu	like a **k** sound	quatre	katre
r	guttural sound	mère	mare
	r is often not pronounced	aimer	aimey
	at the end of a word		
s	between vowels, as in **rose**	maison	maizon
	at the start of a word, like the **s** in **sit**	sur	sur
au	like final sound of **show**	chaud	show
eu		peu	pö
ou	like vowel sound in **true**	foux	fue
in	nasal sound		
an			
en			
gn	like **ny** in **canyon**	champagne	champan

The 11 Most Important Words

yes **Oui**

no **Non**

please **S'il vous plaît**

Thank you!/Thanks! **Merci**

I'm sorry!/Sorry! **Pardon !**

Don't mention it! **De rien**

Good-bye! **Au revoir !**

How are you? **Comment allez-vous ?/Comment vas-tu ?**

Fine, thanks. **Ça va merci.**

Help! **Au secours !**

Hello!
Bonjour !

The 22 Most Important Expressions

My name is ...
Je m'appelle ...

I'm from the United States/Canada.
J'habite aux États-Unis/au Canada.

Can you please help me?
Pouvez-vous m'aider, s'il vous plaît ?

Pardon?
Comment ?

What is that?
Qu'est-ce que c'est ?

How much does that cost?
Ça coûte combien ?

Do you speak French?
Parlez-vous français ?

I don't understand you.
Je ne vous comprends pas.

I only speak a little bit of French.
Je parle un peu français.

Please speak slowly.
Parlez lentement, s'il vous plaît.

Can you please repeat that?
Pouvez-vous répéter, s'il vous plaît ?

Can you write that down?
Pouvez-vous me l'écrire ?

How do you say that in French?
Comment dit-on cela en français ?

Please show me that in this book.
Montrez-le-moi dans ce livre, s'il vous plaît.

Just a minute.
Un instant.

I'm hungry.
J'ai faim.

I'm thirsty.
J'ai soif.

Leave me alone!
Laissez-moi tranquille !

Get out!
Va te faire foutre ! (Vulgar)

What would you recommend?
Que me conseillez-vous ?

Where are the toilets?
Où sont les toilettes ?

I've gotten lost.
Je me suis perdu(e).

If you are not too familiar with the various forms of address, you can keep things simple when you greet people and say *ça va?*

What You Often Hear

Can I help you?
Puis-je vous aider ?

With pleasure.
Avec plaisir.

Don't mention it.
De rien.

I'm sorry.
Je regrette.

We are completely full.
On est complet. Tout est complet.

Doesn't matter./That's all right.
Ce n'est pas grave ; ne vous inquiétez pas.

Where are you from?
D'où venez-vous ?

Too bad!
Dommage !

If you want to convey your regrets, you can also say, *Je suis désolé(e)* or *infiniment désolé*, in which case you are terribly sorry.

The 33 Most Important Verbs

work **travailler**

get **recevoir**

think **penser**

recommend **conseiller**

tell **raconter**

eat **manger**

find **trouver**

ask **demander**

feel **sentir**

give **donner**

go **aller**

believe **croire**

have **avoir**

hear **entendre**

buy **acheter**

come **venir**

can **pouvoir**

let **laisser**

read **lire**

like **aimer/plaire**

must / have to ... **devoir**

take **prendre**

smell **sentir**

say **dire**

taste **goûter**

write **écrire**

see **voir**

speak **parler**

look for ... **chercher**

do **faire**

sell **vendre**

know **savoir**

listen **écouter**

Constructing Sentences

Even if you don't know much about languages you can easily construct the easiest sentences. These formulas will help you. Plug in the words you need to replace the underlined words. It's courteous to begin questions and requests by saying, "Pardon me..."

Excuse me, do you have ...
Excusez-moi, avez-vous ...

I'm hungry.
J'ai faim.

I would like to have a pair of sunglasses.
Je voudrais des lunettes de soleil.

I would like a double room.
Je voudrais une chambre double.

Do you have track shoes/running shoes?
Avez-vous des baskets ?

Are there any oranges?
Avez-vous des oranges ?

I would rather have bananas.
Je préfère des bananes.

Can I have some mineral water?
Pouvez-vous m' apporter de l'eau minérale ?

I need a band-aid.
J'ai besoin d'un pansement.

I'm looking for a hotel.
Je cherche un hôtel.

Can you tell me what time it is?
Quelle heure est-il, s'il vous plaît ?

Do you please bring me a fork?
Pouvez-vous m' apporter une fourchette, s'il vous plaît ?

hear **entendre**

In addition to *de rien* as a response to "Thank you," you can also use the formula *pas de quoi* or *je vous en prie*.

Everyday Conversation

Achoo!
Atchoum !
Bless you!
A vos/tes souhaits !

Have a nice day!
Bonne journée !
Same to you!
Vous de même.

I'll have the special of the day.
Je voudrais le plat du jour.
So will I.
Moi aussi.

I don't feel well today.
Je ne me sens pas très bien aujourd'hui.

Get well soon!
Bon rétablissement !

Have fun!
Amusez-vous bien !
You, too!
Vous de même !

In French negatives are generally constructed with *ne...pas. Je ne fume pas*: I don't smoke.

Comparatives

old, older, oldest
vieux, plus vieux, le plus vieux

good, better, best
bon, meilleur, le meilleur

hot, hotter, hottest
chaud, plus chaud, le plus chaud

high, higher, highest
haut, plus haut, le plus haut

young, younger, youngest
jeune, plus jeune, le plus jeune

cold, colder, coldest
froid, plus froid, le plus froid

short, shorter, shortest
court, plus court, le plus court

long, longer, longest
long, plus long, le plus long

slow, slower, slowest
lent, plus lent, le plus lent

bad, worse, worst
mauvais, plus mauvais, le plus mauvais

fast, faster, fastest
rapide, plus rapide, le plus rapide

beautiful, more beautiful, most beautiful
beau, plus beau, le plus beau

deep, deeper, deepest
profond, plus profond, le plus profond

far, further, furthest
distant, plus distant, le plus distant

Opposites

all – nothing
tout – rien

old – young
vieux – jeune

old – new
vieux – nouveau

outside – inside
dehors – dedans

early – late
tôt – tard

big – small
grand – petit

nice – naughty
gentil – méchant

right – wrong
juste – faux

fast – slow
rapide – lent

beautiful – ugly
beau – laid

strong – weak
fort – faible

expensive – cheap
cher – bon marché

much – little
beaucoup – peu

full – empty
plein – vide

warm – cold
chaud – froid

Comparatives in French are normally constructed using *plus*, and superlatives using *le/la/les plus*; one exception is good: (*bon – meilleur – le/la/les meilleur[e][s]*).

Important Vocabulary

all **tout-tous/toutes-toutes**

as **quand/que**

other **d'autres**

on **sur**

out (of) **dehors/de**

at **chez**

then **puis**

that **celui/celle**

therefore **c'est pourquoi/c'est la raison pour laquelle**

these **ces**

through **à travers**

a, an **un/une**

some/a few **certains/certaines**

for **pour**

same **même/pareil**

their **son/sa/ses**

in **dans/en**

each **chacun/chacune**

now **maintenant**

with **avec**

still **encore**

only **seulement**

although **même si**

or **ou, ou bien**

without **sans**

very **très**

this, these **ce(s)/cette (ces)**

and **et**

of/from **de**

before **avant/devant**

because **parce que**

little **peu**

if **si**

like **comme**

again **de nouveau**

Questions About Questions

when? **quand ?**

what? **quoi/comment ?**

why? **pourquoi ?**

who? **qui ?**

where? **où ?**

how? **comment ?**

how much? **combien ?**

how many? **combien de ?**

how far? **à combien de km/m ?**

how long? **combien de temps ?**

This and That

this one **celui-ci**

that one **celui-là**

here **ici**

there **là**

The question "how far?" is not so easy to formulate in French; if you are asking about the railroad station, for example, you can say, *Est-ce que la gare est loin d'ici?*

Cardinal Numbers

zero **zéro**

one **un**

two **deux**

three **trois**

four **quatre**

five **cinq**

six **six**

seven **sept**

eight **huit**

nine **neuf**

ten **dix**

twenty **vingt**

thirty **trente**

forty **quarante**

fifty **cinquante**

sixty **soixante**

seventy **soixante-dix**

eighty **quatre-vingts**

ninety **quatre-vingt-dix**

one hundred **cent**

one thousand **mille**

ten thousand **dix mille**

one hundred thousand **cent mille**

one million **un million**

one billion **un milliard**

Ordinal Numbers

first (1st) **premier**

second (2nd) **deuxième**

third (3rd) **troisième**

fourth (4th) **quatrième**

fifth (5th) **cinquième**

sixth (6th) **sixième**

seventh (7th) **septième**

eighth (8th) **huitième**

ninth (9th) **neuvième**

tenth (10th) **dixième**

twentieth (20th) **vingtième**

thirtieth (30th) **trentième**

Fractions and Quantities

one eighth **un huitième**

one quarter **un quart**

one half **un demi**

three quarters **trois quarts**

once **une fois**

twice **deux fois**

three times **trois fois**

half **demi**

half **la moitié**

double **le double**

a little **un peu de**

a pair **une paire**

a dozen **une douzaine**

enough **assez**

too much **trop**

more **beaucoup de**

many **beaucoup de**

The page numbers in this book are written out. That way it's easy for you to find any number you may need.

Weights

gram **le gramme**

pound **le demi-kilo/la livre**

kilo **le kilo**

ounce **la tonne**

ton **la tonne**

Fluids

liter **le litre**

one half liter **le quart de litre**

one quarter liter **le quart de litre**

Length

millimeter **le millimètre**

centimeter **le centimètre**

meter **le mètre**

kilometer **le kilomètre**

inch **le pouce**

foot **le pied**

yard **le yard**

mile **le mile**

Area

square meter **le mètre carré**

square kilometer **le kilomètre carré**

Conversions

1 ounce (oz)		= 28,35 g
1 pound (lb)	= 16 ounces	= 453,59 g
1 ton	= 2000 pounds	= 907 kg
¼ pound		= 113 g
½ pound		= 227 g
100 g	= 3.527 oz	
1 kg	= 2.205 lb	
1 inch (in)		= 2,54 cm
1 foot (ft)	= 12 inches	= 0,35 m
1 yard (yd)	= 3 feet	= 0,9 m
1 mile (mi)	= 1760 yards	= 1,6 km
1 cm	= 0.39 in	
1 km	= 0.62 mi	
1 square foot (ft²)		= 930 cm²
1 acre (A)		= 4047 m²
1 m²	= 0.386 mi²	
1 ha	= 2.471 acres	
1 pint (pt)		= 0,47 l
1 quart (qt)	= 2 pints	= 0,95 l
1 gallone (gal)	= 4 quarts	= 3,79 l
¼ l	= 0.26 qt	
½ l	= 0.53 qt	
1 l	= 1.057 qt	
	= 0.264 gal	

A pound is *une livre*, but nowadays all price designations are given per half-kilo (*demi-kilo*).

Date and Time

When will you arrive?
Quand arrivez-vous ?

We will arrive on the 15th of July.
Nous arrivons le 15 juillet.

That is, in two weeks.
C'est-à-dire dans 15 jours.

What is the date today?
On est le combien aujourd'hui ?

Today is the 1st of July.
Aujourd'hui, c'est le 1er juillet.

At what time must we be there?
A quelle heure devons-nous être là ?

At 3 o'clock (in the afternoon).
A trois heures.

How long will you stay?
Combien de temps restez-vous ?

We will stay until the 12th of August.
Nous restons jusqu'au 12 août.

In French two weeks or fourteen days is expressed as 15 (*quinze*) *jours*. One week consists of "8 (*huit*) days."

Days of the Week

Monday **lundi**
Tuesday **mardi**
Wednesday **mercredi**
Thursday **jeudi**
Friday **vendredi**
Saturday **samedi**
Sunday **dimanche**

Months

January **janvier**
February **février**
March **mars**
April **avril**
May **mai**
June **juin**
July **juillet**
August **août**
September **septembre**
October **octobre**
November **novembre**
December **décembre**

Holidays

New Year's Day **le Nouvel An**
Good Friday **le Vendredi Saint**
Easter **Pâques**
Whitsun, Pentecost **la Pentecôte**
Christmas **Noël**
Happy Easter! **Joyeuses Pâques !**
New Year's eve **la Saint-Sylvestre**
Merry Christmas! **Joyeux Noël !**
Happy New Year! **Bonne année !**

Times

in the evening **le soir**
That is too early. **c'est trop tôt**
That is too late. **c'est trop tard**
earlier **autrefois**
yesterday **hier**
today **aujourd'hui**
in fourteen days **dans quinze jours**
year **l'année/l'an**
now **maintenant**
at noon **à midi**
midnight **à minuit**
month **le mois**
tomorrow **demain**
afterward **après**
in the afternoon **dans l'après-midi**
at night **la nuit**
sunrise **l'aube**
sunset **le crépuscule/le coucher de soleil**
later **plus tard**
hourly **toutes les heures**
day **le jour**
daily **quotidien/quotidiennement**
the day after tomorrow **après demain**
the day before yesterday **avant hier**
previously **avant**
in the morning **le matin**
weekend **le week-end**

Seasons

spring **le printemps**
summer **l'été**
autumn/ fall **l'automne**
winter **l'hiver**
in season/high season **la pleine saison**
off season/low season **l'hors saison**

January 6 is a holiday throughout France and is known as *l'Epiphanie*.

Telling Time

Can you tell me what time it is?
Quelle heure est-il, s'il vous plaît ?

Ten minutes past three.
Il est trois heures dix.

Does your watch
have the right time?
**Votre montre est à
l'heure ?**

Of course.
Bien sûr.

My watch is slow.
Ma montre retarde.
I am sorry, I'm late.
Excusez-moi, je suis en retard.

Instead of "every day" you can also say *chaque jour* (literally *each day*) or *tous les jours.*

two o'clock
deux heures

five past two
deux heures cinq

ten past two/two-ten
deux heures dix

quarter past two
deux heures et quart

two-thirty
deux heures et demie

two-thirty-five
**deux heures trente-cinq/trois heures
moins vingt-cinq**

If the clock is fast rather than slow, it is said that *la montre avance.*

twenty to four
**trois heures quarante/quatre heures
moins vingt**

quarter to four
**trois heures quarante-cinq/quatre
heures moins le quart**

five to three
**deux heures cinquante-cinq/trois
heures moins cinq**

12 noon
midi

Can you please tell me the time?
Quelle heure est-il, s'il vous plaît ?

hour
l'heure

minute
la minute

second
la seconde

in ten minutes
en/dans dix minutes

in an hour
en/dans une heure

in half an hour
en/dans une demi-heure

Noon is *midi*, and midnight is *minuit*.

The Weather

Stormy

The weather remains stormy due to a depression located along Brittany. A southwesterly wind continues pushing warm air toward France. For Brittany, the Loire Region, and Lower Normandy, after a morning of mixed clouds and clearing skies, the afternoon brings a threatening sky with localized storms. Temperatures should be between 21 and 25 degrees Celsius. For the north of Picardy, Ile-de-France, the Central Region, Upper Normandy, and the Ardennes, a few storm fronts moved toward Belgium in early morning, leaving behind variable skies with variable haziness. In the afternoon storms are again breaking out in certain regions. Temperatures will be around 23 and 27 degrees Celsius.

Orageux

La situation reste orageuse avec une dépression située au large de la Bretagne. Un flux de sud-ouest continue de véhiculer de l'air chaud sur la France. Bretagne, Pays de Loire, Basse-Normandie: Après une matinée partagée entre nuages et éclaircies, l'après-midi se déroule sous un ciel parfois plus menaçant avec un risque d'orage ponctuel. Les températures s'inscrivent entre 21 et 25 degrés. Nord-Picardie, Ile-de-France, Centre, Haute-Normandie, Ardennes: Quelques foyers orageux s'évacuent vers la Belgique en début de matinée, laissant place à l'arrière à un ciel variable, parfois brumeux. L'après-midi, des orages éclatent de nouveau par endroits. Il fera de 23 à 27 degrés.

How will the weather be today?	**Quel temps fera-t-il aujourd'hui ?**
It will stay nice.	**Le temps restera beau.**
It will become nice.	**Il fera beau.**
It's supposed to rain.	**La météo a annoncé de la pluie.**
How long has it been raining?	**Depuis combien de temps pleut-il ?**
How much longer will it rain?	**La pluie durera encore combien de temps ?**
What is the temperature today?	**Quelle est la température aujourd'hui ?**
It is 15 degrees Celsius.	**(Il fait) 15 degrés C.**
Is it always so hot?	**Il fait toujours si chaud ?**
It was freezing at night.	**La nuit, il a gelé.**
The streets are ...	**Les routes sont ...**
wet	**mouillées**
slippery	**verglacées**
snow-covered	**recouvertes de neige**
dry	**sèches**

In speaking of the weather, such as "It is hot/cold, etc." the French use the verb *faire*: *il fait chaud*, *il fait froid*, etc.

clearing **l'éclaircie**

lightning **l'éclair**

thunder **le tonnerre**

ice **le verglas**

frost **le gel**

regional **régional**

thunderstorm **l'orage**

sheet ice **le verglas**

sleet **la neige fondue**

hail **la grêle**

heat **la chaleur**

high **la haute pression**

maximum (values) **les valeurs maximum**

high tide **la marée haute**

air **l'air**

humidity **l'humidité**

moderately warm **tempéré**

fog **le brouillard**

drizzle **la pluie fine**

ozone **l'ozone**

puddle **la flaque**

powder (snow) **la neige poudreuse**

rain **la pluie**

showers **l'ondée**

snow **la neige**

snow chains **les chaînes à neige**

sun **le soleil**

storm **l'orage**

typhoon **le typhon**

thaw **le dégel**

low **la basse pression**

minimum (values) **les valeurs minimum**

flood **l'inondation**

little change **assez stable**

wind **le vent**

tornado **la tornade**

clouds **les nuages**

Fahrenheit and Celsius

Temperatures in the United States are measured in degrees Fahrenheit, but in France they measure in degrees Celsius. To convert degrees Fahrenheit to degrees Celsius, deduct 32 and multiply by $5/9$. To convert degrees Celsius to degrees Fahrenheit, multiply by $9/5$ and add 32.

°F	°C	°F	°C
0	−17.8	78	25.6
10	−12.2	79	26.1
15	−9.4	80	26.7
20	−6.7	81	27.2
25	−3.9	82	27.8
30	−1.1	83	28.3
32	0.0	84	28.9
35	1.7	85	29.4
40	4.4	86	30.0
45	7.2	87	30.6
50	10.0	88	31.1
60	15.6	89	31.7
61	16.1	90	32.2
62	16.7	91	32.8
63	17.2	92	33.3
64	17.8	93	33.9
65	18.3	94	34.4
66	18.9	95	35.0
67	19.4	96	35.6
68	20.0	97	36.1
69	20.6	98	36.7
70	21.1	99	37.2
71	21.7	100	37.8
72	22.2	101	38.3
73	22.8	102	38.9
74	23.3	103	39.4
75	23.9	104	40.0
76	24.4	105	40.6
77	25.0	106	41.1

There are several types of éclairs.

Don't Forget!

rubber boots
les bottes en caoutchouc

It is ... **Le temps est ...**
cloudy **nuageux**
hazy **maussade**
hot **il fait très chaud**
cold **il fait froid**
foggy **il y a du brouillard**
muggy **il fait lourd**
sunny **il y a du soleil**
stormy **il y a de l'orage dans l'air**
dry **le temps est sec**
warm **il fait chaud**
variable/changeable **le temps est instable**
windy/breezy **il vente/il y a du vent**

It is ... **Il ...**
raining **pleut**
snowing **neige**

umbrella
le parapluie

sun glasses
les lunettes de soleil

parasol/sun umbrella
le parasol

Pronunciation

apple **Antoine**	jam **Julien**	snow **Sabine**
ball **Béatrice**	kitten **K**	toy **Théodore**
cat **Carole**	lamb **Luc**	umbrella **Ulysse**
dog **Denise**	money **Martine**	victory **Victor**
elephant **Emile**	nut **Nadine**	wing **W**
fox **Ferdinand**	orange **Oscar**	xylophone **X**
golf **Gustave**	paper **Paule**	yellow **Y**
house **Hubert**	queen **Quintilien**	zebra **Zoë**
ice **Isabelle**	rabbit **Richard**	

The word *glace* is a real trap; it can mean *ice, ice cream, mirror,* or *car window.*

Conversation

First Contact

At one point in his novel *Tender Is the Night*, F. Scott Fitzgerald says that everyone in Paris wants to be Napoleon. If that's intended to suggest the French people's sense of superiority over foreigners, regardless of what country they come from, he's not far off the mark.

The French have a strong sense of confidence. They are always conscious of belonging to the *grande nation* that introduced *esprit* (an intellectual life style) to European culture. As a result, they may also have developed a certain disinclination to learn foreign languages. And they might sometimes act as if they don't understand you because they are waiting to see if you can speak French. If you can, that's an effective way of breaking the ice.

The normal greeting is *bonjour* during the daytime and *bonsoir* in the evening. These are followed by either the formal *Comment allez-vous?* (How are you?) or the more familiar *Comment ça va?* (How's it going?), or simply *Ça va?* In departing, it's customary to say *Au revoir*, which corresponds to our *Good-bye*, or *A bientôt* (See you later).

In France it's important to treat strangers with politeness. Therefore it's better to thank someone too much rather than too little. You say either *Merci* or *Merci beaucoup*, followed by the form of address *monsieur* or *madame*. If your French acquaintance introduces you to his wife, for example, the word *Enchanté* corresponds to our *Pleased to meet you*.

Concerning invitations: the French are rather reserved about strengthening acquaintances made during vacations. So an invitation to their house is a sign that they really like you.

Hello!
Salut !

Good morning.
Bonjour.

Good day.
Bonjour.

Good evening.
Bonsoir.

Good night.
Bonne nuit.

How are you?
Comment allez-vous ?

Fine, thank you.
Ça va merci.

What is your name?
Comment vous appelez-vous ?

Good-bye.
Au revoir.

Pardon me?
Comment ?

Do you speak French?
Parlez-vous Français ?

I have not understood you.
Je n'ai pas compris.

Unfortunately, I speak only a little bit of French.
Je parle un peu français.

Can you please repeat that?
Pouvez-vous répéter, s'il vous plaît ?

Can you please write that down?
Pouvez-vous me l'écrire, s'il vous plaît ?

Salut is a familiar greeting. It's used in greeting friends or acquaintances, but not people you are meeting for the first time.

Hello!
Salut !

Good day!
Bonjour !

How are you?
Comment allez-vous ?

Fine, thanks.
Ça va merci.

Nice meeting you.
Je suis heureux (heureuse) de faire votre connaissance.

Same here!
Moi aussi.

Good-bye!
Au revoir !

Nice to meet you.
Ça m'a fait plaisir de vous rencontrer.

In saying good-bye to someone, if you want to indicate that you will see each other again soon, you can also say, *à bientôt.*

What You Hear

D'où venez-vous ?
Where are you from?

Vous êtes ici depuis combien de temps ?
How long have you been here?

Ça vous plaît ?
Do you like it?

C'est la première fois que vous venez ici ?
Is it your first time here?

Combien de temps restez-vous ici ?
How long are you staying?

Puis-je vous présenter ?
May I introduce you?

Familiar Greetings

How is it going?
Comment ça va ?

What's happening?/What's going on?
Qu'est-ce qu' il y a ?

Hi, there!
Salut à tous !

Hi folks!
Salut à tous !

Hi pal!
Salut mon vieux!

Good to see you!
Je suis content (contente) de te voir !

What's new?
Quoi de neuf ?

Great!
Très bien !

Okay.
Comme ci, comme ça

Have a nice day.
Bonne journée !

See you later!
A plus tard !

Take care!
Bonne continuation !

Bye!
Salut !

Set Phrases

Oh, really?
Oh, vraiment ?

That's right.
C'est juste.

That's interesting.
C'est intéressant.

I agree.
Je suis d'accord.

I don't agree.
Je ne suis pas d'accord.

I like that.
Ça me plait.

That would be nice.
Ce serait sympa.

Great!
Très bien !

Could be.
C'est possible.

Maybe.
Peut-être.

Probably.
C'est probable.

I don't know.
Je ne sais pas.

Just a minute, please.
Un instant, s'il vous plaît.

May I?/ Excuse me!
Vous permettez ?

Good luck!
Bonne chance !

Have fun!
Amusez-vous bien !

All the best!
Meilleurs vœux !

A hearty welcome!
Bienvenue !

Unfortunately, I have no time.
Je regrette, je n'ai pas le temps.

Excuse me, I'll go to the restroom for a minute.
Excusez-moi, je dois aller aux toilettes.

Depending on the context of a conversation, you can also say *bonne chance* (in the sense of "good luck").

Excusez Me!

Excuse me, how much do
these shoes cost?
**Pardon, combien coûtent ces
chaussures ?**

I'm sorry, I don't work here.
**Je regrette, je ne fais pas partie du
personnel.**

Excuse me please!
Oh, pardon !

No problem!
De rien !

In order to express agreement, as with the brief "OK," the French say *d'accord*
or *entendu*.

Introductions

My name is ...
Je m'appelle ...

What is your name?
Comment vous appelez-vous ?

How old are you?
Quel âge avez-vous ?

I am 25 years old.
J'ai 25 ans.

Are you married?
Etes-vous marié(e) ?

I am single.
Je suis célibataire.

Do you have any children?
Avez-vous des enfants ?

What do you do for a living?
Quel est votre métier ?

Where are you travelling to?
Où allez-vous ?

How long will you stay?
Combien de temps restez-vous ?

I am on ...
Je suis ici en ...
a business trip
voyage d'affaires
vacation
vacances
I am travelling on to ...
Je continue vers ...

I would like to visit the following cities.
Je voudrais visiter les villes suivantes.

I am spending the night ...
Je loge ...
in a hotel
à l'hôtel
with friends
chez des amis

It was very nice to have met you.
Ça m'a fait plaisir de vous rencontrer !

May I introduce?
Puis-je vous présenter ?

Forms of Address

	Singular	Abbreviation	Plural	Abbreviation
Mr.	monsieur	M.	messieurs	MM.
Mrs.	madame	Mme	mesdames	Mme
Miss	mademoiselle	Mlle	mesdemoiselles	Mlles
Ladies and Gentlemen			messieurs	MM.

The titles *Monsieur* and *Madame* are very useful. If you try to attract someone's attention without using them, it sounds very impolite.

Where are you from?

Where are you from?
D'où venez-vous ?

I'm from the United States.
J'habite aux États-Unis.

I'm from Switzerland.
J'habite en Suisse.

I'm from Canada.
J'habite au Canada.

Because of its shape on the map, the French call their country the *Hexagone*.

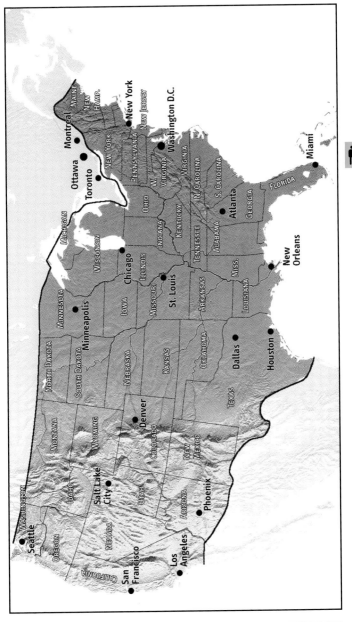

Names of continents and countries are accompanied by the definite article: la France, le Portugal, etc. Exception: Israël.

Relatives

husband **le mari/l'époux**	aunt **la tante**
wife **la femme/l'épouse**	grandson, granddaughter **le petit-fils/la petite-fille**
friend **l'ami**	
friend/acquaintance **la connaissance**	cousin **la cousine**
fiancée **la fiancée**	cousin **le cousin**
fiancé **le fiancé**	nephew **le neveu**
daughter **la fille**	niece **la nièce**
son **le fils**	
brother **le frère**	
sister **la sœur**	
father **le père**	
mother **la mère**	
grandfather **le grand-père**	
grandmother **la grand-mère**	
son-in-law **le gendre**	
daughter-in-law **la belle-fille**	
father-in-law **le beau-père**	
mother-in-law **la belle-mère**	
uncle **l'oncle**	

Occupations

What do you do for a living?
Quel est votre métier ?

I work in a factory.
Je travaille dans une usine.

I work for the XYZ company.
Je travaille chez XYZ.

I work in retail sales.
Je travaille dans le commerce au détail.

I'm still at school.
Je suis encore à lécole.

What are you studying?
Quelles études faites-vous ?

I'm studying architecture.
J'étudie l'architecture.

I am an official/a civil servant.
Je suis fonctionnaire.

French also uses the word *fabrique* for factory, but it's more common to use the word *usine*, which also connotes the workplace.

Professions

doctor
le docteur

construction worker
l'employé du bâtiment

cook
le cuisinier

painter
le peintre en bâtiment

mason
le maçon

chimney sweep
le ramoneur

department head **le chef de département/de service**

geriatric nurse **l'aide soignant pour personnes âgees**

employee **l'employé(e)**

lawyer **l'avocat**

worker **le travailleur**

unemployed **le chômeur**

architect **l'architecte**

architecture **l'architecture**

army **l'armée**

doctor's assistant **la secrétaire médicale**

trainee **l'apprenti(e)**

car mechanic **le mécanicien**

author **l'auteur**

baker **le boulanger**

official/civil servant **le fonctionnaire**

management expert **l'économiste**

biologist **le biologiste**

bookkeeper **le comptable**

bookseller **le libraire**

chemistry **la chimie**

chemist **le chimiste**

roofer **le couvreur**

decorator **le décorateur**

druggist **le droguiste**

computer expert **l'expert EDP**

retail **le commerce au détail**

In French the same word is often used for druggist and pharmacist: *le pharmacien*. But the word *droguiste* does exist for druggist.

Professions

electrician **l'électricien**

teacher **l'instituteur/trice**

skilled worker/specialist **le travailleur spécialisé**

photographer **le photographe**

free-lancer **j'exerce une profession libérale**

hairdresser **le coiffeur**

management-level **le niveau de la direction**

gardener **le jardinier**

hotelier **l'hôtelier**

French language & literature **la langue et la littérature françaises**

glazier **le vitrier**

craftsperson **l'artisan**

housewife **la femme au foyer**

lawyer **le licencié en droit**

jeweler **le bijoutier**

businessman/merchant **le commerçant**

waiter **le garçon de café ou de restaurant**

motor vehicle mechanic **le mécanicien**

nurse **l'infirmière**

artist **l'artiste**

homemaker **l'homme au foyer**

midwife **la sage-femme**

healer ("alternative medicine") **le médecin en médecines douces**

college **l'université**

industry **l'industrie**

engineer **l'ingénieur**

plumber **le plombier**

journalist **le journaliste**

law **le droit**

farmer **l'agriculteur**

teacher **l'enseignant**

broker/agent **le courtier**

manager **le manager**

mechanic **le mécanicien**

medicine **la médecine**

master **le chef**

butcher **le boucher/le charcutier**

musician **le musicien**

notary **le notaire**

government service/public service **le service public**

optician **l'opticien**

A good housekeeper is referred to as *une bonne ménagère.*

Professions

locksmith **le forgeron**
tailor **le couturier**
carpenter **le menuisier**
author **l'écrivain**
shoemaker **le cordonnier**
student **l'écolier**
tax advisor **le conseiller fiscal**
student **l'étudiant**
taxi driver/cab driver **le chauffeur de taxi**
veterinarian **le vétérinaire**
watchmaker **l'horloger**
retraining **le reclassement professionnel**
entrepreneur/businessman **l'entrepreneur**
salesperson **le vendeur**
administration **l'administration**
scientist **le scientifique**
dentist **le dentiste**
dental technician **le mécanicien-dentiste**
carpenter **le charpentier**

priest **le prêtre**
pharmacy **la pharmacie**
philosophy **la philosophie**
physics **la physique**
policeman **le policier**
president **le président**
production **la production**
professor **le professeur**
programmer **le programmateur**

psychologist **le psychologue**
psychology **la psychologie**
lawyer **l'avocat**
retired person **le retraité**
judge **le juge**
actor **l'acteur**

Retail is known as *commerce au detail*; wholesale is *commerce en gros*.

How Are You?

How are you?
Comment allez-vous ?

So-so.
Comme ci, comme ça.

Super!
Très bien.

I feel terrific!
Je suis en pleine forme.

On top of the world!
Je me sens euphorique.

I am in love.
Je suis amoureux/amoureuse.

I'm not feeling very well.
Je ne me sens pas très bien.

I am ...
Je suis ...
   depressed
   déprimé(e)
   frustrated
   frustré(e)

tired
fatigué(e)
sick
malade
angry
contrarié(e)
annoyed
stressé(e)

I am feeling cold.
J'ai froid.

I am feeling warm.
J'ai chaud.

I am worried.
Je suis inquiet/inquiète.

Terms of Endearment

sweetheart
trésor

darling
chéri/chérie

In speaking of *elation*, note the English and French cognates *euphoric* and *euphorique*.

Congratulations

All the best!
Meilleurs vœux !

Lots of success!
Bonne chance !

Good luck!
Bonne chance !

Get well soon!
Meilleurs vœux !

Heartiest congratulations!
Félicitations
  on your birthday
  pour votre anniversaire
  on your promotion
  pour la promotion
  on the birth of your son/daughter
  pour la naissance de votre
  fils/fille
  on your engagement
  pour les fiançailles
  on your wedding
  pour un mariage heureux
  on your silver wedding
  anniversary
  pour les noces d'argent
  on your golden wedding
  anniversary
  pour les noces d'or

Opinion

What is your opinion?
Qu'en pensez-vous ?

I totally agree with you.
Je suis d'accord avec vous.

I have a different opinion.
Je ne suis pas d'accord avec vous.

In my opinion ...
D'après moi ...
  we should go back.
  il faut revenir en arrière.
  we should turn back.
  il faut revenir en arrière.
  we should drive home.
  il faut rentrer chez nous.
  that is wrong.
  ce n'est pas juste.
  that is right.
  c'est juste.

That is shameless!
Quel culot!

Enthusiasm

amazing
splendide

fantastic
fantastique

gorgeous
magnifique

great
excellent/remarquable

super
génial

terrific
formidable

Indignation

Nonsense!
C'est n'importe quoi !

Stop that!
Laissez tomber !

Leave me alone!
Laissez-moi tranquille !

Don't you dare!
Gare à vous !

What nerve!
Quelle impertinence !

How disgusting!
Quelle grossièreté !

That's the limit! is expressed as *Ça, c'est raide tout de même!*

Problems

Can you please help me!
Aidez-moi, s'il vous plaît !

I don't see well.
Je ne vois plus rien.

I don't hear well.
Je n'entends plus très bien.

I feel sick.
Je me sens mal.

 I am dizzy.
J'ai des vertiges.

Please call a doctor.
Appelez un docteur, s'il vous plaît.

Insults

Fool!
Imbécile !

Shit!
Merde !

Idiot!
Idiot !

Imbecile!
Abruti !

Nonsense!
Idiot !

Dumb bitch!
Vieille mégère !

First Approach

May I join you?
Puis-je m'asseoir ici ?

Are you travelling alone?
Vous voyagez tout(e) seul(e) ?

Are you married?
Etes-vous marié(e) ?

Do you have a boyfriend?
Etes-vous avec un(e) ami(e) ?

I think you're very nice.
Vous êtes vraiment sympathique, vous savez ?

You are really sweet.
Tu es vraiment un trésor.

Do you have anything planned for this evening?
Avez-vous déjà quelque chose de prévu pour ce soir ?

Shall we do something together?
Voulez-vous qu'on sorte ensemble ?

Shall we go out together this evening?
Voulez-vous sortir avec moi ce soir ?

May I invite you lunch/dinner?
Puis-je vous inviter à déjeuner/dîner ?

When should we meet?
On se donne rendez-vous à quelle heure ?

At 8 o'clock in front of the movie theatre.
A huit heures devant le cinéma.

I can pick you up.
Je passe vous prendre.

I am looking forward to it.
D'accord.

Thank you for a wonderful evening.
Merci pour l'agréable soirée.

I would be very happy if we could see each other again.
J'aimerais vous revoir.

Can I bring you home?
Puis-je vous accompagner chez vous ?

In order to express that they are *stressed out* the French use the term *stressé(e)s*. That's an easy cognate to use.

Agreement

May I join you?
Puis-je m'asseoir ici ?

Sure, why not?
Bien sûr !

Would you like something to drink?
Voulez-vous boire quelque chose ?

Yes, that's a good idea.
Oui, volontiers.

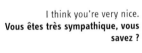

I think you're very nice.
Vous êtes très sympathique, vous savez ?

Do you have anything planned for this evening?
Avez-vous déjà quelque chose de prévu pour ce soir ?

I am meeting my husband.
Oui, j'ai rendez-vous avec mon mari.

An acquaintance is *une connaissance*. It's more common to use *un(e) ami(e)* with no further connotation.

Polite but Firm

I am waiting for ...
J'attends ...
　my husband.
　mon mari.
　my wife.
　ma femme.
　my (boy)friend.
　mon compagnon/mon ami.
　my (girl)friend
　ma compagne/mon amie.

It was nice meeting you, but unfortunately I have to go now.
Ça m'a fait plaisir de vous rencontrer mais maintenant je dois partir.

Unfortunately, I have no time.
Je regrette, je n'ai pas le temps.

I already have something else planned.
Je regrette, j'ai déjà autre chose de prévu.

Leave me alone please!
Je vous en prie, laissez-moi tranquille !

Please go now.
Allez-vous en maintenant, s'il vous plaît.

You are being pushy.
Vous êtes un casse-pieds.

Impolite and Very Firm

Stop that!
Laissez-moi tranquille !

Stop that immediately!
Arrêtez tout de suite !

Clear off!
Allez-vous-en !

Get out!
Débarrassez le plancher !

Take your hands off me!
Bas les pattes !

I'll call the police!
Attention je vais appeler la police !

This person is becoming offensive.
Au secours ! Il est en train de m'importuner !

This person is threatening me.
Au secours ! Il m'a menacé !

Things Are Getting Serious!

I have fallen in love with you.
Je suis tombé(e) amoureux (amoureuse) de toi.

I would like to go to bed with you.
J'ai envie de faire l'amour avec toi.

Your place or mine?
On va chez toi ou chez moi ?

But only with a condom!
Oui, mais seulement si tu as un préservatif !

If you are head-over-heels in love, you are said to be *éperduement amoureux (amoureuse)*.

On the Phone

Good day. This is the Barron's Publishing House. May I help you?
Bonjour. C'est la maison d'édition Barron's. Que puis-je faire pour vous ?

I would like to speak to Mr. Dupond.
Je voudrais parler à M. Dupond.

Who is calling?
C'est de la part de qui ?

My name is Robert Wilson.
Je m'appelle Robert Wilson.

Just a minute, I'll connect you.
Attendez un instant, s'il vous plaît.

Unfortunately, the line is busy. Would you like to hold?
Il est occupé. Pouvez-vous attendre ?

I'll call again later.
Non, je rappellerai plus tard.

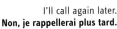

In France, people say *Allô* (Hello) when they answer the phone.

Using the Telephone

Is Paul there?
Est-ce que Paul est là, s'il vous plaît ?

Paul speaking.
C'est moi.

To whom am I speaking?
Qui est à l'appareil ?

Could you connect me with Mr. Dupond?
Pouvez-vous me passer M. Dupond ?

Please stay on the line/Please hold.
Bien sûr, ne quittez pas.

There is no reply.
Personne ne répond.

He is on another line.
Il est en ligne.

Can I leave a message?
Est-ce que je peux laisser un message ?

Can you please repeat the phone number slowly?
Pouvez-vous répéter lentement le numéro de téléphone, s'il vous plaît ?

I'm sorry, I have dialed the wrong number.
Pardon, je me suis trompé(e) de numéro.

Excuse me, I haven't understood your name.
Pardon, je n'ai pas compris votre nom.

Can I call you back?
Est-ce que je peux vous rappeler ?

Thanks for your phone call.
Merci d'avoir appelé.

There is no such number.
Le numéro que vous avez composé n'est pas attribué.

cell phone, cellular
le portable

receiver
le combiné

dial tone **la tonalité libre**

phone call **l'appel téléphonique**

answering machine **le répondeur automatique**

information **les informations**

busy signal **la tonalité occupée**

classified directory/yellow pages **les pages jaunes**

direct dialing **le numéro direct/de poste**

unit **l'unité**

long distance call **la communication extra urbaine**

charge **le tarif**

card telephone **le téléphone à carte**

telephone connection/telephone line **la ligne**

pay phone/coin-operated telephone **le téléphone à pièces**

emergency **l'appel d'urgence**

local call **la communication urbaine**

collect call **l'appel en PCV**

telephone book **l'annuaire**

phone card **la carte téléphonique**

telephone booth/phone booth **la cabine téléphonique**

switchboard **la centrale**

area code **l'indicatif**

You can also express *speaking* by *à l'appareil*.

A Personal Letter

Pierre Leblanc
10 Avenue des Ecoles
83600 Fréjus
France

June 6, 2001

Dear Pierre,
We thank you for your kind invitation.
As agreed, we'll arrive at your place next Thursday at 6 P.M. We look forward to seeing you.

Best regards,

Marie

Leblanc Pierre
10 Avenue des Ecoles
83600 Fréjus
France

6 juin 2000

Cher Pierre,
Je te remercie pour la lettre où tu nous invites gentiment.
Comme convenu, nous arriverons chez toi jeudi prochain vers 18 heures. Il nous tarde de te voir !

Grosses bises,

Marie

In French letters, the salutation is followed by a comma, and then a capital letter is used at the start of the first sentence.

A Business Letter

June 6, 2001
Re: Your letter of July 4, 2001

Dear Mr. Schmitt,

Thank you for your letter.
We confirm our appointment for this Thursday at about 6 P.M. Please find attached a few documents which will be useful in preparing for our discussions.
If you have any further questions, please feel free to call on me at any time.

Sincerely,

Maria Meier
Manager

6 juin 2000
Réf. : Votre lettre du 4 juillet 2001

Monsieur,

Je tiens à vous remercier pour votre lettre.
Je confirme notre entrevue pour jeudi prochain à 18 heures. Je joins à la présente certains documents qui vous permettront de préparer notre rencontre.
Si vous avez des questions à me poser, vous pouvez me contacter par téléphone à tout moment.

Salutations distinguées

Administratrice
Marie Pelevoizin

In business letters, the recipient is addressed in the salutation merely as *Monsieur* or *Madame*, even if you know the person's name.

Salutations

Dear Ms. Leblanc ...
Mme Leblanc ...

Dear Mr. Leblanc ...
M. Leblanc ...

Dear Ms. Leblanc ...
Chère Mme Leblanc ...

Dear Sirs/To whom it may concern
Messieurs ...

Greetings

Good day, Mr. .../Mrs. ...
Monsieur/Madame

Hello, Mr. .../Mrs. ...
Cher.../Chère...

Hi ...
Cher .../Chère ...
Mon cher. ../Ma chère ...
Très cher .../Très chère ..

Hi there!
Salut

Important Vocabulary

sender
l'expéditeur

address
l'adresse

enclosure
la pièce jointe

salutation
le titre

address
l'adresse

reference
la référence

letterhead
l'en-tête

envelope
l'enveloppe

date
la date

registered mail
la lettre recommandée

recipient
le destinataire

greeting
la formule de salutations

post office box (P.O. Box)
la boîte postale

zip code
le code postal

stamp
le timbre

Only in personal correspondence is the recipient addressed directly: *Monsieur Spoerry, Madame Desaulles*, etc.

Subjects

ballet **le ballet**	opera **l'opéra**
television **la télévision**	politics **la politique**
film **le film**	press **la presse**
jazz **le jazz**	radio **la radio**
cinema **le cinéma**	religion **la religion**
concert **le concert**	sports **le sport**
culture **la culture**	theater **le théâtre**
literature **la littérature**	economy/finance **l'économie**
music **la musique**	magazine **la revue/le magazine**
news **les nouvelles**	newspaper **le journal**

Politics

Before the current Fifth Republic in France, there were four other republics and two empires.

The First Republic gave way to the First Empire under Napoleon I. The Second Empire under Napoleon III came after an interlude of monarchy. The Third Republic was launched after the war with Prussia in 1870-1871. The Fourth Republic followed after the end of the Second World War; it was superceded by the Fifth Republic under Charles de Gaulle.

France is best described as a presidential republic, since the national president, who historically has been elected directly by voters, originally for seven years and now for five, occupies a crucial role. The country's lawmaking body is the National Assembly, the *Assemblée nationale.*

The government is led by a prime minister, whose coexistence with the national president (the so-called *cohabitation*) can be particularly difficult if they belong to different parties.

President **le Président**

Chancellor **le Chancelier**

The House of Representatives **la Chambre des représentants**

Federal Council **le Conseil fédéral**

representative/congressman **le député**

vote **le vote**

political refugee **le demandeur d'asile politique**

citizens' action/citizens' initiative **le comité municipal**

democracy **la démocratie**

immigration **l'immigration**

coalition **la coalition**

kingdom **la monarchie**

parliament **le parlement**

government **le gouvernement**

taxes **les impôts**

constitution **la constitution**

elections **les élections**

The voting regulations were changed in September of 2000 by referendum, and they took effect with the presidential election of 2002.

At the Border

Your passport, please!
Votre passeport, s'il vous plaît !

Your passport has expired
Votre passeport est périmé.

How long are you staying?
Combien de temps restez-vous ici ?

How much money do you have with you?
Combien d'argent avez-vous ?

Do you have anything to declare?
Avez-vous quelque chose à déclarer ?

Please open your suitcase.
Ouvrez votre valise, s'il vous plaît.

Can you show me a receipt?
Avez-vous une facture à me montrer ?

There are no more border checks within the European Union. However, spot checks may occur. So always keep your personal identification papers or passport and your auto insurance papers with you. If you arrive by plane, you still have to go through customs and border control. You will see a special counter set aside for citizens of European Union countries.

You have to declare that.
Il faut déclarer ceci.

You can go through.
Vous pouvez passer.

If your passport is no longer valid, the word *expiré* may be used.

Customs Regulations

Within the European Union, you may transport goods for personal use in practically unlimited quantities. If you exceed the following quantities, in the case of a spot check you may have to prove convincingly that the items are really for your personal use, which may prove difficult considering how generous these limits are:

Alcoholic drinks

20 liters of liquor under 22% vol.
10 liters of liquor over 22% vol.
90 liters wine (including a maximum of 60 liters of sparkling wine)
110 liters of beer

Tobacco
800 cigarettes
400 cigarillos
200 cigars
1 kg tobacco

Coffee, tea, and perfume
No limit

Customs

I have nothing to declare.
Je n'ai rien à déclarer.

These are gifts.
Ce sont des cadeaux.

These are personal belongings.
Ce sont des objets personnels.

I want to declare merchandise in the value of ...
Je dois déclarer des marchandises pour une valeur de ...

departure
la sortie

arrival
l'entrée

export
l'exportation

import
l'importation

declarable goods
les marchandises à déclarer

customs
la douane

customs declaration
la déclaration douanière

customs regulations
les réglementations douanières

customs check
le contrôle douanier

duty-free
exempt du droit de douane

dutiable
passible du droit de douane

You probably "would not like" to declare any goods, and the French is more precise, for you say *je dois* (*I must*—by obligation).

Booking a Flight

I would like to make a
reservation to Paris.
**Je voudrais réserver un vol
pour Paris.**

For when?
Pour quel jour ?

Next Tuesday.
Mardi prochain.

One way?
Un aller seulement ?

Round trip.
Un aller retour.

The flight leaves at 3:40
p.m.
Il y a un avion vers 15h40.

Is there an earlier
flight?
**Il n'y a pas de vol
plus tôt ?**

I'm sorry, that flight is booked
full.
**Je regrette, le vol précédent
est complet.**

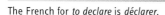

The French for *to declare* is *déclarer*.

Booking a Flight

Where is the Air France counter?
Où se trouve le guichet de l'Air France ?

When is the next flight to Paris?
Quand décolle le prochain vol pour Paris ?

Are seats still available?
Y a-t-il encore des places libres ?

What does the flight cost?
Combien coûte le billet ?

I would like to confirm my flight to Paris.
Je voudrais confirmer mon vol pour Paris.

Is there a connecting flight?
Est-ce que je dois prendre un vol de correspondance ?

My flight number is ...
Mon numéro de vol est ...

How much baggage can I take?
Combien de bagages puis-je emmener ?

Can I take this as hand baggage?
Est-ce que je peux le prendre comme bagage à main ?

Is there an extra charge for this?
Est-ce qu'un supplément est prévu pour cela ?

I would like to change my flight to Paris.
Je voudrais changer la réservation de mon vol pour Paris.

At what time must I be at the airport?
A quelle heure dois-je arriver à l'aéroport ?

How long is the flight?
Combien de temps dure le vol ?

Is there a stopover?
Est-ce qu'une escale est prévue ?

Are there any reduced rates?
Y a-t-il des offres plus intéressantes?

Do children pay the full fare?
Est-ce que les enfants paient le billet plein tarif ?

If the flight is overbooked, I would be prepared to take the next flight.
Si le vol est complet, je suis prêt(e) à prendre le vol suivant.

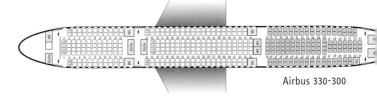

Airbus 330-300

If you're in a hurry, you say, *Je suis pressé(e)*; you are probably familiar with the term *pressing* (or urgent) matters.

Security Check

Last call for flight LH465 to Paris.
Dernier appel du vol LH465 pour Paris.

Excuse me, my flight leaves in a few minutes. Would you please let me through?
Excusez-moi, mon vol part dans quelques minutes. Pouvez-vous me laisser passer ?

I am in a hurry myself.
Moi aussi je suis pressé(e).

Put all objects into this receptacle.
Mettez tous les objets dans cette boîte.

Open your bag.
Ouvrez votre sac.

Switch on your notebook.
Allumez votre notebook.

Passenger Meier, booked to Paris, is requested to proceed immediately to gate 12.
Le passager Meier, du vol pour Paris, est prié de se rendre d'urgence à la porte d'embarquement n°12.

If you turn on your notebook computer, in a sense you make it light up—and that's the literal translation of *allumer* (*allumer une cigarette*, to light up a cigarette).

On the Plane

Please stop smoking.
Vous êtes prié d'éteindre votre cigarette.

Please fasten your seat belts!
Attachez vos ceintures de sécurité !

Where can I put this?
Où est-ce que je peux mettre ceci ?

Could I please have something to drink?
Pouvez-vous m'apporter à boire, s'il vous plaît ?

Could you please pour me another coffee?
Pouvez-vous me verser encore un peu de café ?

Could you please bring me a blanket?
Pouvez-vous m'apporter une couverture, s'il vous plaît ?

Do you have any toys for my children?
Est-ce que vous avez des jouets pour mes enfants ?

Can you heat up the baby food?
Est-ce que vous pouvez chauffer le lait pour le petit, s'il vous plaît ?

Do you also have vegetarian meals?
Y a-t-il des aliments végétariens ?

Can you give me something for my nausea?
Pouvez-vous me donner un cachet pour le mal au cœur ?

What is our cruising altitude?
On vole à quelle altitude ?

Will we arrive on time?
Est-ce que nous arriverons à l'heure ?

When can I use my notebook?
A partir de quel moment puis-je utiliser mon notebook ?

Arrival

When does my connecting flight leave?
Quand est-ce que part mon vol de correspondance ?

I have missed my flight.
J'ai manqué mon vol.

I can't find my baggage.
Je n'arrive pas à trouver mes bagages.

My baggage has been lost.
On a perdu mes bagages.

My suitcase has been damaged.
Ma valise a été endommagée.

Aliments are general types of foods. Foods in the sense of prepared meals are *repas*.

Important Vocabulary

flight schedule **l'horaire du vol**
plane ticket **le billet d'avion**
gate **la porte d'embarquement**
aisle seat **la place près du couloir**
luggage/baggage **le bagage**
baggage claim **la remise des bagages**
baggage carts **le chariot porte-bagages**
belt **la ceinture**

suitcase
la valise

travel bag
le sac de voyage

backpack/knapsack
le sac à dos

takeoff **le décollage**
departure time **l' heure de décollage**
arrival time **l' heure d'arrivée**
connecting flight **le vol de correspondance**
crew **l'équipage**
boarding pass **le ticket d'embarquement**
landing/disembarkation form **le formulaire d'entrée**

hand baggage **le bagage à main**
landing **l'atterrissage**
non-smoking section **le non-fumeur**
passenger **le passager**
smoking section **le fumeur**
return flight **le vol de retour**
counter **le guichet**
life jacket **le gilet de sauvetage**
security check **le contrôle de sécurité**
meeting place **le point de rencontre**
excess baggage **le bagage en excédent**
delay **le retard**
stop-over **l'escale**

window-seat **la place à côté de la fenêtre**
flight number **le numéro du vol**

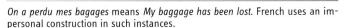

On a perdu mes bagages means *My baggage has been lost.* French uses an impersonal construction in such instances.

Taxi

Where is the nearest taxi stand?
Où se trouve la prochaine station de taxi ?

Taxi!
Taxi !

I would like to order a taxi for 10 o'clock.
Je voudrais réserver un taxi pour 10 heures.

Can you please send a taxi immediately?
Pouvez-vous envoyer immédiatement un taxi, s'il vous plaît ?

Please take me...
Emmenez-moi ...

to the hotel ...
à l'hôtel ...

to this street...
dans cette rue ...

downtown.
dans le centre ville.

to the airport.
à l'aéroport.

to the railway station.
à la gare.

What will the fare cost, approximately?
Combien coûte le trajet, plus ou moins ?

Take the shortest/fastest route.
Prenez la route la plus courte/la plus rapide.

Straight ahead here, please.
Continuez tout droit

Turn right/left here.
Tournez ici à droite/gauche.

Please stop here.
Arrêtez-vous ici.

Stop at the next intersection.
Arrêtez-vous au prochain croisement.

Please wait for me here.
Attendez-moi ici.

How much do I owe to you?
Je vous dois combien ?

We agreed on another amount.
Ce n'est pas le montant convenu !

That seems too much!
C'est un peu trop cher !

I would like a receipt.
Je voudrais un reçu, s'il vous plaît .

Keep the change!
Gardez le reste !

That is for you.
C'est pour vous.

You can keep the change.
Vous pouvez garder le reste.

Could you please put our luggage into the trunk?
Est-ce que vous pouvez mettre nos bagages dans le coffre, s'il vous plaît ?

Could you please help me to get in?
Pouvez-vous m'aider à monter, s'il vous plaît ?

Do you know a reasonably priced hotel in the neighborhood?
Est-ce que vous connaissez un hôtel bon marché près d'ici ?

Tout de suite and *immédiatement* are frequently used equivalents for *right away*.

Renting a Car

I would like to rent a car for a week.
Je voudrais louer une voiture pour une semaine.

Which price category would you like?
Quelle est la catégorie qui vous intéresse ?

A medium-size car.
Une voiture de petite cylindrée.

Let's see what we have. That will cost 200 dollars per week.
Voyons les prix, ça coûte 200 euros par semaine.

May I see your driver's license?
Pouvez-vous me montrer votre permis de conduire ?

Please sign here.
Signez ici, s'il vous plaît.

A driver's license is often referred to simply as a *permis*; to learn to drive or to take a driver's test is *passer son permis*.

Renting a Car

Do you have weekend rates?
Est-ce que vous avez des tarifs week-end ?

Do you have any special offers?
Y a-t-il des offres spéciales ?

Do you have any better offers?
Y a-t-il des offres plus avantageuses ?

Can I return the car elsewhere?
Est-ce que je peux rendre le véhicule dans une autre agence ?

At what time do I have to return the vehicle?
A quelle heure dois-je rendre le véhicule ?

Is this with unlimited mileage?
Est-ce que le kilométrage est illimité ?

Do I have to leave a deposit?
Est-ce que je dois laisser une caution ?

Is the gas tank full?
Le réservoir est-il plein ?

Do I have to return the car with a full tank?
Est-ce que je dois rendre la voiture avec le plein ?

Could you explain to me what the different types of insurance are?
Pouvez-vous m'expliquer les différentes assurances existantes ?

I would like comprehensive insurance.
Je voudrais une assurance tous risques.

How much is the deductible?
Quel est le montant de la franchise ?

Can my partner drive the car too?
Est-ce que mon partenaire peut conduire la voiture ?

Does the car have ...
Est-ce que le véhicule est équipé ...
air-conditioning?
de la climatisation?
power-steering?
de la direction assistée ?
ABS?
de l'ABS ?

anti-theft device?
de l'immobilisateur ?

Do you have a map?
Est-ce que vous avez une carte routière ?

What's the fastest way through the city?
Par où dois-je passer pour traverser rapidement la ville ?

Can I bypass the city center?
Est-il possible d'éviter le centre ?

What's the best way to go downtown?
Par où dois-je passer pour arriver au centre ville ?

Usually the French word for *door* is *porte*; however, with automobiles, the word is *portière*.

The Car

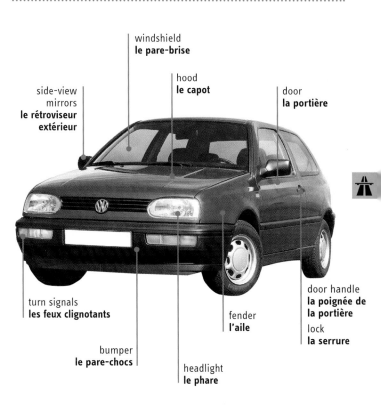

windshield
le pare-brise

hood
le capot

door
la portière

side-view mirrors
le rétroviseur extérieur

turn signals
les feux clignotants

door handle
la poignée de la portière

fender
l'aile

lock
la serrure

bumper
le pare-chocs

headlight
le phare

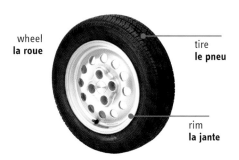

wheel
la roue

tire
le pneu

rim
la jante

Since the mirror helps you see to the rear, it is called a *rétroviseur*.

The Car

steering wheel
le volant

gearshift lever
le levier de vitesse

exhaust
le pot d'échappement

brake
le frein

tachometer
le compte-tours

gas pedal
l'accélérateur

hand brake/emergency brake
le frein à main

glove compartment
la boîte à gants

rear
la partie arrière

rear windshield
la lunette arrière

trunk
le coffre

clutch
l'embrayage

motor
le moteur

rearview mirrors
le rétroviseur

windshield wiper
l'essuie-glace

seat belt
la ceinture de sécurité

speedometer
le compteur de vitesse

fuel guage
le témoin du carburant

emergency flashers
**les feux de
détresse/warnings**

The usual term for *coupling* is *accouplement* or *attelage*; the clutch of a car is *l'embrayage*.

The Motorcycle

exhaust **le pot d'échappement**
flasher/blinker **les feux clignotants**
brake light **les feux de stop**
brake cable **le câble des freins**
motor **le moteur**
tail light **les feux de recul**
headlight **le phare**
tank **le réservoir**
drum brake **le frein à tambour**
carburetor **le carburateur**

A motorcycle, properly termed *une motocyclette*, is called *une moto* for short.

On the Move

Excuse me, how do I get to ...?
Excusez-moi, pour aller à ... ?

Can you show me that on the map?
Pouvez-vous m'indiquer l'endroit sur la carte ?

Can you show me where I am on the map?
Pouvez-vous m'indiquer sur la carte l'endroit où je me trouve ?

Is that the street which goes to ...?
C'est la bonne route pour ... ?

How far is it to ...?
A combien de kilomètres se trouve ... ?

Where is the nearest gas station?
Où se trouve la prochaine station service ?

Where is the nearest repair shop?
Où se trouve le prochain garage ?

traffic light
le feu

turnpike
l'autoroute

national highway
la route nationale

crossroad
le croisement

country road
la route départementale

Directions

You are in the wrong place.
Vous n'êtes pas sur la bonne route.

You must drive back.
Vous devez faire demi-tour.

Straight ahead.
Continuez toujours tout droit.

Go to the first crossroad.
Allez jusqu'au premier croisement.

Turn right at the next corner.
Puis tournez à droite au prochain tournant.

Follow the signs.
Suivez les panneaux de signalisation.

Turn left at the traffic lights.
Tournez à gauche au feu.

Careful! There are some nasty rumors in circulation that say that the French believe that in a conflict the right has the right of way.

Notices and Traffic Signs

Caution! **Attention !**

exit **Sortie**

keep driveway clear **Interdiction de stationner**

construction **Travaux en cours**

one-way street **Sens unique**

junction **Issue**

form lanes **Placez-vous sur une seule voie**

single-lane traffic **Route pouvant être parcourue sur une seule voie**

end of no parking zone **Fin d'interdiction de stationner**

road narrows **Chaussée rétrécie**

pedestrian crossing **Passage piéton**

pedestrian zone **Zone piétonne**

danger **Danger**

dangerous curve **Virage dangereux**

gradient **Descente**

speed limit **Limitation de vitesse**

hairpin bend **Virage à 180 degrés**

no stopping **Arrêt interdit**

no entry **Accès interdit**

rotary traffic **Rond-point**

crossing **Croisement**

slow lane **Voie pour véhicules lents**

drive slowly **Ralentir**

slow down **Ralentir ultérieurement**

trucks **Camions**

no parking **Interdiction de stationner**

parking garage **Garage**

parking lot **Parking**

automatic ticket vending machine **Distributeur automatique du ticket de parking**

radar control **Contrôle radar**

bicycle path **Piste cyclable**

keep right **Conduisez à droite**

right lane has right of way **Priorité à droite**

no right turn **Interdiction de tourner à droite**

gravel **Pierraille**

road slippery when wet **Chaussée glissante**

dead end **Voie sans issue**

turn on headlights **Allumez vos phares**

danger of skidding **Chaussée glissante**

expressway **Voie rapide**

school-bus stop **Arrêt ramassage scolaire**

traffic jam **Embouteillage**

road construction **Travaux en cours**

street parking charge **Péage**

underground parking garage **Parking sous-terrain**

no passing **Interdiction de dépasser**

by-pass **Rocade**

detour **Déviation**

traffic light **Feu**

heed right of way **Priorité**

yield right of way **Céder le passage**

no u-turn **Interdiction de faire demi-tour**

toll booth **Péage**

The toll you pay on a highway is referred to as *le péage*.

Parking

Can I park here?
Est-ce que je peux me garer ici ?

How long can I park here?
Pendant combien de temps puis-je rester garé ?

Where is there ...
Pouvez-vous m'indiquer ...
a parking lot?
un parking ?
an underground parking garage?
un parking sous-terrain ?
a parking garage?
un garage ?

What are the parking charges ...
Le parking coûte combien ...
per hour?
à l'heure ?

per day?
par jour ?

Is the parking lot attended?
Est-ce que le parking est surveillé ?

During what hours is the parking garage open?
Pendant combien de temps le garage reste-t-il ouvert ?

Is the parking garage open all night?
Est-ce que le garage est ouvert la nuit ?

Where is the cashier?
Où se trouve la caisse ?

Where is the automatic ticket vending machine?
Où se trouve le distributeur automatique de ticket de parking ?

Can you give me change?
Pouvez-vous me donner de la monnaie ?

I have lost my parking ticket.
J'ai perdu mon ticket.

Parking meter
le parcomètre

At the Gas Station

gas pump
la station service

gas can
le bidon d'essence

gas
l'essence

oil
l'huile

super
l'essence Super

regular
l'essence normale

unleaded
sans plomb

diesel
le Diesel

brake fluid
le liquide des freins

Service stations are also called *stations d'essence* (but this is not commonly used); the gas station attendant is usually called *un pompiste*.

Filling Up

Where is the nearest gas station?
Où se trouve la prochaine station service ?

Please fill it up.
Le plein, s'il vous plaît.

Give me 10 euros worth please.
Je voudrais 10 euros d'essence/gasoil.

I need one quart of oil.
Je voudrais un litre d'huile.
Can you check ...
S'il vous plaît, pouvez-vous contrôler ...
the oil?
le niveau de l'huile ?
the tire pressure?
la pression des pneus ?
the coolant?
l'eau de refroidissement ?

Please fill the windshield washer fluid.
Est-ce que vous pouvez me remplir le réservoir à eau ?

Can you do an oil change?
Pouvez-vous faire la vidange ?

Would you please clean the windshield?
Pouvez-vous me nettoyer le pare-brise ?

Octane Ratings

In the US, gasolines have the following octane ratings:

Regular: 89

Mid-grade: 91

Super: 94

Compare these ratings with those of France.

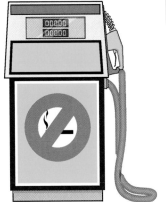

Can I have the car washed?
Pouvez-vous me laver la voiture ?

How much do I owe you?
Je vous dois combien ?

Do you have a map?
Avez-vous une carte routière ?

Where are the toilets?
Où se trouvent les toilettes ?

Full in French is *plein*; *Fill it up* is *faites le plein.*

Breakdowns

Can you help me? I've
had a breakdown.
**Pouvez-vous m'aider ?
Ma voiture est en panne.**

What is wrong?
**Qu'est-ce qui s'est
passé ?**

The motor won't start.
Le moteur ne démarre pas.

Let me have a look.
Voyons un peu.

I think you have to take it
to the repair shop.
**Il va falloir aller au
garage.**

Can you tow my car?
Pouvez-vous me remorquer ?

If you head for the next repair shop, you are going to *un garage*.

I've had a breakdown.
Ma voiture est en panne.

I have a problem ...
J'ai des problèmes avec ...
  with the battery.
  la batterie.
  with the steering.
  la direction.
  starting.
  le démarrage.
  with the lights.
  les feux
  with the brakes.
  les freins
  with changing gears
  la boîte de vitesse.

I have a flat tire.
J'ai une roue crevée.

It won't start.
La voiture ne démarre pas.

The motor splutters/misses.
Le moteur tourne par secousses.

I'm out of gas.
Il n'y a plus d'essence dans le réservoir.

Do you know of a repair shop nearby?
Est-ce qu'il y a un garage près d'ici ?

Can you take me to the nearest gas station?
Pouvez-vous m'emmener à la prochaine station service ?

Can you tow me?
Pouvez-vous me remorquer ?

Can you give me a push?
Pouvez-vous pousser ma voiture ?

Can you repair it?
Pouvez-vous le réparer ?

Can I drive any further with the car?
Est-ce que je peux continuer en voiture ?

When will it be ready?
Quand sera-t-elle prête ?

Can I phone from here?
Est-ce que je peux téléphoner ?

Please connect me with my car rental agency.
Pouvez-vous me mettre en contact avec mon agence de location de voitures ?

gas can
le bidon d'essence

warning-triangle
le triangle

tool
les outils

breakdown/towing service **le service de remorquage**

towing cable **le câble de remorquage**

breakdown assistance **l'assistance mécanique**

jumper-cables **le chargeur de câble à batterie**

jack **le cric**

emergency flashers **les feux de détresse**

The verb *crever*, which is used in speaking about a flat tire, also means *to die* or *to croak*.

In the Repair Shop

There's something wrong with the brakes.
Les freins sont défectueux.

My car is losing oil.
Ma voiture perd de l'huile.

The warning light is on.
Le témoin est allumé.

Change the spark plugs please.
Pouvez-vous me changer les bougies ?

Can you recharge the battery?
Pouvez-vous charger la batterie ?

Can you fix the tire?
Pouvez-vous réparer la roue crevée ?

Can you take a look at it?
Pouvez-vous jeter un coup d'œil ?

Can you repair it?
Pouvez-vous le réparer ?

Something is wrong with the motor.
Le moteur ne tourne pas rond.

How long will it take?
Vous en avez pour combien de temps ?

What will it cost?
Combien coûte la réparation ?

starter **le démarreur**	gears/transmission **la boîte de vitesse**
brake lining **la garniture de frein**	light bulb **l'ampoule**
brakes **les freins**	heater **le chauffage**
brake fluid **le liquide du frein**	rear axle **l'essieu arrière**
brake light **les feux stop**	horn **le klaxon**
gaskets **la garniture**	cable **le câble**
fuel injector pump **l'injecteur**	v-belt **la courroie trapézoïdale**
spare wheel **la roue de secours**	air-conditioning **la climatisation**
spare tire **la roue de secours**	radiator **le radiateur**
spare parts **les pièces de rechange**	coolant/water **l'eau de refroidissement**
backfire **l'allumage défectueux**	short circuit **le court-circuit**

A flashing of the headlights is called *un avertisseur lumineux* or *un appel de phares*.

battery
la batterie

distributor
le distributeur

pistons
le piston

water pump
la pompe à eau

shock absorber
le pare-chocs

spark plug
la bougie

steering
la direction

fuse
le fusible

headlight flasher
le clignotant

seat
le siège

dynamo
la dynamo

valve
la soupape

motor
le moteur

carburetor
le carburateur

oil filter
le filtre à huile

front axle
l'essieu avant

tail-light
le feu arrière

ignition
l'allumage

cylinder head
la culasse de cylindres

sunroof
le toit ouvrant

Auto can be used in French, but the term *voiture* is more common.

Traffic Regulations, Violations

Like so many things in the European Union, even the traffic regulations are *harmonized*, as the official usage would have it. Just the same, France, like every other country, has maintained its own special characteristics. Here are some traffic regulations to which you need to pay particular attention: Green lines at the edge of the traveled portion of a road indicate no parking. Headlights must be turned on in rain or snow, and in tunnels. Traffic in a rotary (of which there are many) has the right of way. Using a telephone while driving is permitted only with a hands-free headset.

Legal alcohol limit
  0.5

Speed limit
  in town, 50 km/h
  outside town, 90
  high-speed roads, 110
  divided highways, 130

Seat belt law in effect.

In France drivers are required to pay promptly in case of traffic violations. The traffic police are likely to deal summarily with tourists.

Current fines
  DWI, up to 4600 euros
  20 km/h over the speed limit, 92 euros and higher
  red light infraction, 92 euros and higher
  passing violation, 92 euros and higher
  parking violation, 13–36 euros

Police emergency: 17

Accident assistance: 17

With cell phone: 112

You were driving too fast.
Vous avez dépassé la limite de vitesse.

You went through a red light.
Vous avez brûlé le feu rouge.

You didn't yield the right of way.
Vous n'avez pas respecté la priorité.

You cannot park here.
Vous vous êtes garé à un endroit interdit.

Passing is not allowed here.
Ici, il y a interdiction de dépasser.

You have had too much to drink.
Conduite en état d'ivresse.

In France, cars always have feminine grammatical gender: *une Renault, une Peugeot* (based on *une voiture*).

Accidents

There has been an accident.
Il y a un accident.

I've had an accident.
J'ai eu un accident.

Please give me your insurance number.
Donnez-moi le numéro de votre police d'assurance.

I need witnesses.
J'ai besoin de témoins.

I have witnesses.
J'ai des témoins

It was my fault.
C'est de ma faute.

It was your fault.
C'est de votre faute.

Some people have been injured.
Il y a des blessés .

Do you have any bandages?
Avez-vous des bandages ?

Please call ...
S'il vous plaît, appelez ...
  the police.
  la police.
  an ambulance.
  une ambulance.
  breakdown assistance.
  le service de remorquage.

My name is ...
Je m'appelle...

I am a tourist.
Je suis un touriste.

What is your name and address?
Quel est votre nom et votre adresse ?

I had the right of way.
J'avais la priorité.

You came too close.
Vous n'avez pas gardé vos distances.

You braked suddenly.
Vous avez freiné tout à coup.

Please inform my family. The number is ...
Pourriez vous informer ma famille ? Voici leur numéro de téléphone : ...

If you need help quickly, call out *Au secours*; if it's not so urgent, you say, *j'ai besoin d'aide.*

The Bicycle

saddle
la selle

handlebars
le guidon

saddlebags
le sac porte-outils

chain
la chaîne

pedal
la pédale

tire
le pneu

derailleur
le dérailleur

reflector
le réflecteur

cable **le câble**

bicycle pump **la pompe de la bicyclette**

rim **les jantes**

repair kit **le kit de réparation des pneus**

hand brake **le frein à main**

chain guard **le carter de chaîne**

cover **l'enveloppe**

mountain bike **le VTT (vélo tout terrain)**

nut **l'écrou**

hub **le moyeu**

wheel **la roue**

racing bike **la bicyclette de course**

tail light **le feu arrière**

inner tube **le tuyau**

mudguard **le garde-boue**

spoke **le rayon**

valve **la vanne**

headlight **le feu avant**

front wheel fork **la fourche roue avant**

tools **les outils**

gear **le roue dentée**

Normally *seventy* in French is *soixante-dix*. But in some parts of France, in Switzerland, and in Belgium, people say *septante*.

Renting a Bicycle

I would like to rent a bicycle.
Je voudrais louer une bicyclette.

Gladly. We have a big selection.
Bien sûr, nous avons un vaste choix.

I would like something more sporty.
Je voudrais une bicyclette sportive.

How is this one?
Celle-ci vous convient ?

How many gears
does the bicycle
have?
**Combien de
vitesses a-t-elle ?**

Twenty-one.
Vingt et une.

La bicyclette and *le vélo* are both used for *bicycle.*

Renting a Bicycle

How much does a bicycle cost per day?
Combien coûte une bicyclette par jour ?

That is too expensive.
C'est trop cher.

Do I have to leave you a deposit?
Est-ce que je dois laisser une caution ?

Do you have also special offers for more than one day?
Est-ce que vous avez aussi des offres spéciales pour une location de plusieurs jours ?

Do you also rent ...
Est-ce que vous louez aussi ...
  saddlebags?
  des sacs porte-outils ?
  rain gear?
  une protection anti-pluie ?
  children's seats?
  des sièges pour enfants ?
  children's bicycles?
  des bicyclettes pour enfants ?
  repair kits?
  un kit de réparation ?
  helmets?
  des casques ?

Can you show us a scenic route from ... to ...?

Est-ce que vous connaissez un bel itinéraire de ...à ... ?

Can you show me an easier route?
Connaissez-vous un itinéraire plus pratique ?

Do you have information about bicycle routes in the area?
Est-ce que vous avez du matériel d'information sur les promenades touristiques de la région ?

Is there a lot of traffic on this route?
Est-ce qu'il y a beaucoup de circulation sur ce trajet ?

I have children with me.
J'ai des enfants avec moi.

Is this bicycle route suitable for children?
Est-ce que ce trajet est approprié aux enfants ?

I have a flat tire.
J'ai crevé.

Can you lend me your repair kit?
Est-ce que vous pouvez me prêter votre kit de réparation ?

I fall off my bike.
Je suis tombé(e).

Do you have some bandages?
Avez-vous des bandages ?

To ride a bike is *faire du vélo.*

Buying Tickets

A ticket to Paris,
please.
**Un billet pour Paris,
s'il vous plaît.**

One-way or round-trip?
**Aller seulement ou aller
retour ?**

Only one way.
Seulement aller.

When does the next
train leave?
**Quand est-ce que
part le prochain
train ?**

At 10:28 on platform 3.
A 10h28 sur le quai n°3.

Un aller simple is a one-way ticket.

At the Ticket Window

I would like to have a timetable.
Pouvez-vous me donner les horaires ?

I would like a ticket for the train from ... to ...
Je voudrais un billet pour le train de ... à ...

When does the next train leave?
Quand est-ce que le prochain train part ?

What does the round trip cost?
Combien coûte le voyage aller retour ?

Are there special offers for tourists?
Est-ce qu'il a des offres spéciales pour les touristes ?

Is there a discount for ...
Est-ce qu'il y a une réduction pour les ...

children?
enfants ?
schoolchildren?
écoliers ?
students?
étudiants ?
senior citizens?
retraités ?
families?
familles ?

I would like to have ...
Je voudrais ...
a place in the sleeping car.
une place dans un wagon-lit.
a sleeping compartment for ... persons.
un compartiment pour ... personnes.
a reclining seat.
une couchette.
a seat in first class.
un billet en première classe.

Do I have to reserve a seat?
Est-ce que je dois réserver une place ?

I would like to reserve a window seat.
Je voudrais une place à côté de la fenêtre.

Is that a nonstop train?
Est-ce que le train est direct ?

Does the train stop at Lyon?
Est-ce que le train s'arrête à Lyon ?

Does the train have a dining car?
Est-ce que le train a un wagon-restaurant ?

Do I have to change trains?
Est-ce que je dois changer de train ?

From which track does the train depart?
Le train part de quel quai ?

Where can I check in my luggage?
Où puis-je laisser mes bagages ?

Can I take my bicycle?
Est-ce que je peux emmener ma bicyclette ?

What does that cost?
Ça coûte combien ?

Signs

Eau non potable
Non potable

Occupé
Occupied

Libre
Vacant

Frein de secours
Emergency brake

Sortie
Exit

Toilettes
Toilets

Since water that's not safe to drink is *eau non potable*, it follows logically that drinking water is *eau potable*.

On the Platform / On the Train

Does the train to Paris leave from
this platform?
**Est-ce que le train pour Paris part
de ce quai ?**

Where does the train to Paris leave?
D'où part le train pour Paris ?

Is this the train to Paris?
C'est le train pour Paris ?

Does the train go via Paris?
Est-ce que le train passe par Paris ?

Is the the train from Paris delayed?
**Est-ce que le train en provenance de
Paris a du retard ?**

How long is the delay?
Combien a-t-il de retard ?

Excuse me, is this seat still
unoccupied?
Excusez-moi, la place est libre ?

Is this seat free?
Est-ce que cette place est libre ?

That is my seat. I have reserved it.
C'est ma place, je l'ai réservée.

May I ...
Est-ce que je peux...
    open the window?
    ouvrir la fenêtre ?
    close the window?
    fermer la fenêtre ?

Is there a smoking compartment?
**Est-ce qu'il y a un compartiment
pour fumeurs ?**

Where are we?
Où sommes-nous ?

How long do we stop here?
**Pendant combien de temps restons-
nous arrêtés ici ?**

Will we arrive on time?
**Est-ce que nous arriverons à
l'heure ?**

Will I make my connecting train?
**Est-ce que j'ai encore le temps pour
prendre la correspondance ?**

From which track does my
connecting train leave?

Sur quel quai part ma
correspondance ?

Where is the dining car?
Où se trouve le wagon-restaurant ?

Where can I buy something to drink?
Où puis-je acheter à boire ?

Where are the toilets?
Où sont les toilettes ?

What You Hear

**Le train pour Paris entre en gare sur
le quai n°3.**
The train to Paris is arriving on
track 3.

**Le train pour Paris qui est attendu
sur le quai n°3 a dix minutes de
retard.**
The train to Paris on track 3 is
delayed by ten minutes.

Montez, s'il vous plaît !
All aboard!

**Est-ce qu'on vous a déjà demandé
votre billet ?**
Did he ask for your ticket?

Votre billet s'il vous plaît.
The tickets, please.

**Vous devez payer la différence pour
le supplément.**
For this special train you have to pay
extra.

**Dans quelques minutes nous serons
à Paris.**
In few minutes, we will arrive in
Paris.

Bon voyage (Have a good trip) is said to people traveling by train; you say *Bonne
route* to people traveling by automobile.

Important Vocabulary

departure **le départ**

compartment **le compartiment**

stopover **l'arrêt**

information **les informations**

shuttle **la navette**

railway station **la gare**

platform **le quai**

express train **le rapide**

direct train **le train direct**

railroad **le chemin de fer**

last stop **le terminus**

reduction/discount **la réduction**

ticket **le billet**

ticket counter **le guichet**

timetable **l'horaire**

family ticket **le billet pour famille**

window seat **la place à côté de la fenêtre**

lost-and-found office **le bureau des objets trouvés**

aisle **le couloir**

baggage **les bagages**

baggage deposit **le compartiment pour bagages**

checkroom **le dépôt de bagages**

group ticket **le billet de groupe**

sleeper car **le wagon avec couchettes**

locomotive **la locomotive**

local train **l'omnibus**

emergency brake **le frein de secours**

ticket **le billet**

reservation **la réservation**

round-trip ticket **le billet aller retour**

ticket clerk **le guichetier**

sleeping car **le wagon-lit**

locker **la petite armoire**

dining car **le wagon-restaurant**

commuter train **le train suburbain**

car number **le numéro du wagon**

waiting room **la salle d'attente**

washroom **les lavabos**

newsstand **le kiosque**

surcharge **le supplément**

porter **le porteur**

platform **le quai**

You say *voyager en train/en voiture/en bus* (to travel by train/car/bus).

Taking the Bus

I would like to travel by bus for two weeks in this area.
Je voudrais visiter cette zone en autobus pendant deux semaines.

Do you any have special offers?
Avez-vous des offres spéciales ?

Do you give a discount for ...
Est-ce qu'il y a une réduction pour les ...

    students?
    étudiants ?
    schoolchildren?
    écoliers ?
    senior citizens?
    retraités ?
    handicapped?
    handicapés ?
    groups?
    groupes ?
    families?
    familles ?

Is it cheaper if I buy a round-trip ticket now?
Est-ce c'est plus interessant de payer l'aller retour ?

Is it possible to reserve seats?
Est-ce qu'on peut réserver des places ?

Where does the bus leave from?
D'où part l'autobus ?

Will the passengers be called for departure?
Est-ce que les passagers sont appelés avec le haut-parleur ?

Does the bus have ...
Est-ce que l'autobus est équipé de ...

    air-conditioning?
    l'air climatisé ?

    reclining seats?
    couchettes ?
    a toilet?
    toilettes ?

When do I have to be at the bus station?
A quelle heure dois-je arriver à la gare routière?

Do I have to transfer?
Est-ce que je dois changer d'autobus ?

Where/when is the next stop?
Le prochain arrêt est dans combien de temps ?

How long does the trip take?
Combien de temps dure le voyage ?

Where does this bus go to?
Où va cet autobus ?

The word *car* can also be used for *bus*. This has nothing to do with the English word *car*.

Traveling by Boat

I would like to have a timetable.
Pouvez-vous me donner les horaires ?

When does the next ship leave for Corsica?
Quand est-ce que part le prochain bateau pour la Corse ?

I would like to have a ticket to Corsica.
Je voudrais un billet pour la Corse.

How much does the trip cost?
Combien coûte le voyage ?

Are there any special offers for tourists?
Est-ce qu'il y a des offres spéciales pour les touristes ?

Is the ticket also valid for the return trip?

Est-ce que le billet est valable pour le retour ?

I would like to take my car along.
Je voudrais emmener ma voiture.

What does that cost?
Ça coûte combien ?

When do we have to board?
Quand devons-nous nous embarquer ?

How long does the crossing take?
Combien de temps dure la traversée ?

In which harbors do we stop?
Dans quels ports y a-t-il des escales ?

I would like a round-trip ticket for 11 o'clock.
Je voudrais un billet pour le bateau de 11 heures.

On Board

I am looking for cabin no. 12.
Je cherche la cabine n°12.

Can I have another cabin?
Est-ce que je peux avoir une autre cabine ?

Can I have an outside cabin?
Est-ce que je peux avoir une cabine externe ?

How much more does that cost?
Quel est le montant du supplément ?

Where is my luggage?
Où sont mes bagages ?

Where is the dining room?
Où se trouve la salle à manger ?

When are the meals served?

A quelle heure les repas sont-ils servis ?

When do we leave port?
Quand sortons-nous du port ?

How long is the stop?
Combien de temps restons-nous ici?

Can I go ashore?
Peut-on descendre du bateau ?

When do I have to be back?
A quelle heure faut-il revenir ?

I am feeling sick.
J'ai mal au cœur/j'ai envie de vomir.

Do you have any medicine for seasickness?
Avez-vous un cachet contre le mal de mer ?

If you become seasick, you need to find *le bastingage* (the ship's rail).

deck chair
la chaise sur le pont

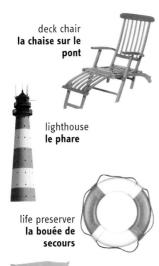

lighthouse
le phare

life preserver
la bouée de secours

life jacket
le gilet de secours

anchor **l'ancre**

mooring **l'embarcadère**

outside cabin **la cabine externe**

car ferry **le ferry-boat**

port **à bâbord**

bow **l'avant**

steamer **le navire à vapeur**

deck **le pont**

single cabin **la cabine individuelle**

ferry **le ferry-boat**

ticket **le billet**

mainland **le continent**

river boat trip **l'excursion sur le fleuve**

freighter **le navire marchand**

harbor **le port**

harbor tour **le tour du port**

stern **l'arrière**

inside cabin **la cabine interne**

yacht **le yacht**

cabin **la cabine**

quay **le quai**

berth/cabin **la cabine**

captain **le capitaine**

cruise **la croisière**

coast **la côte**

shore excursion **l'excursion à terre**

jetty **la passerelle**

reclining seat **la couchette**

rubber raft/rubber dinghy **l'aéroglisseur**

crew **l'équipage**

sailor **le marin**

motorboat **le bateau à moteur**

hurricane **l'ouragan**

lifeboat **le bateau de sauvetage**

rowing boat **la barque à rames**

round-trip **le tour**

swell **la houle**

seasickness **le mal de mer**

sail **la voile**

sailboat **le bateau à voile**

starboard **à tribord**

steward **le steward**

storm **la tempête**

hydrofoil **l'hydroptère**

wave **la vague**

double cabin **la double cabine**

Monter un bateau à quelqu'un is a slang term for to pull someone's leg.

Asking for Directions

Excuse me, how do I get to the Arc de Triomphe?
Excusez-moi, par où dois-je passer pour arriver à l'Arc de Triomphe ?

Straight ahead, take the second street on the left, then the third on the right.
Continuez tout droit, tournez dans la deuxième rue à gauche puis à droite dans la troisième.

The third left?
La troisième à gauche ?

No, the second left. There is a gas station, then a supermarket and after that you'll get to a traffic light.
Non, la deuxième à gauche, il y a une station service, ensuite vous passez devant le supermarché et vous arrivez au feu.

So you mean left at the gas station?
Alors, je tourne à gauche après la station service ?

No, you must get to the traffic light!
Non, vous devez arriver au feu !

Maybe ten minutes.
Il faut compter dix minutes.

Is it far?
C'est loin ?

Ah, thank you. I should be able to find it.
OK, merci. Je pense que je vais trouver.

The French start multiplying at 80 and say *quatre-vingts* (4 x 20).

What You Hear

Je regrette, je ne sais pas.
I'm sorry, I don't know.

Je ne suis pas d'ici.
I am not from here.

C'est loin.
It is far.

Ce n'est pas loin.
It is not far.

Traversez la rue.
Cross the street.

Vous ne pouvez pas vous tromper.
You cannot miss it.

Demandez encore une fois.
Ask once again.

Traveling on Foot

Excuse me, can you help me?
Pardon, pouvez-vous m'aider ?

I am looking for De Gaulle Street.
Je cherche la Rue De Gaulle.

Can you show me that on the map?
Pouvez-vous me l'indiquer sur la carte ?

How far is it to the Eiffel Tower?
A quelle distance se trouve la Tour Eiffel ?

traffic light
le feu

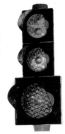

bridge
le pont

pedestrian zone
la zone piétonne

alley
la ruelle

building
l'édifice/le bâtiment

street number
le numéro de la rue

downtown
le centre ville

crossing
le croisement

park
le parc

square/place
la place

street
la route

Can I take a bus?
Est-ce que je peux y aller en autobus ?

Where are the nearest toilets?
Est-ce qu'il y a des toilettes dans les environs ?

The complete French term for the traffic light is *le feu de signalisation*.

Directions

left
à gauche

right
à droite

straight ahead
tout droit

the first left
la première à gauche

the second right
la deuxième à droite

before
avant

behind
derrière

after
après

The French refer to traffic signs as *panneaux de signalisation*.

Local Traffic

Where is the nearest ...
Où se trouve ...
  subway station?
  la prochaine station de métro ?
  bus stop?
  le prochain arrêt de bus ?
  streetcar stop?
  le prochain arrêt du tramway ?

When does the next bus leave?
Quand est-ce que le prochain autobus part ?

When does the last subway train leave?
Quand est-ce que le dernier métro part ?

Where can I buy a ticket?
Où est-ce qu'on achète les billets ?

Can you help me? I don't know how to use the automatic vending machine.
Pouvez-vous m'aider ? Je n'arrive pas à utiliser le distributeur automatique.

What is this button for?
A quoi sert ce bouton ?

I would like to go to ... Which ticket must I buy?
Je voudrais aller à ... Quel billet dois-je acheter ?

Can you give me change for this?
Pouvez-vous me faire de la monnaie ?

How much does a trip cost?
Combien coûte un voyage ?

How much does the round trip cost?
Combien coûte le voyage aller retour ?

Do you also have ...
Est-ce que vous avez aussi ...
  multiple ride tickets?
  des billets pour plusieurs voyages ?
  day tickets?
  des billets journaliers ?
  weekly tickets?
  des billets hebdomadaires ?
  monthly tickets?
  des billets mensuels ?
  tourist tickets?
  des billets pour touristes ?

How long is this ticket valid?
Combien de temps ce billet est-il valable ?

Can I travel as often as I like with this ticket?
Est-ce que ce billet est valable pour un nombre illimité de voyages ?

Is this ticket valid for just one trip?
Est-ce que ce billet n'est valable que pour un voyage ?

Is this ticket also valid for the return trip?
Est-ce que ce billet est valable pour le retour ?

Is this ticket also valid for the bus/the subway?
Est-ce que ce billet est aussi valable pour l'autobus/le métro ?

Which line goes to ...?
Quelle est la ligne pour ... ?

In which direction do I have to go?
Quelle direction dois-je prendre ?

The best way to get around Paris is the *métro*. A side benefit is getting to see some old Art Nouveau subway stations.

Where do I have to transfer?
A quel arrêt dois-je changer de bus/tramway ?

What is the next station?
Quelle est la prochaine station ?

How many stops are there?
Combien y a-t-il d'arrêts en tout ?

Can you please tell me when we reach the stop?
Pouvez-vous m'avertir quand on arrive à mon arrêt, s'il vous plaît ?

What do I have to do when I want to get off?
Qu'est-ce que je dois faire pour descendre ?

I did not know that the ticket was not valid here.
Je ne savais pas que le billet n'était pas valable sur ce moyen de transport.

I have lost my ticket.
J'ai perdu mon billet.

I have left something behind in the bus.
J'ai oublié quelque chose dans l'autobus.

Can you tell me where the lost-and-found office is?
Pouvez-vous m'indiquer où se trouve le bureau des objets trouvés ?

subway
le métro

bus
l'autobus/le bus

streetcar
le tramway

last stop
le terminus

driver
le conducteur

ticket
le billet

automatic ticket vending machine
le distributeur automatique de billets

timetable
l'horaire

stop
l'arrêt

ticket inspector
le contrôleur

ticket clerk
le guichetier

day ticket
le billet journalier

one week ticket
le billet hebdomadaire

season ticket
l'abonnement

If you travel a lot, perhaps you'll make le *tour du monde* (a trip around the world).

Overnight Accommodations

Where Can One Spend the Night?

Every year France draws millions of tourists from all over the world, and its infrastructure for tourists is accordingly well developed. In addition to hotels of every kind, there are many other possibilities for overnight accommodations.

There are, for example, the *Relais et Chateaux* (accommodations in castles and former relay stations from the days of the mail coaches), the *auberges de jeunesse* (youth hostels), private lodging, and a great many campgrounds.

farm
la ferme

bungalow
le bungalow

campsite
le camping

YWCA
l'Union chrétienne de jeunes femmes

YMCA
l'Union chrétienne de jeunes gens

vacation house
la maison de vacances

vacation apartment
l'appartement (pour les vacances)

hotel
l'hôtel

youth hostel
l'auberge de jeunesse

motel
le motel

private guest house/bed and breakfast
la chambre chez l'habitant

single room
la chambre individuelle

double room
la chambre pour deux personnes

suite
la suite

breakfast
le petit déjeuner

half board
la demi-pension

full board/American plan
la pension complète

room only/European plan
uniquement des chambres

Signs

Chambres à louer
Rooms available/Vacancies

Complet
No vacancy

Offre spéciale
Special offer

In southern France a farmhouse is also known as *un mas*.

Finding a Room

Do you know of a good hotel in this area?
Est-ce que vous connaissez un bon hôtel dans les environs ?

What is the hotel like?
Comment est-il (l'hôtel) ?

I am looking for a room for ...
Je voudrais une chambre pour ...
one night.
une nuit.
three days.
trois nuits.
a week.
une semaine.

Do you still have rooms available?
Avez-vous des chambres libres ?

How much are the rooms?
Combien coûtent les chambres ?

Is there a discount for children?
Est-ce qu'il y a une réduction pour les enfants ?

That is too expensive for me.
C'est un peu trop cher.

Do you have something less expensive?
Est-ce qu'il y a quelque chose de plus abordable ?

Do you have a list of private guest houses?
Avez-vous une liste d'appartements privés ?

Where else can I find a vacant room in vicinity?
Où puis-je trouver des chambres libres dans les environs ?

What is the address?
Quelle est l'adresse ?

Can you please write down the address?
Pouvez-vous m'écrire l'adresse ici ?

How can I get there?
Par où faut-il passer ?

Is it far?
Est-ce que c'est loin ?

Written Inquiry

Dear Sir/Madam,

We would like to reserve a room for two persons with attached bath, with an ocean view and balcony if possible, from August 7–15.

Please give us the rates for a double room, and also the rates for breakfast, half board and full board.

Sincerely,

Messieurs,

Nous voudrions réserver une chambre pour deux personnes du 7 au 15 août avec douche ou baignoire, si possible avec vue sur mer et un balcon.

Nous vous prions de bien vouloir nous fournir la liste des prix pour une chambre pour deux personnes, éventuellement avec le petit déjeuner, la demi-pension et la pension complète.

Salutations distinguées

One very good type of accommodation in France is the youth hostels, *les auberges de jeunesse.*

Reserving by Phone

Would you connect me to reservations, please?
Pouvez-vous me passer le bureau de réservation, s'il vous plaît ?

One moment, please.
Un instant, s'il vous plaît.

Grand Hotel, room reservations. May I help you?
Grand Hôtel, réservation des chambres. Que puis-je faire pour vous ?

I would like to have a room for tonight.
Je voudrais une chambre pour cette nuit.

About 5 P.M.
Vers 17 heures.

When will you arrive?
Vous arriverez à quelle heure ?

We will reserve your room until 6 p.m. If you will be arriving later, please let us know.
Nous pouvons vous garder la chambre jusqu'à 18 heures. Si vous arrivez plus tard, vous devez téléphoner.

To get off at the hotel is *descendre à l'hôtel.*

At the Reception Desk

Good day, I would like a room for one night.
Bonjour, je voudrais une chambre pour une nuit.

We have a double room for 120 euro.
Nous avons une chambre pour deux personnes à 120 euro.

That's fine. Can I pay by credit card?
Très bien. Est-ce que je peux payer avec ma carte de crédit ?

Of course.
Bien sûr.

Can I look at the room?
Pouvez-vous me montrer la chambre ?

No problem.
Oui, bien sûr.

Good, I will take it.
D'accord, je la prends.

The key is here. The room number is 212 on the second floor.
Voici la clé. Votre chambre est au n° 212 au deuxième étage.

When you go to reserve a room, you end up at *la réception*.

I have reserved a room.
J'ai réservé une chambre.

Can I look at the room?
Est-ce que je peux voir la chambre ?

I will take it.
Je la prends.

I don't like the room.
Cette chambre ne me plaît pas.

The room is ...
La chambre est ...
  too small.
  trop petite.
  too noisy.
  trop bruyante.
  too dark.
  trop sombre.

Can I have another room?
Pouvez-vous me donner une autre chambre ?

Do you have something ...
Est-ce que vous avez une chambre ...
  quieter?
  plus calme ?
  bigger?
  plus grande ?
  cheaper?
  moins chère ?
  with a balcony?
  avec un balcon ?

Do you have non-smoking rooms?
Est-ce que vous avez des chambres pour non-fumeurs ?

Do you also have rooms with three beds?
Est-ce que vous avez des chambres avec trois lits ?

Could you put in a third bed?
Est-il possible d'ajouter un troisième lit ?

Is there an elevator?
Est-ce qu'il y a un ascenseur ?

Is breakfast included?
Est-ce que le petit déjeuner est compris ?

Where can I park my car?
Où puis-je garer ma voiture ?

Do you have a garage?
Est-ce que vous avez un garage ?

I will stay for two nights.
Je reste ici deux nuits.

I don't yet know how long we will stay.
Nous n'avons pas encore décidé combien de temps nous resterons ici.

Can we still get something to eat in the neighborhood?
Est-ce qu'il y a des restaurants encore ouverts dans les environs ?

Please bring the luggage to the room.
Pouvez-vous porter les valises dans ma chambre, s'il vous plaît ?

What You Hear

Nous sommes complet./Tout est complet.
We are full.

Quel est votre nom, s'il vous plaît ?
In whose name?

Combien de temps voulez-vous rester ?
How long would you like to stay?

Remplissez ce formulaire, s'il vous plaît.
Fill in the registration form please.

Pouvez-vous me montrer votre passeport, s'il vous plaît ?
May I see your passport?

Signez ici.
Please sign here.

A double room is *une chambre à deux lits*. To designate a double bed, you can use *un lit à deux personnes*, and twin beds are *lits jumeaux*.

Requests and Desires

I would like to extend my stay by one night.
Je voudrais réserver encore pour une nuit.

The key for room 212, please.
Pouvez-vous me donner la clé de la chambre 212, s'il vous plaît ?

I have locked myself out of my room.
J'ai laissé les clés dans ma chambre.

I have lost my key.
J'ai perdu le clé.

Can you put that into your safe?
Est-ce que vous pouvez mettre ceci dans le coffre-fort ?

When is breakfast served?
A quelle heure servez-vous le petit déjeuner ?

Where is breakfast served?
Où servez-vous le petit déjeuner ?

Is the hotel open the whole night?
Est-ce que l'hôtel est ouvert toute la nuit ?

When must I check out of the room?
A quelle heure dois-je quitter la chambre ?

Can you wake me at 8 o'clock?

DO
NOT
DISTURB!

Pouvez-vous me réveiller à 8 heures ?

Is there any mail for me?
Y a-t-il du courrier pour moi ?

I am expecting a phone call.
J'attends un coup de fil.

Please inform them that I ...
Pouvez-vous répondre que ...
  will call them back.
  je rappellerai ?
  will be back in the evening.
  je serai là dans la soirée ?

I would like to leave a message for Mr. Leblanc.
Je voudrais laisser un message pour M. Leblanc.

Can you please bring me a towel?
Pouvez-vous m'apporter une serviette de bain, s'il vous plaît ?

Can I have an extra blanket?
Pouvez-vous me donner une autre couverture, s'il vous plaît ?

Can you get a typewriter for me?
Pouvez-vous me procurer une machine à écrire, s'il vous plaît ?

Can I send a fax from here?
Est-ce que je peux utiliser votre fax ?

Mathematics in French: 4 x 20 + 10 = 90 (*quatre-vingt-dix*).

The Hotel Staff

manager
le directeur

receptionist
**la personne chargée
de l'accueil**

bell boy
le groom

porter
le portier

chambermaid
le personnel de service

room service
le service en chambre

Complaints

The key doesn't fit.
La clé ne fonctionne pas.

The door won't open.
Je n'arrive pas à ouvrir la porte.

The room has not been made.
La chambre n'a pas été faite.

The bathroom is dirty.
La salle de bain est sale.

There are no towels.
Il n'y a pas de serviette de bain.

The window can't be opened/closed.
**Je n'arrive pas à ouvrir/fermer la
fenêtre.**

Departure

We are leaving tomorrow morning.
Nous partons demain matin.

We are leaving now.
Nous partons maintenant.

I would like the bill.
**Je voudrais mon compte, s'il vous
plaît.**

Can I pay by credit card?
**Est-ce que je peux payer avec ma
carte de crédit ?**

I am paying cash.
Je paie comptant.

This does not add up right.
Votre calcul n'est pas exact.

Can I leave my luggage with you for
the day?
**Est-ce que je peux laisser mes
bagages ici pour aujourd'hui ?**

Could you call me a taxi?
Pouvez-vous m'appeler un taxi ?

We were very pleased.
Nous sommes satisfaits.

Please get my luggage.
**Est-ce que vous pouvez prendre mes
bagages, s'il vous plaît ?**

The bill in a hotel is *le compte* in French; in a restaurant, though, it's *l'addition*.

Accessories

adapter
l'adaptateur

child's bed
**le lit pour
enfants**

ashtray
le cendrier

suitcase
la valise

iron
le fer à repasser

pillow
l'oreiller

TV
la télévision

refrigerator
le frigidaire/frigo

light bulb
l'ampoule

sewing kit
**le nécessaire de
couture**

hand towel
la serviette

lock
la serrure

comb
le peigne

key
la clé

Hors saison is *off-season*. Another word for that is *arrière-saison*.

telephone
le téléphone

bathroom
les toilettes

alarm clock
le réveil

toothbrush
**la brosse à
dents**

reception desk **l'enregistrement**
elevator **l'ascenseur**
bath **la salle de bain**
bathrobe **le peignoir**
bath towel **la serviette de bain**

bed **le lit**
blanket **la couverture**
bed sheet **le drap**
stationery **le papier à lettre**
double bed **le lit à deux places**
shower **la douche**
single bed **le lit à une place**
ice cube **le glaçon**
electricity **l'électricité**
floor/story/level **l'étage**
window **la fenêtre**
hairdryer **le sèche-cheveux**
breakfast **le petit déjeuner**
luggage **les bagages**
half board **la demi-pension**
high season **la pleine saison**
electric blanket **la couverture
chauffante**
heating **le radiateur**
cold water **l'eau froide**
babysitting/child care **l'encadrement
pour les enfants**

hanger **le portemanteau/le cintre**
locker room **le vestiaire**
air-conditioning **la climatisation**
lamp **la lampe**
mattress **le matelas**
ocean view **la vue sur la mer**
mini-bar **le mini-bar**

bathtub **la baignoire**
balcony **le balcon**

Some expressions are used only in the plural in French: *les toilettes, les alentours* (the surroundings), and so on.

low season **hors saison**
night table **la table de chevet**
off season **hors saison**
waste paper basket **la corbeille**
radio **la radio**
bill **le compte**
reservation **la réservation**
restaurant **le restaurant**
reception **la réception**
shutters **le volet**
quiet **tranquille**
safe **le coffre-fort**
wardrobe/closet **l'armoire**
desk/writing table **le bureau**

toilet paper **le papier-toilette**
door **la porte**
fan/ventilator **le ventilateur**
extension cord **la rallonge**
full board **la pension complète**
curtain **le rideau**
pre-season **hors saison**
warm water **l'eau chaude**
wash basin **le lavabo**
water **l'eau**
valuables **les objets de valeur**
toothpaste **le dentifrice**
room **la chambre**
room number **le numéro de chambre**
to the street **sur la rue**

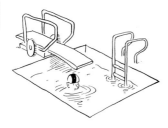

swimming pool **la piscine**
soap **le savon**
armchair **le fauteuil**
mirror **le miroir**
socket **la prise de courant**
plug **la fiche**
floor **l'étage**
plug/stopper **le bouchon**
beach **la plage**
chair **la chaise**
terrace **la terrasse**

Le bureau is a *writing desk* and an *office.*

Reserving a Vacation Home

Vacation apartment
l'appartement (pour les vacances)

Vacation house
la maison de vacances

We are looking for a vacation apartment for three weeks.
Nous cherchons un appartement pour trois semaines.

We have rented a vacation apartment for three weeks.
Nous avons loué un appartement pour trois semaines.

There are four of us.
Nous sommes quatre personnes.

We need two bedrooms.
Nous voulons deux chambres.

We need four beds.
Nous voulons quatre lits.

How many beds are there available?
Combien y a-t-il de lits disponibles ?

Where do I pick up the keys?
Où dois-je retirer les clés ?

Is the vacation apartment completely furnished?
Est-ce que l'appartement est complètement meublé ?

Do we have to bring bed linen?
Est-ce que nous devons emmener les draps et les couvertures ?

What does it cost to rent bed linen?
Combien coûte la location des draps et des couvertures ?

Does the house have central heating?
Est-ce que la maison est équipée du chauffage central ?

Does the apartment have a phone?
Est-ce qu'il y a un téléphone dans l'appartement ?

Can I make outgoing telephone calls, or only receive incoming calls?
Est-ce que je peux téléphoner ou simplement recevoir des appels ?

Is the final cleaning included?
Est-ce que le nettoyage final est compris ?

What does the final cleaning cost?
Combien coûte le nettoyage final ?

ocean view
la vue sur la mer

The French people love their countryside, and they often own *une résidence secondaire*, a second home where they spend their vacation.

Vacation Home: Practical Matters

Where are the garbage cans/trash cans?
Où se trouvent les poubelles ?

Do I have to separate the garbage?
Est-ce que je dois séparer les différents types d'ordures ?

When is the trash/garbage picked up?
A quelle heure retire-t-on les ordures ?

Whom should I contact if there are problems?
A qui dois-je m'adresser en cas de problèmes ?

Can you give me the phone number?
Pouvez-vous me laisser votre numéro de téléphone ?

During our stay, a glass broke.
Nous avons cassé un verre durant notre séjour.

How much do I owe you for it?
Je vous dois combien pour cela ?

The window pane broke.
Nous avons cassé une vitre.

Where can I have it repaired?
Où puis-je la faire réparer ?

Where can one ...
Où puis-je ...
  shop?
  faire des courses ?

make a phone call?
téléphoner ?
do the laundry?
faire ma lessive ?
hang up the laundry?
étendre ma lessive ?

The toilet is clogged.
Les toilettes sont bouchées.

The heating isn't working.
Le chauffage ne fonctionne pas.

There is no water.
Il n'y a pas d'eau.

There is no hot water.
Il n'y a pas d'eau chaude.

The faucet is dripping.
Le robinet goutte.

→ Also see HOUSEWARES, p. 159; TOOLS, p. 164; CAMPING EQUIPMENT, p. 165.

The waste basket *(la poubelle)* owes its name to Monsieur Poubelle, the Parisian prefect who first introduced this item.

Equipment

cutlery/silverware
les couverts

refrigerator
le frigidaire/frigo

TV
la télévision

light switch
l'interrupteur

gas range
le poêle à gaz

frying pan
la poêle

dishes
la vaisselle

lock
la serrure

glass
le verre

key
la clé

grill
le barbecue

vacuum cleaner
l'aspirateur

saucepan/pot
la casserole

socket
la prise de courant

Le poêle is the stove; *la poêle* is the frying pan.

chair
la chaise

telephone
le téléphone

plate/dish
l'assiette

VCR
le magnétoscope

faucet
le robinet

bath **la salle de bain**
balcony **le balcon**
bed **le lit**
hot water heater **le chauffe-eau**
shower **la douche**
electric range **le four électrique**
electric heating **le chauffage électrique**
window **la fenêtre**
window pane **la vitre**
dishwasher **le lave-vaisselle**
heating **le chauffage**
coffee machine **la cafetière**
chimney **la cheminée**
coal heating **le chauffage au charbon**
kitchen **la cuisine**
microwave **le four à micro-ondes**
radio **la radio**
bedroom **la chambre**
terrace **la terrasse**
table **la table**
toaster **le grille-pain**
door **la porte**
hot water **l'eau chaude**
clothes dryer **le séchoir à linge**
washing machine **la machine à laver**
living room **la salle de séjour**
central heating **le chauffage central**

Important Vocabulary

. . . .

date of departure **le jour de départ**
date of arrival **le jour d'arrivée**
apartment **l'appartement**
bungalow **le bungalow**
vacation spot **la résidence hôtel**
vacation house **la maison de vacances**
vacation apartment **l'appartement (pour les vacances)**

garage **le garage**
ocean view **la vue sur la mer**
rent **le loyer**
garbage **les ordures**
garbage can **la poubelle**
extra costs **les frais supplémentaires**
power **le courant**
voltage **la tension électrique**
landlord **le locataire**

La radio is the device you listen to. *Le radio*, on the other hand, is the radio operator.

Youth Hostels

Do you still have rooms available?
Est-ce qu'il y a encore des chambres libres ?

Do you have rooms only for women?
Est-ce qu'il y a encore des chambres seulement pour femmes ?

What is the cost of...
Combien...
an overnight stay?
coûte la nuit ?
bed linen?
coûtent les couvertures et les draps ?
a lockable cupboard?
coûte une armoire que l'on peut fermer à clé ?

Are there any other reasonably priced accomodations?
Est-ce qu'il y a d'autres possibilités abordables pour la nuit ?

Can I use my own sleeping bag?
Est-ce que je peux utiliser mon sac de couchage ?

Do you have bed linen?
Est-ce qu'il y a des couvertures et des draps ?

Where is ...
Où se trouve ...
the washroom?
la salle de bains ?
the shower?
la douche ?
the toilet?
les toilettes ?

Do you have lockers?
Est-ce qu'il y a des petites armoires fermant à clé ?

When do you close for the night?
A quelle heure fermez-vous la nuit ?

Do you close during the day?
Est-ce que vous êtes fermé la journée ?

Is there breakfast in the morning?
Est-ce que vous servez le petit déjeuner ?

What does the breakfast cost?
Combien coûte le petit déjeuner ?

When is breakfast served?
A quelle heure servez-vous le petit déjeuner ?

Are there reduced rates for longer stays?
Est-ce qu'il y a des prix plus intéressants si l'on reste plus longtemps ?

Where can I leave a message?
Où puis-je laisser les messages ?

Can I leave a message?
Est-ce que je peux laisser un message ?

Can I have mail sent here?
Est-ce que je peux me faire envoyer du courrier ici ?

Has any mail come for me?
Est-ce qu'il y a du courrier pour moi ?

Is the area safe at night?
Est-ce que cet endroit/cette région est sûr(e) la nuit ?

Which bus lines go from here ...
Quelles lignes de bus faut-il prendre pour aller ...
to the railway station?
à la gare ?
to the harbor?
au port ?
to the beach?
à la plage ?
to the airport?
à l'aéroport ?
downtown?
dans le centre ville ?

Can I have another room tomorrow night?
Est-ce que vous pouvez me donner une autre chambre pour la prochaine nuit?

Can I leave my luggage here until 12 o'clock?
Est-ce que je peux laisser mes bagages ici jusqu'à 12 heures ?

The youth hostel pass is *la carte d'hébergement.*

At the Campground

Do you still have vacant camping spots?
Est-ce qu'il y a encore des places libres ?

Do I have to register in advance?
Est-ce que je dois réserver ?

How far in advance?
Combien de temps à l'avance ?

What does it cost per night for ...
Combien doit-on payer par nuit pour ...

a tent?
une tente ?
a trailer?
une caravane ?
a camper?
un camping-car ?
one person?
une personne ?
a car?
une voiture ?
a cottage?
un bungalow ?

We will stay for three days/weeks.
Nous resterons trois jours/semaines.

Can you tell me how to get to my camping spot?
Par où dois-je passer pour rejoindre ma place ?

Where is/are the ...
Où se trouve(nt) ...
toilets?
les toilettes ?

washrooms?
les lavabos ?
showers?
la douche ?
garbage cans?
les poubelles ?

What voltage is used here?
Quelle tension électrique utilisez-vous ?

Is there a grocery store?
Y a-t-il un magasin d'alimentation ?

Are we allowed to light fires?
Est-ce qu'on peut allumer un feu ?

Is there someone on duty at night?
Est-ce que le camping est surveillé la nuit ?

Where can I speak to the ranger?
Où puis-je joindre le garde forestier ?

Which is the weather-side?
Quel est le côté exposé au vent ?

Can you please lend me a tent peg?
Pouvez-vous me passer un piquet de tente, s'il vous plaît ?

Where can I rent/exchange gas cylinders?
Où puis-je me procurer de bouteilles de gaz/changer la bouteille de gaz ?

A neologism for *campground* has been coined: *une campière*.

kerosene lamp/hurricane lamp
la lampe à pétrole

plug
la fiche

electrical connection
le branchement électrique

gas cylinder
la bouteille de gaz

gas stove
le fourneau à gaz

tent peg
le piquet de tente

children's playground
l'aire de jeu

grocery store
le magasin d'alimentation

rental fee
le tarif de location

coins
la monnaie

propane
le gaz propane

drinking water
l'eau potable

washing machine
la machine à laver

washroom
les lavabos

water connection
le branchement de l'eau

camper
le camping-car

trailer
la caravane

tent
la tente

tent pole
le mât d'une tente

→ Also see HOUSEWARES, p. 159; TOOLS, p. 164; CAMPING EQUIPMENT, p. 165

La caravane can mean either a *camping trailer* or a *caravan*.

On the Farm

tractor
le tracteur

harvester
**la moissonneuse-
batteuse**

field
le champ

grain
le blé

ear of grain
l'épi

In France if you can't "see the forest for the trees," it's said that *Les arbres cachent la forêt.*

straw
la paille

hay
le foin

horse
le cheval

donkey
l'âne

pig
le cochon

A large forest is *une forêt*; a small woods is *un bois*.

goat
la chèvre

chick
le poussin

sheep
le mouton

goose
l'oie

cow
la vache

duck
le canard

calf
le veau

turkey
le dindon

rooster/cock
le coq

cat
le chat

dog
le chien

chicken
le poulet

Le chat is the general term for cat; *le matou* is the male cat, and *la chatte* is the female cat. With dogs there is a distinction between *le chien* and *la chienne*.

Cuisine

By definition, French people are gourmets, and French cuisine is the best, or at least one of the best in the world. There's a reason that French culinary terms can be found on menus in other countries, from *aperitifs* to *entrecote* and *cordon bleu*.

For us French cuisine conjures up many exotic dishes such as snails and frog's legs, but that doesn't take into account the great variety of delicious hors d'oeuvres, fish, and meat dishes and desserts that it offers, not to mention the abundant variety of wines.

France is not an inexpensive country, and that's also true of restaurant dining. In addition to the various classes of restaurants, there are other establishments where you can eat more cheaply. These include the *brasseries* and *bistros*, where you usually don't have to dig as deep into your wallet, and the *crêperies*.

France is also the land of crêpes, and that doesn't necessarily imply a *flambé* dessert. Crêpes can also be very good in the form of pockets filled with ham, cheese, or egg.

You can also order cold meals and sandwiches in cafés.

The French eat a hot meal in the evening, as people in other southern countries do. The northern European custom of evening sandwiches with bread and cold cuts is not known.

Where to Turn

Le self-service is clearly a restaurant where you help yourself.

Le bar, good for breakfast, light meals, and of course all types of coffee.

La pâtisserie, a pastry shop second to none.

Le café-glacier for ice cream.

Le restoroute, a restaurant on a divided highway.

Le fast food restaurant requires no translation.

Le kiosque à sandwiches is excellent for simple, take-out meals such as salads and sandwiches.

Le grill-room is for everything involving meat.

Le pub, **l'auberge**, **la taverne** are fairly simple restaurants.

If someone asks you, *Comment trouvez-vous cela?* or *C'est bon?* you are being asked if you like the way something tastes.

Meals

breakfast
le petit déjeuner

lunch
le déjeuner

dinner
le dîner

Meal Times

breakfast
7 – 9 a.m.

lunch
12:30 – 2 p.m.

dinner
7:30 – 10 p.m.

What You Hear

Avez-vous réservé ?
Do you have a reservation?

Une place pour fumeurs ou non-fumeurs ?
Smoking or non-smoking?

Voulez-vous un apéritif ?
Would you like a drink before your meal?

Voulez-vous commander ?
Would you like to order?

Voici les plats du jour ...
Today's specials are ...

Je vous conseille...
I recommend ...

Je regrette, mais nous n'en avons plus.
I'm sorry, we're out of that.

Que voulez-vous boire ?
What would you like to drink?

Vous en voulez encore ?
Can I give you another?

Tout va bien ?
Is everything okay?

Voulez-vous autre chose ?
Would you like anything else?

Est-ce que c'était bon ?
Did you enjoy your meal?

What You Often Need

Where are the restrooms?
Où sont les toilettes ?

Can you please pour me another one?
Pouvez-vous m'en verser encore, s'il vous plaît ?

Can I please have the menu (again)?
Pouvez-vous m'apporter (me rapporter) le menu, s'il vous plaît ?

I would like to order.
Est-ce que je peux commander ?

Can you bring the wine menu?
Pouvez-vous m'apporter la carte des vins ?

No thank you, I'm full/that's all.
Non merci, c'est tout.

Signs and Posters

Plats à emporter
Take-out

Dernière commande à ...
Last orders at ...

Attendez pour des places assises
Please wait to be seated

Payez à la caisse
Please pay the cashier

Plat du jour
Today's/Daily Special

If you don't recall the differences between lunch *(le déjeuner)* and dinner *(le dîner)*, you can manage by saying, *Je voudrais manger.*

In a Restaurant

As in other Mediterranean countries, eating is an important part of everyday life in France, and a meal can take up to two to three hours. The main meal usually begins at 7:30 in the evening.

In addition to satisfying the palate, eating also functions as a social event that involves a good deal more than merely eating and drinking.

When you go to a restaurant, you should wait to be seated, rather than simply going directly to a table. This rule is not ironclad in fairly simple restaurants such as *brasseries*, but for reasons of politeness, it doesn't hurt to observe it.

Service is generally included in the bill, but the server still expects a tip; there is no hard and fast rule, but 5–10% should suffice. Anyone who feels particularly well served can of course give more than that.

There is no special dress code in French restaurants. Businesspeople and business occasions (and private events such as baptisms, communion, birthdays) tend to be rather conservative; in other words, if you are invited to such an occasion or attend a business meeting in a restaurant, you should come in a jacket and tie.

I am hungry.
J'ai faim.

Can you recommend a good restaurant?
Pouvez-vous me conseiller un bon restaurant ?

I would like something to eat.
Je voudrais manger quelque chose.

I would just like a bite of something.
Je voudrais manger un morceau.

I would just like something to drink.
Je voudrais seulement boire quelque chose.

I would like to have breakfast.
Je voudrais prendre mon petit déjeuner.

I would like to have dinner.
Je voudrais dîner.

I would like to have lunch.
Je voudrais déjeuner.

A dish that's a meal or a course in a restaurant is *un plat*.

Ordering

Excuse me!
Excusez-moi !

Yes, Sir?
Oui ?

Can I please have
the menu?
**Pouvez-vous
m'apporter le
menu, s'il vous
plaît ?**

Of course. Just a
minute.
**Bien sûr, un
petit instant.**

Would you like to you order?
Voulez-vous commander ?

Thank you!
Merci !

Don't mention it.
De rien

What do you recommend?
Que me conseillez-vous ?

I recommend the day's special.
Je vous conseille le plat du jour.
Thanks! I would like ...
Merci ! Je voudrais ...

When you order, you can start by saying, *Je voudrais* or *Je prends* (*I'll have...*).

Making a Reservation

I would like to reserve a table ...
Je voudrais réserver une table ...
  for 6 persons.
  pour six personnes
  for tonight.
  pour ce soir
  for 5 p.m.
  pour 17 heures.

I have reserved a table in the name of Meier.
J'ai réservé une table au nom de M. Meier.

I would like a table ...
Je voudrais une table ...
  at the window.
  près de la fenêtre.
  in a quiet corner.
  dans un coin tranquille.

Do you have a smoking/non-smoking area?
Avez-vous une place pour fumeurs/non-fumeurs ?

Where can we wait?
Où pouvons-nous attendre ?

How long will we have to wait for a table?
Combien de temps faut-il attendre pour avoir une table ?

Ordering

The menu/beverage menu, please.
Pouvez-vous m'apporter le menu, s'il vous plaît ?

What do you particularly recommend?
Que me conseillez-vous ?

Can we order the beverages right now?
Est-ce qu'on peut commander les consommations tout de suite ?

Do you also have children's/senior citizens' portions?
Est-ce qu'il y a aussi des portions pour les personnes âgées/enfants ?

Are there also vegetarian dishes?
Est-ce qu'il y a des aliments végétariens ?

Is there any alcohol in this dish?
Est-ce que les aliments contiennent des substances alcoolisées ?

I am a diabetic.
J'ai le diabète.

I am not very hungry. Can I have a small portion?
Je n'ai pas tellement faim. Pouvez-vous m'apporter une petite portion ?

I will have ...
Je prends ...

Can you prepare the dish without garlic?
Est-ce que je peux commander des aliments sans ail ?

Would you bring me a bottle of wine, please.
Pouvez-vous m'apporter une bouteille de vin, s'il vous plaît ?

Naturally, you can pay your compliments to the chef; in that case you say, *Mes compliments au chef.*

Paying

The bill, please.
Pouvez-vous m'apporter l'addition ?

I am in a hurry.
Je suis pressé(e).

Is the tip included in the bill?
Est-ce que le pourboire est compris dans l'addition ?

Everything on one bill, please.
Est-ce que vous pouvez faire une seule addition ?

Separate bills, please.
Est-ce que vous pouvez faire des additions séparées ?

Do you take ...
Est-ce que vous acceptez ...
credit cards?
les cartes de crédit ?
travelers checks?
les chèques de voyage ?
checks?
les chèques ?

I think there is a mistake on the bill.
Je crois que le compte n'est pas juste.

I did not have that.
Je n'ai pas pris ceci !

Keep the change.
Gardez la monnaie.

Praise

I liked it.
J'ai beaucoup aimé.

Thank you very much, the service was excellent.
Mes compliments pour le service !

We will recommend you.
Nous saurons vous recommander.

The meal was excellent.
Le repas était excellent.

Complaints

I didn't order that.
Je n'ai pas commandé cela.

The meat is tough.
La viande est dure.

Excuse Me! We've been waiting quite a while!
Excusez-moi ! On attend depuis un bout de temps !

I am sorry, but I didn't like it.
Je regrette, je ne suis pas satisfait.

The service was ...
Le service était ...
sloppy.
négligé.
unfriendly.
désagréable.

The meal was ...
La nourriture ...
too salty.
était trop salée.
cold.
était froide.

If you say that the service was *mauvais*, it was lousy; if you want to stress how unfriendly it was, you can also mention *peu aimable* or *brusque*.

On the Table

ashtray
le cendrier

cup
la tasse

silverware
les couverts

plate
l'assiette

fork
la fourchette

beverage **la boisson**

pepper **le poivre**

salt **le sel**

bowl **le bol**

glass
le verre

mustard **la moutarde**

teaspoon **la cuillère à café**

tablecloth **la nappe**

sugar **le sucre**

highchair
la chaise haute

Is Something Missing?

Can you bring me some pepper?
**Pouvez-vous m'apporter le poivre,
s'il vous plaît ?**

Would you please pass me the
sugar?
**Pouvez-vous me passer le sucre, s'il
vous plaît ?**

spoon
la petite cuillère

How Was It?

knife
le couteau

The food is ... **La nourriture est ...**
 simple **simple**
 hearty **substantielle**
 sweet **sucrée**
 sour **acide**
 spicy **épicée**
 very spicy **très relevée**
 hot **piquante**
 hellishly hot **très piquante**

napkin
la serviette de table

In France the salad bowl is called *le saladier.*

The Menu

A complete French menu consists of a first course (*une entrée*), a main course (*un plat*) of fish or meat, the usual side dishes including both vegetables and pasta (*les pâtes*) or rice (*le riz*), plus a sweet dessert (*un dessert*), cheese (*le fromage*), or fruits (*fruits*). A cup of coffee generally concludes the meal.

If you missed the appetizers in this list—the famous hors d'oeuvres—you can relax, for naturally they are included in the menu. You can also select one or more appetizers and skip the entrée.

Concerning drinks, of course wine is commonly served in France; you can order it by the 33-cl or 50-cl carafe (*vin en carafe*). Around Lyon a carafe is called *un pot*, and it holds just a half-liter.

Of course you can also drink mineral water (*eau minérale*), and order it in addition to wine. There are two types of mineral water: with or without carbonation (*gazeuse* or *naturelle*, respectively). Naturally, you can also have beer instead of wine.

cold appetizers
les hors d'œuvres froids

hot appetizers
les hors d'œuvres chauds

soups
les soupes

salads
les salades

egg dishes
les plats à base d'œufs

fish
le poisson

seafood
les fruits de mer

meat
la viande

poultry
la volaille

side-dishes
les garnitures

vegetables
les légumes

cheese
le fromage

dessert
le dessert

soft drinks
les boissons non alcoolisées

alcoholic beverages
les boissons alcoolisées

hot beverages
les boissons chaudes

Petits-fours are an exquisite pastry served with coffee after a meal.

Breakfast

In every French city there are numerous cafés and bistros where you can breakfast fairly economically.

French people, who are dashing off to catch the *metro* or some other type of transportation to get to work, generally have a frugal breakfast consisting of a *café noir* (black coffee) or *café au lait* (coffee with milk) plus a croissant or a piece of baguette.

People who are accustomed to a sumptuous breakfast won't get their fill in France: the standard repertory at a French breakfast is limited (except of course at buffets in the better hotels).

A cup of coffee.
Une tasse de café.

A glass of milk.
Un verre de lait.

A slice of ham.
Une tranche de jambon.

Breakfast is *le petit déjeuner;* the morning coffee break is the *pause-café.*

Drinks

coffee
le café

milk
le lait

tea
le thé

orange juice
le jus d'orange

cocoa **le cacao**
herbal tea **la tisane**

 ## Eggs

scrambled eggs **les œufs brouillés**
poached eggs **les œufs pochés**
bacon and eggs **les œufs avec du lard fumé**
ham and eggs **les œufs avec du jambon**
omelet **l'omelette**

fried eggs
les œufs à la poêle

soft-boiled egg
l'œuf à la coque

hard-boiled egg **l'œuf dur**

Herbal teas are also known as *infusions*.

Bread and Rolls

roll
le petit pain

white bread
le pain blanc/la baguette

whole wheat bread
le pain complet

croissant
le croissant

toast
le toast

bread **le pain**

wheat **le blé**

caraway seed **le cumin**

rye **le seigle**

butter **le beurre**

honey **le miel**

crispbread/cracker **le pain de seigle croustillant**

jam **la confiture**

syrup **le sirop**

Zwieback **la biscotte**

Miscellaneous

French toast
la soupe au pain

fried potatoes/hash browns
les pommes de terre sautées

cornflakes
les corn-flakes

oatmeal/porridge
la bouillie d'avoine

cheese
le fromage

müsli/granola
le bouillie de flocons d'avoine et de fruits/le musli

fruit
les fruits

pancake
la crêpe

ham
le jambon

bacon
le lard

saccharin/sugar substitute
la saccharine

waffles
la gaufrette

sausage
la saucisse

sausage link
la petite saucisse

yogurt
le yaourt

sugar
le sucre

For quite a while you could scarcely find whole-grain bread in France, but now it is becoming popular throughout the country.

Appetizers

artichokes **les artichauts**
oysters **les huîtres**
prawn **les crevettes**
scallop **le vénéricarde**
crab cocktail **le cocktail de crevettes**
crayfish **les écrevisses**
melon **le melon**
mussels **les moules**
smoked salmon **le saumon fumé**
sardines **les sardines**
clams **les palourdes**

Soups

soup of the day **le potage du jour**
vegetable soup **la soupe de légumes**
noodle soup **le potage avec des pâtes**
tomato soup **la soupe de tomates**
chicken broth **le bouillon de poulet**
beef broth **le bouillon de bœuf**

Salads

green salad **la salade verte**
mixed salad/tossed salad **la salade composée**
potato salad **la salade de pommes de terre**
garden lettuce salad **la laitue**
tomato salad **la salade de tomates**

Salad Dressings

Roquefort dressing **la sauce Roquefort**
vinaigrette dressing **la vinaigrette**
Italian dressing **italien**
French dressing **français**
Russian dressing **russe**

Vinegar and Oil

olive oil **l'huile d'olive**
sunflower oil **l'huile de tournesol**
balsamic vinegar **le vinaigre balsamique**
herb vinegar **le vinaigre aromatisé aux herbes**
fruit vinegar **le vinaigre de fruits**
wine vinegar **le vinaigre de vin**
lemon vinegar **le vinaigre de citron**
soy sauce **la sauce de soja**
mayonnaise **la mayonnaise**

One specialty from Nice is the *salade niçoise*: olives, tuna, and tomatoes over green lettuce.

From Ocean and Lake

eel **l'anguille**
grayling **l'ombre**
perch **la perche**
blue fish **le poisson bleu**
flounder **le flet**
trout **la truite**
golden perch **la rascasse du Nord**
golden bream **la dorade**
shark **le requin**
pike **le brochet**
halibut **le flétan**
herring **le hareng**
codfish **la morue**
carp **la carpe**
salmon **le saumon**
mackerel **le maquereau**
mullet **le rouget**
ray/skate **la race**
roe **les œufs de poisson**
red perch **le sébaste**
anchovies **les anchois**
sardines **les sardines**
haddock **l'églefin**
flounder **la sole**
swordfish **l'espadon**
sea-bream **le loup de mer**
sea-pike **le merluche**
anglerfish **la lotte de mer/la baudroie**
sole **la sole**
turbot **le turbot**
smelt **l'éperlan**
salt cod **la morue**
tuna **le thon**
squid **le calamar**
catfish **le silure**
wolf perch **le bar**
pike-perch **le sandre**

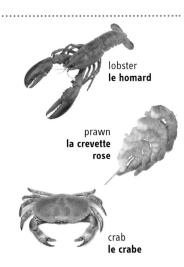

lobster
le homard

prawn
la crevette rose

crab
le crabe

oyster **l'huître**
scallop **la coquille Saint-Jacques**
scallop **la coquille**
shrimp **la crevette grise**
crayfish **l'écrevisse**
spiny lobster **la langouste**
mussel **la moule**
sea snail **l'escargot de mer**
spider crab **l'araignée de mer**
clam **la palourde**

In French crab is called *crabe*.

Types of Meat

mutton
le mouton

veal
le veau

rabbit
le lapin

lamb
l'agneau

beef
le bœuf

pork
le cochon

suckling pig
le cochon de lait

kid
le cabri

goat
la chèvre

Steaks

rare **saignant**
medium **à point**
well done **bien cuit**

Specialties

Daube provençale pot roast with vegetables and olives.

Choucroute à l'alsacienne sauerkraut with pork belly, pork knuckle, and sausages.

Blanquette de veau fricasseed veal, pot-au-feu, beef stew, veal knuckle, marrow bones, and vegetables.

Pork is *viande de porc*.

Cuts of Meat

steak **le bifteck**

round steak **la jambe**

sweetbread **le ris**

tip **l'épaule**

fillet steak **le bifteck dans le filet**

neck **le cou**

leg **le jarret**

brain **la cervelle**

prime rib **la côte**

cutlet **la côtelette**

tripe **les tripes**

liver **le foie**

loin **la longe**

loin steak **le bifteck de longe**

kidneys **les reins**

roast filet **la noix**

spare ribs **la côte**

roast beef **le rosbif**

saddle of lamb/chine of beef **le dos**

rump steak **la côte de bœuf**

ham **le jambon**

deep-fried cutlet **l'escalope**

tail **la queue**

bacon **le lard fumé**

tongue **la langue**

rib steak **l'entrecôte**

Ways to Prepare

browned **passé à la poêle**

roast **le rôti**

low cholesterol **pauvre en cholestérol**

low-fat **pas trop gras**

deep fried **frit**

for diabetics **pour les diabétiques**

baked **cuit au four**

fried **rôti**

steamed **cuit à la vapeur**

stuffed **farci**

grilled **grillé**

chopped/ground **haché**

boiled **bouilli**

smoked **fumé**

shaken/stirred **battu**

braised **cuit à l'étouffée**

stewed **tailladé**

larded **entrelardé**

glazed **glacé**

stew **ragoût**

meat loaf **rouleau de viande hachée**

low-calorie **pauvre en calories**

breaded **pané**

raw **cru**

tangy **piquant**

For roasting, you can also say *rôtir à petit feu*–literally, to cook over a small fire.

Poultry

duck
le canard

chicken
le poulet

goose
l'oie

turkey
le dindon

pigeon
le pigeon

Wild Game

pheasant
le faisan

hare
le lièvre

stag
le cerf

partridge
la perdrix

venison
le chevreuil

wild duck
le canard sauvage

boar
le sanglier

pullet **le poulette**

capon **le chapon**

guinea fowl **la pintade**

young fattened hen **le poulet d'engrais**

quail **la caille**

grilled chicken **le poulet rôti**

The French like to eat frogs' legs *(cuisses de grenouille)*, preferably with lots of garlic.

Potatoes

french fries
les frites

roasted potatoes **les pommes de terre sautées**

baked potatoes **les pommes de terre cuites au four**

potatoes au gratin **le gratin de pommes de terre/le gratin dauphinois**

mashed potatoes **la purée**

pan-fried potatoes **les pommes de terre à la bernoise**

boiled potatoes **les pommes de terre cuites à l'eau**

sweet potatoes/yams **les patates douces**

Noodles

flat noodles **les taglitesses**
macaroni **les macaronis**

spaghetti **les spaghettis**

Rice

wild rice **riz sauvage**
cooked rice **riz cuit**
fried rice **riz frit**
whole-grain/brown rice **riz complet**

Bread

rolls
le petit pain

black bread
le pain noir

whole wheat bread
le pain complet

white bread
le pain blanc/la baguette

corn **le maïs**
wheat **le blé**
rye **le seigle**
barley **l'orge**
oats **l'avoine**

The French eat two hot meals a day.

Vegetables

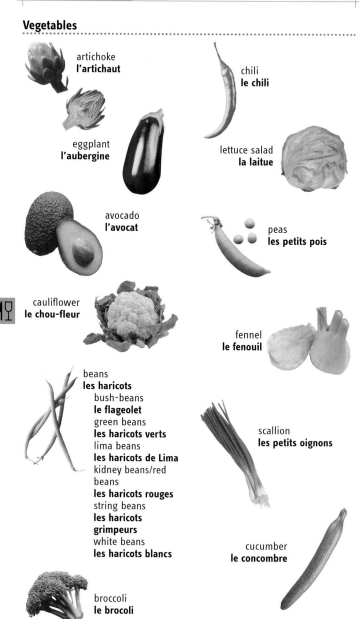

artichoke
l'artichaut

chili
le chili

eggplant
l'aubergine

lettuce salad
la laitue

avocado
l'avocat

peas
les petits pois

cauliflower
le chou-fleur

fennel
le fenouil

beans
les haricots
  bush-beans
  le flageolet
  green beans
  les haricots verts
  lima beans
  les haricots de Lima
  kidney beans/red beans
  les haricots rouges
  string beans
  les haricots grimpeurs
  white beans
  les haricots blancs

scallion
les petits oignons

cucumber
le concombre

broccoli
le brocoli

In southern France, people cook up a delicious *ratatouille* using eggplant, zucchini, and tomatoes.

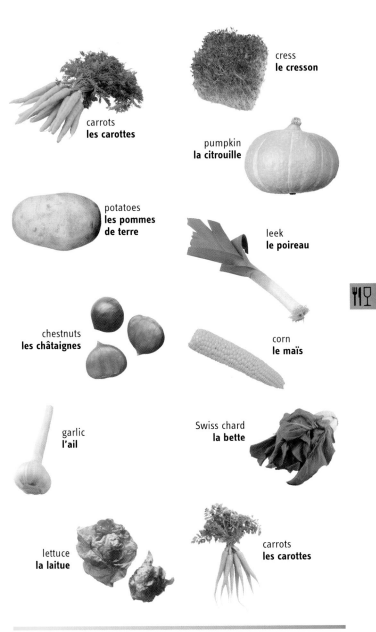

cress
le cresson

carrots
les carottes

pumpkin
la citrouille

potatoes
**les pommes
de terre**

leek
le poireau

chestnuts
les châtaignes

corn
le maïs

garlic
l'ail

Swiss chard
la bette

lettuce
la laitue

carrots
les carottes

La choucroûte (sauerkraut) is a specialty from Alsace. It is eaten garnished with all kinds of sausages and meats.

Vegetables

okra
gombo

black radish
le radis noir

pepper
le poivron

brussels sprouts
le chou de Bruxelles

green pepper/bell pepper
le peperoni

red beets
le navet rouge

mushrooms
les champignons

red cabbage
le chou rouge

radishes
les radis

turnips
le navet

People make a distinction among *poivrons rouges/verts/jaunes* (red, green, and yellow peppers).

zucchini
les courgettes

asparagus
les asperges

spinach
les épinards

tiny green peas
les petits pois doux

celery
le céleri

onions
les oignons

tomatoes
les tomates

watercress **le cresson**
chicory **la chicorée**
endive **l'endive**
garden salad **la salade des champs**
chick-pea **le pois chiche**
cabbage **le chou**
lentils **les lentilles**
sauerkraut **la choucroute**
black salsify **le scorsonère/salsifis noir**
celery **le céleri**
rutabaga **le navet**

cabbage
le chou blanc

savoy cabbage
le chou frisé

The typical southern *ratatouille* is seasoned with a *bouquet garni* (a bundle of herbs).

Herbs and Spices

basil
le basilique

sage
la sauge

dill
l'aneth

thyme
le thym

ginger
le gingembre

cinnamon
la cannelle

mint
la menthe

oregano
l'origan

parsley
le persil

rosemary
le romarin

vinegar **le vinaigre**
tarragon **l'estragon**
capers **la câpre**
chervil **le cerfeuil**
caraway **le cumin**
bayleaves **les feuilles de laurier**
marjoram **la marjolaine**
horseradish **le raifort**
nutmeg **la noix de muscat**
clove **le clou de girofle**
pepper **le poivre**
saffron **le safran**
salt **le sel**
chive **la ciboulette**
mustard **la moutarde**
vanilla **la vanille**
sugar **le sucre**

The French word for *cumin* is *le cumin*. *Kummel* is a cumin liqueur whose name is based on the German word for cumin.

Cheese

fresh cheese
le fromage frais

grated cheese
le fromage râpé

sheep's milk cheese
le fromage de brebis

goat's milk cheese
le fromage de chèvre

France is a cheese country par excellence. France truly has everything for cheese lovers: from cream cheese to hard cheese, and made with milk from sheep, goats, or cows.

Specialties include Camembert from Normandy and Brie, which is available so perfectly aged only in France, as well as Roquefort, a blue mold cheese.

France is also famous for its many varieties of goat cheeses. There are all kinds, from creamy to hard, and true connoisseurs are not put off by an unappetizing exterior.

There are reportedly 370 types of cheese in France, and an immense assortment of them can be found in the specialty cheese shops, small markets, and even supermarkets.

Fruit

pineapple
l'ananas

apple
la pomme

apricot
l'abricot

banana
la banane

pears
la poire

blackberries
les mûres

strawberries
les fraises

Une salade de fruits is a fruit salad.

Fruit

figs
les figues

cherries
les cerises

pomegranate
la grenade

kiwi fruit
les kiwis

grapefruit
le pamplemousse

coconut
la noix de coco

blueberries
les myrtilles

lime
la limette

raspberries
les framboises

mango
la mangue

persimmon
les kakis

carambola
carambolier

melon
le melon

If the word for *watermelon—pastèque*—doesn't spring to your lips, you can also say *melon d'eau.*

orange
l'orange

watermelon
la pastèque

papaya
la papaye

lemon
le citron

peach
la pêche

dates **les dattes**
Spanish chestnuts **les châtaignes**
elderberries **le sureau**
currants **les groseilles rouges**
cactus-fruit **le fruit du cactus**
litchee **la litchi/la prune chinoise**
tangerine **la mandarine**
mulberries **les baies du mûrier**
mirabelle/yellow plum **la mirabelle**

plum
la prune

medlar **le nèfle**
passion-fruit **les fruits de la passion**
cranberries **les myrtilles rouges**
quince **le coing**
ramboutan **la ramboutan**
rhubarb **la rhubarbe**
raisins **les raisins secs**

pomelo
la pamplemousse

gooseberry **la groseille à maquereau**
tamarind **le tamarin**

grape
le raisin

Blackcurrants are *cassis*–many people may be familiar with it from the drink of the same name.

Nuts

peanut
les cacahouètes

pecan nut
la noix de pecan

hazelnut
les noisettes

pistachios
les pistaches

coconut
la noix de coco

walnut
la noix

almond
les amandes

Brazil nuts **la noix du Parà**

pine nuts **le pignon**

sunflower seeds **les graines de tournesol**

A nutcracker is a *casse-noisettes*; a walnut tree is *un noyer*.

Cakes

apple pie **la tarte aux pommes**

cheesecake **la tarte au fromage frais**

blueberry pie **la tarte aux myrtilles**

carrot nut cake **la tarte aux noix et aux carottes**

cherry pie **la tarte aux cerises**

lemon cake **la tarte au citron**

fruit tart/pie **la tarte aux fruits**

petits fours **les petits fours**

chocolate cake **le gâteau au chocolat**

vanilla cream pie **la tarte à la vanille**

cream **la crème Chantilly**

Desserts

a scoop of ice cream **la glace à une boule**

assorted ice creams **glace mixte**

ice cream cone **le cornet**

ice cream in a cup **la glace dans une coupe**

ice cream on a stick **le cornet de glace**

coffee with ice cream **le café liégeois**

flavor **le parfum**

with cream **avec de la crème Chantilly**

vanilla pudding **le flan à la vanille**

almond pudding **le flan aux amandes**

chocolate pudding **le flan au chocolat/la mousse au chocolat**

bread pudding **le flan au pain**

In France most bakeries (*boulangeries*) also sell pastries (*pâtisseries*). Most French bakers offer a wide assortment of *tartelettes* (fruit pastries) and *flans* made of egg, flour, and milk baked in the oven and sold in square or triangular slices.

At the bakery you will also find the delightful éclairs, plus cream tarts, which are often too sweet for many people's taste. On the other hand, you won't find sumptuous cream *gateaux*.

Only whipping cream is *crème Chantilly*; cream is simply *crème*.

Snacks

A classic between-meals snack in France is the *croque-monsieur*, a hot, toasted sandwich made with ham and melted cheese.

Anyone who wants to get to know France's delicious snacks will also buy a *baguette* and keep a watch out for a cheese shop or a *traiteur*, where you can get *pâtés*, *terrines*, hams, and many kinds of prepared meals—and enjoy it all on a shady park bench.

Pizza

Pizza has been known as an inexpensive snack in Naples for 200 years. Pizza's worldwide conquest began in 1895 when a homesick Neapolitan living in New York opened the first pizzeria. As late as the 1960s the rest of Italy knew of pizza only through hearsay.

Pizza Margherita tomatoes, mozzarella, basil

Pizza alla napolitana tomatoes, mozzarella, anchovies, oregano, olive oil

Pizza calabrese tomatoes, tuna, anchovies, olives, capers

Pizza alle vongole tomatoes, oregano, mussels, parsley, garlic

Pizza quattro stagioni tomatoes, mozzarella, mushrooms, baked ham, artichoke hearts

Pizza al prosciutto tomatoes, mozzarella, baked ham

Pizza con funghi tomatoes, mozzarella, mushrooms, garlic, parsley

Pizza alla siciliana tomatoes, mozzarella, paprika, salami, mushrooms

Pizza alla Pugliese tomatoes, mozzarella, onions

Pizza Romana tomatoes, mozzarella, anchovies, capers, olives

Pizza alla diavola tomatoes, mozzarella, salami, pepperoni

Pilla alla "Re Ferdinando" tomatoes, mozzarella, crab, garlic, parsley

Pizza puttanesca tomatoes, mozzarella, bacon, olives, capers, anchovies

Calzone folded-over pizza with ham, mozzarella, often with ricotta

In addition to small slices of pizza, at every street corner there are the typical *pans bagnas*—large, round sandwiches made with tomatoes, tuna, lettuce.

What Would You Like?

a cup of coffee
une tasse de café

a pot of tea
une théière

a glass of orange juice
un verre de jus d'orange

a bottle of milk
une bouteille de lait
hot milk
le lait chaud
cold milk
le lait froid

a can of cola
une boîte de coca cola

Coffee

coffee **le café**
with milk **avec du lait**

with sugar **avec du sucre**
with cream **avec de la crème Chantilly**
with foamed milk **le café crème**
black **noir**
small **serré**
medium **normal**
large **allongé**
decaffeinated coffee **café décaféiné**
espresso **l'express**
cappuccino **le café crème**
mocha **le moka**

Tea

black tea **le thé noir**
peppermint tea **l'infusion de menthe**
fennel tea **le thé au fenouil**
camomile tea **la camomille**
fruit tea **le thé aux fruits**
herbal tea **la tisane**
flavored tea **le thé aromatisé**
unflavored tea **le thé non aromatisé**
with lemon **le thé au citron**

A *can* is normally *une boîte*. A can of food is *une boîte de conserve*.

Refreshments

mineral water **l'eau minérale**
carbonated **gazeuse**
non-carbonated **plate**
fruit juice **le jus de fruits**
apple juice **le jus de pomme**
orange juice **le jus d'orange**
grape juice **le jus de raisin**
tomato juice **le jus de tomate**
lemonade **la limonade**

Miscellaneous

cocoa **le cacao**
milk **le lait**
hot/cold chocolate **le chocolat**

Beer

beer **la bière**
on tap **à la pression**
low alcohol **pas trop alcoolisée**
non-alcoholic **sans alcool**
bottle **la bouteille**
can **la boîte**

Liquors

without ice **sans glaçons**
with ice **avec des glaçons**
schnapps **l'eau de vie**
herbal schnapps **l'eau de vie aux plantes**
liqueur **la liqueur**
cognac **le cognac**

Specialties

Pastis, the classic aperitif made from anise. Pastis is never served with ice, which is used only in the water added to the liqueur.

Crème de cassis (liqueur made from red currants) is mixed with white wine.

Cognac, the brandy from the region north of Bordelais. The highest grades (aged in casks over six years) are Napoléon, Extra, XO, and Vielle Réserve.

Armagnac is the brandy from Gascogne. Classification similar to that of cognac.

Cidre is apple wine from Normandy. Thoroughly fermented it's referred to as brut.

Calvados: apple schnapps from Normandy, made from cider. Napoléon, Extra, and Hor d'Age are aged longer than six years.

Marc (grape residue) is burnt schnapps, similar to grappa. *Marc de champagne* is well known.

The French prefer non-carbonated mineral water, *de l'eau plate*; there are countless brands to choose from: Evian, Thonon, and Volvic, to name just a few.

Wine and Champagne

Can I please see the wine list?
Pouvez-vous me monter la carte des vins ?

cork
le bouchon

corkscrew
le tire-bouchon

cooler
le seau à champagne

I would have like to have a bottle of wine.
Je voudrais une bouteille de vin.

What will go best with the meal?
Quel est le vin qui convient à notre menu ?

Is this a good year?
C'est une bonne année ?

Can I taste the wine?
Est-ce que je peux goûter le vin ?

The wine tastes like cork.
Le vin a un goût de bouchon.

The wine is too warm.
Le vin est trop chaud.

Can you please cool the wine?
Pouvez-vous mettre le vin au frais ?

wine-growing area **le vignoble**

rosé **le vin rosé**

red wine **le vin rouge**

vineyard **la vigne**

vintage **les vendanges**

wine tasting **la dégustation du vin**

white wine **le vin blanc**

smooth **onctueux**

light **doux**

fruity **fruité**

dry **sec**

sweet **sucré**

To pull the cork is *déboucher une bouteille.*

Wine-Producing Regions

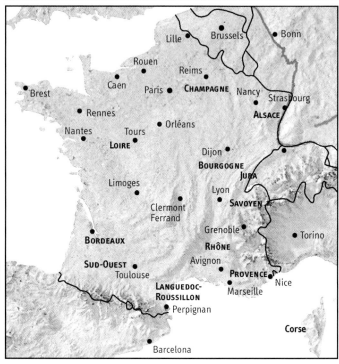

France is Europe's wine-growing country. Wines such as Beaujolais and Chablis (both from Burgundy) have become fashionable drinks for us as well.

Every region has its typical wines. The noblest wines come from Burgundy and Bordeaux; they are esteemed worldwide and often overpriced.

Alsace produces primarily earthy white wines, Provence fruity rosés. For a long time Languedoc-Roussillon was the source of modest mass-produced wines, but here too higher quality wines are increasingly being cultivated.

The *appellations contrôlées* are an assurance of quality origin, type of vine, and cultivation method, but only in part a guarantee of quality. Wine connoisseurs have to be informed about vintners and vintages.

A *vin de pays* is not necessarily a pedestrian *vin ordinaire*. This class also includes many outstanding wines.

Widespread types of vines include Cabernet Sauvignon (southwest, Bordeaux, here blended with Merlot and others), Chardonnay, and Pinot Noir (Burgundy), Gamay (Beaujolais), and Sauvignon Blanc (Loire).

A glass of wine is *un verre de vin*; a bottle of wine, *une bouteille de vin*.

Shopping

What's Most Important

Do you have toothbrushes?
Pouvez-vous me donner une brosse à dent ?

Where do I find a shoe-store?
Pouvez-vous m'indiquer un magasin de chaussures ?

working hours/open hours
les horaires d'ouverture

closed
fermé

I would just like to look around.
Je regarde simplement.

How much does that cost?
Combien est-ce que ça coûte ?

That is too expensive.
C'est trop cher.

Do you have something cheaper?
Avez-vous quelque chose de plus abordable ?

Can I try on the shoes?
Est-ce que je peux essayer les chaussures ?

That is too big.
Cette pointure/taille est trop grande.

That is too small.
Cette pointure/taille est trop petite.

Forget Something?

hairbrush
la brosse à cheveux

underwear
la lingerie

comb
le peigne

toothbrush
la brosse à dents

band-aid
le pansement

towel
la serviette de bain

soap
le savon

pajamas
le pyjama

shoelaces
les lacets (chaussures)

sunblock
la crème solaire

toothpaste
le dentifrice

The French make distinctions among types of sizes: with reference to shoes, the term is *pointure*; with clothing, it's *taille*; and with shirts and collars, *encolure*.

Have you already been
served/waited on?
Puis-je vous aider ?

Thanks, I'm just
looking around.
**Non merci, je jette
juste un coup
d'œil.**

Can I help you?
Puis-je vous aider ?

Yes, I would like a pair of
pants.
**Oui, je voudrais un
pantalon.**

These pants are on
sale.
**Ces pantalons sont
en solde.**

Which size is
that?
**C'est quelle
taille ?**

That is size 38.
**C'est un trente-
huit.**

Ah, I think that is
too small.
**Oh, je pense qu'il
est trop petit.**

Would you like to try
it on?
**Voulez-vous
l'essayer ?**

Yes. Where are the
changing rooms?
**Oui, où se trouve la cabine
d'essayage ?**

I need is a commonly used expression; you can avoid it by saying instead *I would
like*: *je voudrais* or even *j'ai besoin de.*

What You Often Need

Thanks, that is all.
Ça va merci.

I would like a pound of cherries.
Je voudrais un demi-kilo de cerises.

Do you have toothbrushes?
Est-ce que vous avez des brosses à dents ?

Where are the neckties?
Où se trouvent les cravates ?

What can you recommend?
Que me conseillez-vous ?

Do you have any special offers?
Est-ce qu'il y a des offres spéciales ?

I have seen a pair of shoes in the display window.
J'ai vu une paire de chaussures en vitrine.

I don't want to spend more than ten euro.
Je ne veux pas dépenser plus de 10 euro.

I like these.
Celles-ci me plaisent.

I don't like these.
Celles-ci ne me plaisent pas.

That is not exactly what I want.
Ce ne sont pas celles que je cherchais.

What do they cost?
Combien coûtent-elles ?

Where is the cashier?
Où se trouve la caisse ?

I would like a receipt.
Je voudrais le bon de caisse.

Can you wrap them for me?
Est-ce que vous pouvez les empaqueter ?

Can you deliver that to me in the hotel?
Est-ce que vous pouvez m'envoyer le paquet à l'hôtel ?

Do you deliver to foreign countries too?
Est-ce que vous faites des livraisons dans le monde entier ?

I would like to exchange this.
Je voudrais échanger ce que j'ai acheté.

I would like to make a complaint.
J'ai une réclamation à formuler.

The product is defective.
Le produit a un défaut.

I would like my money back.
Pouvez-vous me rendre l'argent ?

I'll take these.
Je prends celles-ci.

Can you show me something else?
Avez-vous autre chose à me montrer ?

Do you have a shopping bag?
Avez-vous un sac ?

One common expression is *something different*: *autre chose.*

What You Hear or Read

Puis-je vous aider ?
Can I help you?

On vous sert ?
Have you already been
served/waited on?

Vous désirez ?
What would you like?

Quelle est votre taille/pointure ?
What is your size?

liquidation, soldes
Sale

Vous voulez autre chose ?
Will there be something else?

Je regrette, nous n'en avons pas.
We don't have that, unfortunately.

Ça fait 10 euro.
That will be 10 euro.

**Vous payez comptant ou avec une
carte de crédit ?**
Are you paying in cash or by credit
card?

Que cherchez-vous ?
What are you looking for?

In a Department Store

department
le rayon

elevator
l'ascenseur

entrance
l'entrée

cash register/cashier
la caisse

customer service
le service clients

emergency exit
la sortie de secours

escalator
l'escalier roulant

floor
l'étage

toilets
les toilettes

stairways
les marches

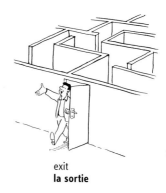

exit
la sortie

If you travel to France in September, you may encounter the end of summer
sales, *les soldes d'été.*

Shops

souvenir shop **le magasin de souvenirs**

antique shop **le commerce d'antiquités**

pharmacy **la pharmacie**

bakery **la boulangerie**

florist **le fleuriste**

book store **la librairie**

computer store **le commerce d'ordinateurs**

drugstore **la pharmacie**

shopping center **la grande surface**

retail sale **la vente au détail**

hardware **la quincaillerie**

electrical appliances store **le commerce d'électroménagers**

bicycle store **le magasin pour bicyclettes**

delicatessen **le traiteur**

fish store **la poissonnerie**

flea market **le marché aux puces**

photo store **le photographe**

hairdresser **le coiffeur**

fresh produce stand **fruits et légumes**

household merchandise **le magasin d'articles ménagers**

jeweler **la bijouterie**

department store **le grand magasin**

clothing store **le commerce d'habillement**

pastry shop **la pâtisserie**

cosmetics store **l'institut de beauté**

art gallery **la galerie d'art**

arts and crafts **les arts décoratifs**

notions **la mercerie**

grocery store **le magasin d'alimentation/l'épicerie**

leather goods **la maroquinerie**

market **le marché**

butcher **la boucherie**

creamery/dairy **le fromager**

furniture **les meubles**

music store **le magasin de disques**

fruit stand **fruits et légumes**

optician **l'opticien**

perfumery **la parfumerie**

furrier **le magasin de fourrures**

pawnbroker **le mont-de-piété**

health food store **produits diététiques**

cleaning/dry cleaning **la blanchisserie/le pressing**

travel agency **l'agence de voyage**

record store **le magasin de disques**

tailor **l'atelier de couture**

stationery **la papeterie**

shoe store **le magasin de chaussures**

shoemaker **le cordonnier**

second-hand store **le magasin de vêtements d'occasion**

toy store **le magasin de jouets**

liquor store **les vins et liqueurs**

sporting goods store **le magasin d'articles de sport**

fabric store **le magasin de tissus**

supermarket **le supermarché**

candy **les friandises**

tobacco store **le bureau de tabac**

pet shop **les animaux**

second-hand dealer **l'antiquaire/le brocanteur**

watchmaker **l'horlogerie**

laundromat **la laverie automatique**

wine store **vins et liqueurs**

news shop **le kiosque à journaux**

The shopping center is also referred to as *le centre commercial* in French.

Colors

■	black **noir**		■	green **vert**
□	white **blanc**		■	blue **bleu**
■	gray **gris**		■	pink **rose**
■	red **rouge**		■	orange **orange**
■	yellow **jaune**		■	purple **mauve**

Designs

colored/colorful
coloré

checkered
à carreaux

mottled
mélangé

printed/patterned
avec des motifs

knotted
bouclé

light
clair

dark
foncé

high-contrast
très contrasté

low-contrast
peu contrasté

matte/dull
opaque

glossy/shiny
brillant

polka-dotted
pointillé

 vertically striped
à raies longitudinales

 diagonally striped
à raies transversales

 black-and-white
noir et blanc

Here are some shades of blue in French: *bleu ciel* (sky blue), *bleu marine* (navy blue), and *bleu vert* (greenish blue).

At the Market

Cherries, beautiful cherries!
Des cerises, mes belles cerises !

They look nice.
Celles-ci sont belles.

Would you like a taste?
Voulez-vous les goûter ?

Mh, delicious. Give me one pound.
Mh, c'est délicieux. J'en voudrais un demi-kilo.

What is that?
Qu'est-ce que c'est ?

Salsify.
Du salsifis noir.

How do you prepare it?
Comment faut-il le préparer ?

You cook it like a vegetable.
Comme des légumes.

To go shopping is *faire le marché/faire son marché.*

Foods

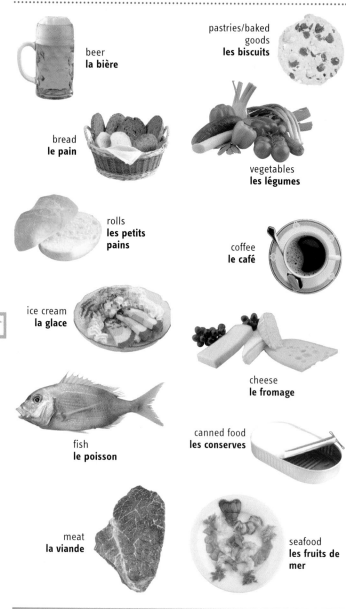

beer
la bière

pastries/baked
goods
les biscuits

bread
le pain

vegetables
les légumes

rolls
**les petits
pains**

coffee
le café

ice cream
la glace

cheese
le fromage

fish
le poisson

canned food
les conserves

meat
la viande

seafood
**les fruits de
mer**

If you are looking to buy dairy products, look for *une laiterie* or *une crémerie*.

organic food **les produits biologiques**

butter **le beurre**

vinegar **le vinaigre**

beverages **les boissons**

spices **les épices**

semolina **la semoule**

honey **le miel**

cake **le gâteau**

margarine **la margarine**

jam **la confiture**

mayonnaise **la mayonnaise**

flour **la farine**

milk products/dairy products **les produits laitiers**

oil **l'huile**

chocolates **le chocolat**

curd **le fromage blanc**

rice **le riz**

salt **le sel**

sour cream **la crème fraiche**

whipped cream **la crème Chantilly**

chocolate **le chocolat**

mustard **la moutarde**

candies **les douceurs/sucreries**

yogurt **le yaourt**

sugar **le sucre**

→ Also see FISH AND SHELLFISH, p. 117; TYPES OF MEAT, p.118; POULTRY, p. 120; VEGETABLES, p. 122; FRUITS, p. 127; and NUTS, p. 130

nuts
les noix

fruit
les fruits

salad
la salade

tea
le thé

wine
le vin

noodles
les pâtes

sausage
la saucisse

If you want jelly, ask for *confiture*.

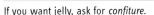

shopping cart
le chariot

shopping
basket
le panier

shopping bag
le sac

Quantities

100 grams
100 grammes

a pound
un demi-kilo/une livre

a kilo
un kilo

a piece
un morceau

a slice
une tranche

a liter
un litre

a packet
un paquet

a bottle
une bouteille

a can
une boîte/un pot

a glassful/a glass of ...
un verre

Sales Conversations

I would like some butter.
Je voudrais du beurre.

Do you have flour?
Avez-vous de la farine ?

A bit more, please.
Encore un peu, s'il vous plaît.

Can I taste it?
Est-ce que je peux goûter ?

Some more?
Vous en voulez encore ?

Anything else?
Avec ceci ?/Voulez-vous autre chose ?

Thanks, that is all.
C'est tout merci.

If you want an undetermined amount, say *je voudrais du beurre, du lait, de la crème.*

Drugs and Cosmetics

bath sponge
l'éponge

perfume
le parfum

batteries
les piles

band-aid
le pansement

hairbrush
la brosse à cheveux

razor
le rasoir

comb
le peigne

razor blades
les lames de rasoir

clothes brush
la brosse pour vêtements

shaving brush
le blaireau

shaving cream
la mousse à raser

condom
le préservatif

lipstick
le rouge à lèvres

safety pin
l'épingle à nourrice

For a Band-Aid, use *un pansement adhésif* or *un sparadrap.*

Drugs and Cosmetics

suntan creme **la crème solaire**

mirror **le miroir**

matches **les allumettes**

bandage **le bandage**

toothbrush **la brosse à dents**

eyeshadow **le fard à paupières**
mouthwash **le collutoire**
nail file **la lime à ongles**
nail polish **le vernis à ongles**
nail polish remover **le dissolvant**
nail scissors **les ciseaux à ongles**

tissues/kleenex **les mouchoirs en papier/kleenex**
tweezers **la pince à épiler**
powder **la poudre**
cleaners/cleaning products **le détergent**
rouge **le fard**
sponge **l'éponge**
soap **le savon**
scrubbing brush **le brosse**
dishwashing liquid **le liquide vaisselle**
tampons **les tampons**
handkerchiefs **les mouchoirs**
toilet paper **le papier-toilette**
face cloths **le gant de toilette**
laundry detergent (powder) **la lessive en poudre**
cotton **le coton**
mascara **le rimmel**
toothpaste **le dentifrice**
dental floss **le fil dentaire**

concealer **le crayon**
eyebrow pencil **le mascara**
sanitary napkins **les serviettes hygiéniques**
deodorant **le déodorant**
disinfectant **le produit pour désinfecter**
stain-remover **le détachant**
shampoo **le shampoing**
hand cream **la crème pour les mains**
insect repellent **l'insecticide**
body lotion **le lait pour le corps**

A washcloth is *un gant de toilette*.

For Children and Babies

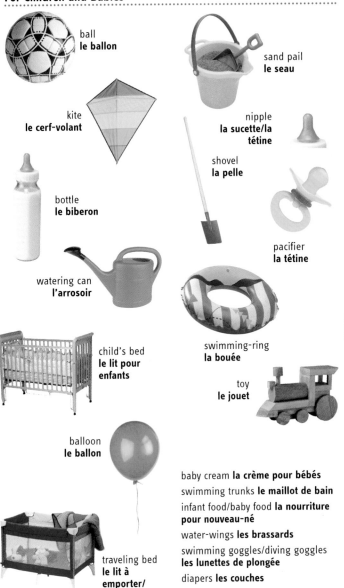

ball
le ballon

sand pail
le seau

kite
le cerf-volant

nipple
la sucette/la tétine

shovel
la pelle

bottle
le biberon

pacifier
la tétine

watering can
l'arrosoir

child's bed
le lit pour enfants

swimming-ring
la bouée

toy
le jouet

balloon
le ballon

baby cream **la crème pour bébés**
swimming trunks **le maillot de bain**
infant food/baby food **la nourriture pour nouveau-né**
water-wings **les brassards**
swimming goggles/diving goggles **les lunettes de plongée**
diapers **les couches**

traveling bed
le lit à emporter/ le lit de camp

An infant is also called *un bébé* or *un nourisson*.

Tobacco Products

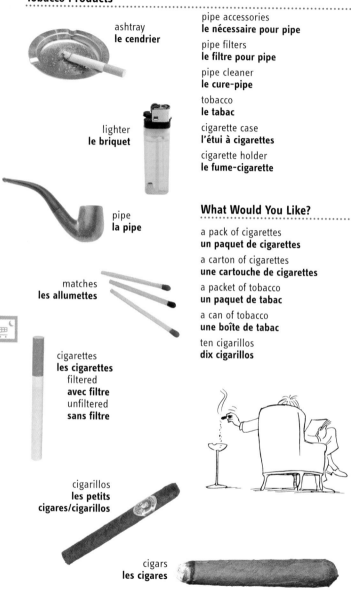

ashtray
le cendrier

pipe accessories
le nécessaire pour pipe

pipe filters
le filtre pour pipe

pipe cleaner
le cure-pipe

tobacco
le tabac

cigarette case
l'étui à cigarettes

cigarette holder
le fume-cigarette

lighter
le briquet

pipe
la pipe

What Would You Like?

a pack of cigarettes
un paquet de cigarettes

a carton of cigarettes
une cartouche de cigarettes

a packet of tobacco
un paquet de tabac

a can of tobacco
une boîte de tabac

ten cigarillos
dix cigarillos

matches
les allumettes

cigarettes
les cigarettes
filtered
avec filtre
unfiltered
sans filtre

cigarillos
**les petits
cigares/cigarillos**

cigars
les cigares

Trains have *des compartiments fumeurs/non-fumeurs* (smoking and non-smoking compartments).

Clothing

I am looking for a skirt.
Je voudrais une jupe.

I am looking for something to go with it.
Qu'est-ce que je pourrais mettre avec ?

Can I try that on?
Est-ce que je peux l'essayer ?

I'll take that.
Je le prends.

I don't like that.
Ça ne me plaît pas.

I don't like the color.
Je n'aime pas la couleur.

Where is the changing room?/dressing room?
Où se trouve la cabine d'essayage ?

Do you have a mirror?
Est-ce qu'il y a une glace ?

The sleeves are too long.
Les manches sont trop longues.

Can you alter it?
Est-ce que vous pouvez faire la retouche ?

How long will the alteration take?
Dans combien de temps sera-t-il prêt ?

What You Hear

Quelle est votre taille ?
What is your size?

Voulez-vous l'essayer ?
Would you like to try it on?

Voulez-vous le changer ?
Should we alter it?

De quelle couleur le voulez-vous ?
Which color?

Sizes

I wear size 38. **Je porte du 38.**

small **petit(e)**

medium **moyen(ne)**

large **grand(e)**

extra large **très grande**

Do you have a larger/smaller one?
Est-ce que vous l'avez plus grand/plus petit ?

That fits well. **Il/elle me va.**

That doesn't fit. **Il/elle ne me va pas.**

That is too ... **Il est...**
    small **petit**
    big **grand**
    tight/narrow **étroit**
    loose/wide **large**
    short **court**
    long **long**

Faire du lèche-vitrines means to go window-shopping (literally, *to lick the display windows*).

Articles of Clothing

 swimsuit
le maillot de bain

 trunks
le slip de bain

 bikini
le bikini

 bowtie
le nœud papillon

 gloves
les gants

 hat
le chapeau

 tie
la cravate

 cap
le bonnet

 scarf
l'écharpe

 baseball cap/cap with visor
la casquette

Size Conversions

Men's Suits

Europe	USA
46	36
48	38
50	40
52	42
54	44
56	46
58	48
60	50

Women's Clothing

Europe	USA
38	10
40	12
42	14
44	16
46	18
48	20

Men's Shirts

Europe	USA
36	14
37	14 1/2
38	15
39/40	15 1/2
41	16
42	16 1/2
43	17
44	17 1/2
45	18

For underpants, you can simply say *un slip*. The ladies' equivalent, panties, is *culottes*.

umbrella
le parapluie

handkerchief
le mouchoir

socks
les chaussettes

underpants
le caleçon

anorak/windbreaker/parka **l'anorak**
suit **le complet**
bathrobe **le peignoir**
blazer **le blazer**
blouse **le chemisier**
brassiere/bra **le soutien-gorge**

suit jacket **la jaquette**
dress **la robe**
outfit **le costume**
coat **le manteau**
housecoat **la robe de chambre**
nightshirt **la chemise de nuit**
sweater/pullover **le pull**
raincoat **l'imperméable**
skirt **la jupe**
pajamas **le pyjama**
apron **le tablier**
shorts **le short**
panties **la culotte**
stockings **les chaussettes**
tights **le collant**
t-shirt **le tee-shirt/le t-shirt**
undershirt **le maillot de corps**
slip/petticoat **le jupon**
vest **le gilet**

belt **la ceinture**
scarf **l'écharpe/le foulard**
shirt **la chemise**
pants **le pantalon**
suspenders **les bretelles**
jacket **la veste**

A suit can also be referred to as *un costume*, which applies to both men's and women's suits.

Sewing

thimble
le dé à coudre

button
le bouton

measuring tape
le mètre

sewing needle
l'aiguille

zipper
la fermeture éclair

safety pin
l'épingle de nourrice

sleeves **les manches**
thread **le fil**
elastic **l'élastique**
collar **le col**
cuffs **les poignées**
pin **l'épingle**

Fabrics

What material is this made from?
C'est en quelle matière ?

I would like something in cotton.
Je voudrais du coton.

Is that machine-washable?
Est-ce qu'on peut le laver en machine ?

Can one put this in the dryer?
Est-ce qu'on peut le mettre dans le séchoir à linge ?

Does that shrink when washed?
Est-ce qu'il rétrécit au lavage ?

wrinkle-free/no ironing
ne pas repasser

lining
la doublure

cambric/batiste **le batiste**
cotton **le coton**
corduroy **le velours**
felt **le feutre**
flannel **la flanelle**
terrycloth **le tissu-éponge**
worsted **le tissu peigné**
crepe **le crêpé**
synthetic fiber **la fibre synthétique**
leather **le cuir**
linen **le lin**
microfiber **la microfibre**
poplin **la popeline**
velvet **le velours**
satin **le satin**
silk **la soie**
wool **la laine**

Fabric is *le tissue* or *l'étoffe.*

Leather Goods

gloves
les gants

handbag
le sac à main

suitcase
la valise

tote bag
le sac de voyage

Dry Cleaning, Laundromat

Please clean this garment.
Ce vêtement est à laver.

Which type of cleaning do you recommend?
Quel type de lavage voulez-vous ?

I would like ...
Je voudrais un ...
dry-cleaning
lavage à sec
gentle cleaning
lavage délicat
thorough cleaning
lavage complet

What will that cost?
Combien est-ce que ça coûte ?

How long will it take?
Il faudra combien de temps ?

When can I pick it up again?
Quand puis-je passer retirer mes vêtements ?

Can you send me the garment?
Pouvez-vous me faire livrer le vêtement ?

Here is my address.
Je vous donne mon adresse.

briefcase **la serviette/le porte-documents**

wallet/billfold **le portefeuille**

purse **le porte-monnaie**

belt **la ceinture**

artificial leather **le similicuir**

leather jacket **la veste en cuir**

leather coat **le manteau en cuir**

shoulder bag **le sac en bandoulière**

suede **le daim**

washing machine **la machine à laver**

dryer **le sèche-linge**

spin-dryer **l'essoreuse**

coins **les pièces**

rinse **rincer**

spin-dry **essorer**

hot wash **laver à 90 degrés**

delicate/gentle wash **le programme délicat**

spin-drying **l'essorage**

colored laundry **les vêtements délicats**

hot-water wash **la lessive lavable à 90 degrés**

When *pièce* is used to mean *coin*, *de monnaie* is left unspoken as long as the context is clear.

Shoes

I wear size 37.
Je fais du 37.

The shoes pinch.
Les chaussures me font mal.

The shoes are ...
Les chaussures sont ...
  too narrow
  trop justes
  too wide
  trop larges
  too small
  trop petites
  too big
  trop grandes

Shoes with a...
Chaussures ...
  flat heel.
  avec un talon bas.
  high heel.
  avec un talon haut.

Can you resole the shoes?
Est-ce que vous pouvez ressemeler les chaussures ?

I need new heels.
Je voudrais refaire le talon.

When will the shoes be ready?
Quand est-ce que les chaussures seront prêtes ?

heel **le talon**
bath slippers **les chaussures de bain**
rubber boots **les bottes en caoutchouc**
slippers **les pantoufles**
children's shoes **les chaussures pour enfants**
sandals **les sandales**
shoelaces **les lacets**

shoe brush **la brosse pour chaussures**
shoe cream/shoe polish **le cirage**
shoes **les chaussures**
sole **la semelle**
boots **les bottes**
track shoes **les baskets**
leather soles **la semelle en cuir**
rubber soles **la semelle en caoutchouc**
walking shoes/hiking boots **les chaussures de marche**
climbing boots **les chaussures de randonnée**

Where Does It Pinch?

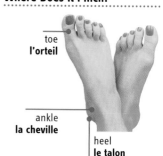

toe
l'orteil

ankle
la cheville

heel
le talon

Size Conversions			
Men's Shoes		Women's Shoes	
Europe	USA	Europe	USA
39	6 1/2	36	5 1/2
40	7 1/2	37	6
41	8 1/2	38	7
42	9	39	7 1/2
43	10	40	8 1/2
44	10 1/2	41	9
45	11		
46	11 1/2		

Doigt de pied can also be used for *toe*.

In the Sporting Goods Shop

swimsuit/bathing suit
le maillot de bain

trunks
le slip de bain

golf clubs
le club de golf

golf bag
le sac de golf

ball
la balle/le ballon

dumb-bell
les haltères

basketball
le basket

backpack/knapsack
le sac à dos

bikini
le bikini

snorkel
le tuba

soccer ball
le ballon de foot

fins
les palmes

golf ball
la balle de golf

sun umbrella/parasol
le parasol

With bathing suits there is a choice between one-piece and two-piece, which are designated as *maillot de bain une pièce* or *maillot deux-pièces*.

In the Sporting Goods Shop

diving goggles/
diving mask
**les lunettes de
plongée**

tennis ball
la balle de tennis

tennis racket
**la raquette de
tennis**

ping-pong ball
la balle de ping-pong

ping-pong rackets/paddles
la raquette de ping-pong

walking shoes/hiking boots
les chaussures de marche

fishing rod
la canne à pêche

bathing cap
le bonnet de bain

hiking boots/climbing boots
les chaussures de montagne

shuttlecock
le volant

badminton rackets
le badminton

inline skates/rollerblades
les Inline-Skates/les patins en ligne

thermal mattress
le tapis de sol

air mattress
le matelas pneumatique

sleeping bag
le sac de couchage

ice skates
les patins à glace

water-wings
les brassards

skateboard
**la planche à roulettes/le skate-
board**

tennis shoes/sneakers
les baskets

track shoes/sneakers
les baskets

windbreaker/parka
l'abri contre le vent

→ Also see TYPES OF SPORTS, p. 179;
AT THE BEACH, p. 183; WATER SPORTS,
p. 186; DIVING, p. 187; HIKING AND
CLIMBING, p. 191

There is a difference between *jouer au golf* (playing golf) and *le Golfe de Saint
Tropez* (the Gulf of Saint Tropez).

Housewares

drain
**le filtre
d'évacuation**

pail/bucket
le seau

broom
le balais

lighter
le briquet

silverware/tableware
les couverts

griddle/frying
pan
la poêle

bottle opener
**l'ouvre-bouteilles,
le décapsuleur**

meat knife
**le couteau à
viande**

ironing
board
**la planche à
repasser**
iron
**le fer à
repasser**

fly-swatter
l'attrape-mouches

can opener
l'ouvre-boîtes

In French *to iron* is *repasser* or *faire le repassage.*

Housewares

hairdryer
le sèche-cheveux

hand-broom
la balayette

dishes
la vaisselle

dishrack
l'égouttoir à vaisselle

coffee mill/coffee grinder
le moulin à café

jug
la cruche

watering can
l'arrosoir

dustpan
la pelle

glass
le verre

candle
la bougie

light bulb
l'ampoule

candlestick
le chandelier

A candle is either *une bougie* or *une chandelle* (*un dîner aux chandelles*).

chain
la chaîne

ladder
l'échelle

clothes brush
la brosse pour vêtements

magnet
l'aimant

saucepan/pot
la casserole

knife
le couteau

corkscrew
le tire-bouchon

creamer/
milk jug
la bouilloire

kitchen sponge
l'éponge

kerosene lamp/
hurricane lamp
la lampe à pétrole

insulated bag
le sac thermique

cleaning rag
le chiffon

In French there are quite a number of verb-noun constructions such as *tire-bou-chon* (corkscrew), *ouvre-boîte* (can opener), and *presse-citron* (lemon squeezer).

Housewares

whisk
le fouet

vacuum cleaner
l'aspirateur

wooden spoon
**la cuillère en
bois**

matches
les allumettes

suction pump
la pompe d'aspiration

cup
la tasse

scissors
les ciseaux

plate
l'assiette

string
la ficelle

pot
la marmite

mirror
le miroir

funnel
l'entonnoir

As in English, scissors are always plural in French: *les ciseaux.*

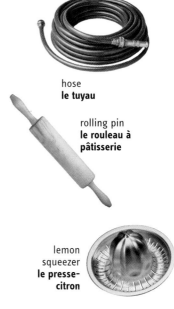

padlock
le cadenas

hose
le tuyau

scale
la balance

rolling pin
le rouleau à pâtisserie

hot water bottle/bed-warmer
la bouillotte

lemon squeezer
le presse-citron

clothes pins
les pinces à linge

laundry-basket
le panier à linge

clothes line
la corde pour étendre le linge

trash bag **le sac-poubelle**

aluminum foil **le papier aluminium**

cup **la tasse**

twine **la ficelle**

plastic wrap **le sachet pour aliments**

paper napkins **les serviettes en papier**

plastic bags **le sachet en plastique**

scrubbing brush **la brosse**

flashlight **la torche**

pocket knife/jacknife **le canif**

immersion heater **le thermoplongeur**

thermos **le bouteille thermos**

fan/ventilator **le ventilateur**

clothes racks **le séchoir/l'étendoir**

For clothesline you can also say *une corde à linge* or un *étendoir* (drying rack).

Tools

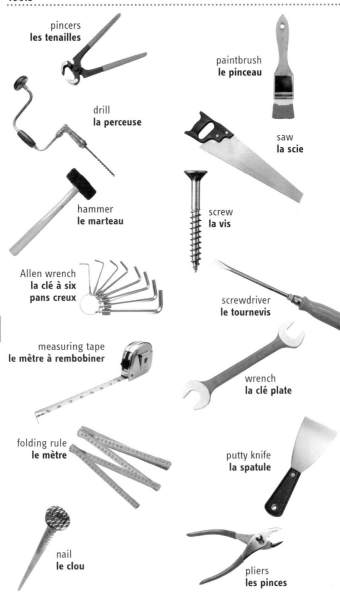

pincers
les tenailles

paintbrush
le pinceau

drill
la perceuse

saw
la scie

hammer
le marteau

screw
la vis

Allen wrench
**la clé à six
pans creux**

screwdriver
le tournevis

measuring tape
le mètre à rembobiner

wrench
la clé plate

folding rule
le mètre

putty knife
la spatule

nail
le clou

pliers
les pinces

Le tuyeau means *pipe*; in a figurative sense it can also be an important tip.

Camping Equipment

grill
le barbecue

cooler
la glacière

deck chair
la chaise longue

air pump
la pompe

kerosene lamp/
hurricane lamp
la lampe à pétrole

string
la corde

butane gas
le gaz butane

gas stove
le fourneau à gaz

hammock
le hamac

tent peg
les piquets

charcoal
le charbon de bois

folding chair
la chaise pliante

folding table
la table pliante

air mattress
le matelas pneumatique

mosquito net
le voile anti-moustiques

propane
le gaz propane

sleeping bag
le sac de couchage

water jug
le bidon d'eau

tent
la tente

tent pole
le mât de tente

→ Also see IN THE CAMPGROUND, p. 100

Les tuyeaux et astuces are "tips and tricks."

The Bookshop

Where can I find a bookstore? **Où puis-je trouver une librairie ?**

Do you also have books in English? **Est-ce que vous avez des livres écrits en anglais ?**

I am looking for a novel. **Je cherche un roman.**

postcards **la carte postale**

illustrated book/coffee-table book **le volume illustré**

picture book **le livre illustré**

stamps **les timbres**

stationery/writing paper **le papier à lettres**

technical book **le livre spécialisé**

wrapping paper/gift wrap **le papier cadeau**

children's book **le livre pour enfants**

cookbook **le livre de cuisine**

mystery/detective novel **le roman policier**

map **la carte**

short novel/novella **les contes**

guide book **le guide touristique**

non-fiction **les essais**

science fiction **la science-fiction**

map of the city **la carte de la ville**

dictionary **le dictionnaire**

magazine **la revue/le magazine**

newspaper **le journal**

calendar **le calendrier**

Writing Implements

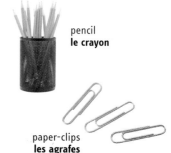

pencil **le crayon**

paper-clips **les agrafes**

colored pen **le crayon de couleur**

fountain pen **le stylo-plume**

ruler **la règle**

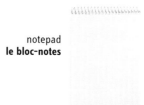

notepad **le bloc-notes**

Policier and *roman policier* are terms for crime novel.

notebook
le cahier

thumb tacks
les petits clous

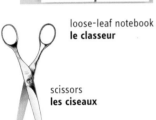

loose-leaf notebook
le classeur

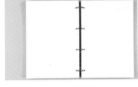

scissors
les ciseaux

string
la corde

playing cards
les cartes à jouer

twine
la ficelle

pencil sharpener
le cutter

labels
l'étiquette

felt tip pen
le feutre

paper clips
les agrafes

glue
la colle

ballpoint pen
le stylo-bille

eraser
la gomme

stationery
le papier à lettres

stationery/office supplies
les articles de papeterie

adhesive tape
le ruban adhésif (scotch)

pocket calculator
la calculette

ink
l'encre

Bic is often used for ballpoint pen, *Kleenex* for tissues—both are brand names.

Painting Supplies

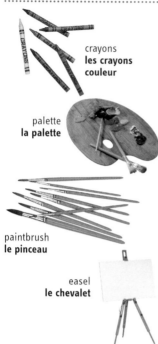

crayons
les crayons couleur

palette
la palette

paintbrush
le pinceau

easel
le chevalet

watercolors **la peinture à l'eau**

watercolor paper **le papier pour peinture à l'eau**

fixative **le fixateur**

canvas stretcher/frame **le cadre de serrage**

charcoal pencils **les crayons de charbon**

chalk/crayon **le craie**

canvas **la toile**

watercolor crayons/chalk **les pastels**

oil paints **les couleurs à l'huile**

oil pastels **les bâtons de craie**

pastels **les teintes pastel**

watercolors **les aquarelles**

sketch pad **le bloc à dessin**

In the Photography Shop

I am looking for a ...
Je cherche un ...
single lens reflex camera.
appareil photo reflex.
35 mm camera
appareil photo pour le format vingt-quatre trente-six.

I would like to spend about 100 euro.
Je ne veux pas dépenser plus de 100 euro.

Is the guarantee valid internationally?
Est-ce que la garantie est valable dans le monde entier ?

I need passport pictures.
Je voudrais des photos d'identité.

What Is Broken?

Something is wrong with my camera.
Mon appareil photo ne fonctionne pas bien.

The film is jammed.
La pellicule se bloque.

Can you repair it?
Pouvez-vous le réparer ?

How much will it cost?
J'en aurai pour combien ?

How long will it take?
Combien de temps faudra-t-il ?

exposure meter/light meter
le posemètre

distance meter
le télémètre

shutter
l'obturateur

Le peintre can designate either an artist or a house painter. *Les travaux de peinture* are paintings.

Accessories

film
la pellicule

lens
l'objectif

battery
la pile

flashbulb
le flash

camera bag
l'étui de l'appareil photo

automatic shutter release/self-timer
le câble du dispositif à retardement

lens shade
le pare-soleil

tripod
le trépied

telephoto lens
le téléobjectif

uv-filter
le filtre ultra violet

wide-angle lens
l'objectif grand-angle

zoom lens
l'objectif zoom

Films

I would like a ...
Je voudrais. ..
    black and white film
    une pellicule en noir et blanc
    color-negative film
    une pellicule couleur
    slide film/transparency film
    une pellicule pour diapositives

100/200/400 ASA.
En 100/200/400 ASA.

36 exposures.
A trente-six photos.

daylight film
pellicule pour la lumière du jour

artificial light film
pellicule pour la lumière artificielle

Can you put the film into the camera?
Pouvez-vous mettre la pellicule dans l'appareil, s'il vous plaît ?

developing
le développement

printing
le tirage/la photo

format
le format

slide frame
le petit cadre pour diapositives

Le photographe prend des photos means *The photographer takes photos.*

Developing Film

Please develop this film.
Pouvez-vous développer cette pellicule ?

In what format?
Dans quel format ?

Four by six.
Dix par quinze.

Glossy or matt?
Brillant ou mat ?

Glossy. When can I pick up the pictures?
Brillant. Quand est-ce que je peux retirer les photos ?

The day after tomorrow.
Après demain.

To develop can be *développer, dessiner,* and, by extension, *étudier.*

Video Cameras

I would like to buy a video camera.
Je voudrais une caméra vidéo.

It should not cost more than 300 euros.
Je ne voudrais pas dépenser plus de 300 euro.

Does the camera have a worldwide guarantee?
Est-ce que la garantie de l'appareil est valable dans le monde entier ?

Is this a discontinued model?
Est-ce un modèle de fin de série ?

Is this the most current model from this company?
Est-ce le modèle le plus actuel ?

I would like ...
Je voudrais ...
   a film for my video camera
   une pellicule
   batteries for my video camera
   des piles
   a charger for my video camera
   un chargeur
   a halogen light for my video camera
   une lumière halogène pour caméra vidéo

Camcorders, DVD

VCR
le magnétoscope

video cassette
la cassette vidéo

DVD player
le lecteur DVD

Do you have cassettes for the PAL system too?
Avez-vous des cassettes vidéo pour le système PAL ?

Can it also run on 110 volts?
Est-ce possible de commuter le bloc d'alimentation sur 110 volt ?

Do I need a transformer for it?
Ou aurais-je besoin d'un transformateur ?

A videographer is un *vidéoiste*.

Electronic Devices

adapter
l'adaptateur

plug
la fiche

battery
la pile

alarm clock
le réveil

iron
le fer à repasser

razor
le rasoir

flashlight
la lampe de poche

extension cord
la rallonge

hair dryer
**le sèche-
cheveux**

light bulb
l'ampoule

fuse
le fusible

socket
la prise de courant

Electroménager are small household appliances.

Stereo

diskman
le lecteur laser

remote control
la télécommande

headphones
le casque

speakers
le haut-parleur

CD player/compact disc player
le lecteur CD

DVD player
le lecteur DVD

stereo system
la chaîne Hi-Fi

cassette recorder
le magnétophone

MD player
le lecteur MD

radio
la radio

record player
le tourne-disques

walkman
le balladeur

Computer

screen/monitor
l'écran

keyboard
le clavier

RAM **la mémoire de travail**

operating system **le système d'exploitation**

CD-writer **le graveur de CD-ROM**

CD-ROM drive **le lecteur de CD-ROM**

hard disk **le disque dur**

graphics card **la carte graphique**

laser printer **l'imprimante laser**

speaker **le haut-parleur**

modem **le modem**

network cable **le câble réseau**

network card **la carte réseau**

paper **le papier**

processor **le processeur**

scanner **le scanneur**

sound card **la carte audio**

control unit **l'unité de commande**

electrical cord **le câble d'alimentation**

inkjet printer **l'imprimante jet d'encre**

toner **le toner**

extension cord **la rallonge**

video card **la carte vidéo**

Since the French are notoriously reluctant to adopt anglicisms, a computer is known as *un ordinateur*.

At the Optician's

My frame is broken.
Ma monture est cassée.

No problem, I can solder that.
Ce n'est pas grave, je peux la souder.

Can I wait for it?
Pouvez-vous le faire tout de suite ?

I'm sorry, it won't be ready until tomorrow.
Non pas avant demain matin.

Don't you have an extra pair of glasses?
Avez-vous des lunettes de rechange ?

As in English, *glasses* in French are always plural: *les lunettes.*

ear-piece
la branche

glass
le verre

frame
la monture

The glass is broken.
Le verre est cassé.

sun glasses
les lunettes de soleil

binoculars
les jumelles

My glasses are broken.
Mes lunettes sont cassées.

Can you repair it?
Pouvez-vous les réparer ?

How long will it take?
Il faudra combien de temps ?

Can you do it right away?
Pouvez-vous le faire tout de suite ?

magnifying glass
la loupe

contact lenses
les lentilles
   hard lenses
   lentilles dures
   soft lenses
   lentilles souples

vision
la tension de l'œil

near-sighted
myope

far-sighted
presbyte

glasses case
l'étui (pour lunettes)

lens cleaner
le produit pour nettoyer les verres

Don't confuse *les lentilles* (contact lenses) with *plat de lentilles* (lentils).

At the Watchmaker's

crown
le bouton pour remonter la montre

hands
l'aiguille

glass
le verre

alarm clock
le réveil

stopwatch
le chronomètre

My watch /clock isn't working.
Ma montre ne fonctionne plus.

My watch/clock is running fast.
Ma montre avance.

My watch/clock is running slow.
Ma montre retarde.

Can you repair it?
Pouvez-vous la réparer ?

How long will it take?
Il faudra combien de temps ?

wristband
le bracelet

wristwatch
la montre-bracelet

pocket watch
la montre de poche

wall clock
l'horloge

waterproof
étanche

Jeweler

I am looking for a gift. **Je voudrais faire un cadeau.**

It is for a man/a woman. **C'est pour un homme/une femme.**

Do you have something less expensive? **Est-ce que vous avez quelque chose de moins cher ?**

What material is that? **C'est en quelle matière ?**

Which gem is that? **Quelle pierre est-ce ?**

pendant **le pendentif**

badge/pin **l'épingle**

bracelet **le bracelet**

brooch **la broche**

necklace **le collier**

tie pin **l'épingle à cravate**

cufflinks **les boutons de manchette**

pearl necklace/string of pearls **le colier en perles**

ring **la bague**

earrings **les boucles d'oreille**

amethyst **l'améthyste**

amber **l'ambre**

diamond **le diamant**

high-grade steel **l'acier spécial**

ivory **l'ivoire**

gold **l'or**
    gold plate(d) **plaqué or**

coral **le corail**

copper **le cuivre**

onyx **l'onyx**

pearl **la perle**

platinum **le platine**

ruby **le rubis**

sapphire **le saphir**

silver **l'argent**
    silver plate(d) **plaqué argent**

emerald **l'émeraude**

Le platine is platinum; *la platine* is *the turntable* and *the record player.*

Hair Stylist

hair setting lotion
le fixateur

elastic
la gomina

hairpins
l'épingle à cheveux

barrette
la barrette

hairspray
la laque

hair conditioner
le lavage

shampoo
le shampooing

curler
le bigoudi

hair dye/hair color
la teinture pour cheveux/la coloration

color rinse/tint
le reflet

hairbrush
la brosse à cheveux

comb
le peigne

la barbe

perm
la permanente

sideburns
les pattes

curls
les boucles

center part
la raie au milieu

part
la raie sur le côté

mustache
les moustaches

dandruff
les pellicules

strands
la mèche

wig
la perruque

eyebrows
les sourcils

beard

In France *le coiffeur* is a hairdresser; his female colleague is *la coiffeuse*.

How Would You Like It?

Are you free, or do I have to make an appointment?
Est-ce que vous avez le temps maintenant ou est-ce que je dois prendre un rendez-vous ?

A wash and set, please.
Je voudrais une mise en pli.

Please color my hair.
Je voudrais teindre mes cheveux.

I want my hair to stay long.
Je voudrais garder mes cheveux longs.

Please cut off only the ends.
Je voudrais seulement couper les pointes.

Somewhat shorter than that.
Coupez-les-moi un peu plus courts.

My ears should stay covered.
Ne dégarnissez pas les oreilles.

Yes, that's right.
Oui ça va.

Would you please trim my beard too?
Je voudrais rafraîchir ma barbe.

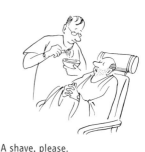

A shave, please.
Je voudrais que vous me rasiez.

color
faire une couleur

blow-dry
sécher avec le sèche-cheveux

set
faire la mise en pli

wash
laver les cheveux

tint
faire des mèches

tease/back-comb
le crêpage

Which Style?

modern
(coupe) moderne

very short
(coupe) très courte

sporty
(coupe) sportive

Je voudrais une nouvelle coupe means *I would like a new hairstyle.*

Beach, Sports, and Nature

What's Happening?

fishing
la pêche

darts
les fléchettes

baseball
le base-ball

hang-gliding
le parapente

basketball
le basket

ice hockey
le hockey sur glace

billiards
le billard

boxing
la boxe

One of the most important sports in France is *boules* (also called *pétanque*).

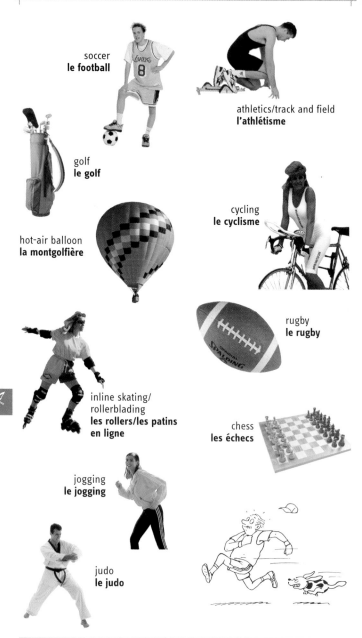

soccer
le football

athletics/track and field
l'athlétisme

golf
le golf

cycling
le cyclisme

hot-air balloon
la montgolfière

rugby
le rugby

inline skating/
rollerblading
**les rollers/les patins
en ligne**

chess
les échecs

jogging
le jogging

judo
le judo

Recreational bicycling is known as *le cyclisme*; professional cycling is called *faire de la bicyclette*.

skiing
le ski

snowboard
le snowboard

diving
la plongée sous-marine

tennis
le tennis

ping-pong/table tennis
le ping-pong

aerobics **l'aérobic**
car racing **la course automobile**
badminton **le badminton**
mountaineering **l'alpinisme**
ice-skating **la patinage artistique**
sky diving/parachute jumping **le parachutisme**
badminton **le badminton**
gymnastics **la gymnastique**
handball **le handball**
canoeing **l'aviron**
karate **le karaté**
bowling **les quilles**
mountain climbing/rock climbing **l'alpinisme**
cricket **le cricket**
horse racing **la course de chevaux**
bicycle racing **la course de bicyclettes**
regatta **la régate**
riding/horseback riding **l'équitation**
wrestling **le catch**
rowing **l'aviron**
swimming pool **la piscine**
sailing **la voile**
squash **le squash**
beach **la plage**
surfing **le surf**
exercise **la gymnastique**
volleyball **le volley-ball**
hiking **la randonnée**
water polo **le water-polo**
waterskiing **le ski nautique**

windsurfing
la planche à voile

→ Also see IN THE SPORTING GOODS SHOP, p. 157

The French use the term *bowling*.

Renting

I would like to rent a tennis racquet.
Je voudrais louer une raquette de tennis.

What does it cost ...
Quel est le prix pour ...
per hour?
une heure ?
per day?
un jour ?
per week?
la semaine ?

That is too expensive for me.
C'est trop cher.

Must I leave a deposit?
Est-ce que je dois laisser une caution ?

Instruction

I would like to take a tennis course.
Je voudrais suivre un cours de tennis.

Are there sailing courses here?
Est-ce qu'il y a des cours de voile par ici ?

I have never been diving.
Je n'ai jamais fait de plongée.

I am a beginner.
Je suis débutant.

I am advanced.
Je ne suis pas débutant.

Creative Vacations

cooking course **le cours de cuisine**

painting course **le cours de peinture**

language course **le cours de langue étrangère**

dance **la danse**

theater **le théâtre**

At the Beach

Where is the nearest beach?
Pouvez-vous m'indiquer la plage la plus proche ?

Where can I rent a sun umbrella?
Où puis-je louer un parasol ?

What does a place on the beach cost per day?
Combien coûte une place sur la plage par jour ?

I am looking for a nudist beach.
Je cherche une plage pour nudistes.

Is it high or low tide?
Sommes-nous à marée haute ou à marée basse ?

How warm is the water?
Quelle est la température de l'eau ?

Are there any dangerous currents?
Est-ce qu'il y a des courants dangereux ?

Is there a lifeguard on the beach?
Est-ce que la plage est surveillée ?

What do the flags mean?
Que signifient les drapeaux ?

Notices and Signs

Baignade interdite !
No swimming!

Avis de tempête
Storm warning

Danger !
Danger!

Plage sans maître nageur (plage non surveillée)
Swim at your own risk.

Seulement pour nageurs
Only for swimmers

Plongeons interdits/Défense de plonger.
Diving prohibited.

Courants dangereux !
Dangerous current!

Plage privée
Private beach

An advanced course is designated *un cours de perfectionnement.*

At the Beach

swimsuit
le maillot de bain

flippers
les palmes

trunks/swimming trunks
le slip de bain

crayfish
l'écrevisse

bathing shoes
les chaussures de plage

beach chair
la chaise longue

bath towel
le drap de plage

motorboat
le canot à moteur

ball
la balle

bikini
le bikini

A motorboat is also called *un bateau à moteur*.

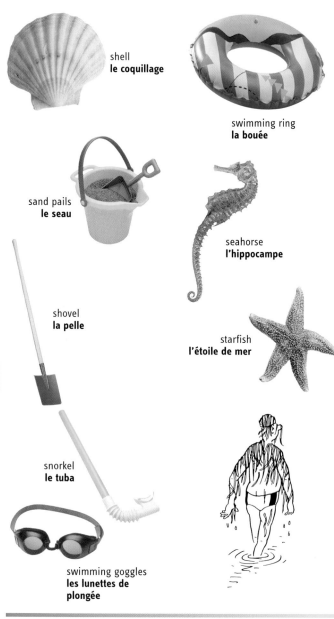

shell
le coquillage

swimming ring
la bouée

sand pails
le seau

seahorse
l'hippocampe

shovel
la pelle

starfish
l'étoile de mer

snorkel
le tuba

swimming goggles
les lunettes de plongée

A swell is *une houle*. A dune is *une dune*.

sun glasses **les lunettes de soleil**

suntan lotion **la crème solaire**

sunburn **le coup de soleil**

sunstroke **l'insolation**

sun umbrella **le parasol**

diving goggles/mask **les lunettes de plongée**

beach ball **le ballon de plage**

seaweed **les algues**

beach cabin/cabana **la cabine**

boat **la barque/le bateau**

boat rental **location de bateaux/de barques**

surf **le ressac**

dune **la dune**

low tide **la marée basse**

shuttlecock **le volant**

rocky shoreline **la côte rocheuse**

river **le fleuve**

high tide **la marée haute**

pebble beach **la plage de galets**

air mattress **le matelas pneumatique**

sea **la mer**

non-swimmer **le non-nageur**

canoe **le canoë**

jellyfish **la méduse**

life guard/beach patrol **le maître nageur**

rowboat **la barque à rames**

sand **le sable**

sandy beach **la plage de sable**

shadows **l'ombre**

swimmer **le nageur**

water wings **les brassards**

sea/ocean **le lac**

beach shoes **les chaussures de plage**

beach towel **le drap de plage**

current **le courant**

surfboard **la planche à surf**

pedal boat **le pédalo**

pollution **la pollution**

waterski **le ski nautique**

wave **la vague**

Gravel that's used for concrete is called *le gravier*; *caillouteux* means *stony*.

Indoor and Outdoor Swimming Pools

I would like two entrance tickets, please.
Pouvez-vous me donner deux billets, s'il vous plaît ?

Is there also a weekly pass/multiple-entry pass?
Est-ce qu'il y a aussi des billets hebdomadaires ou multiples ?

There is a discount for ...
Est-ce qu'il y a une réduction pour les ...

children?
enfants ?
teenagers?
adolescents ?
students?
étudiants ?
the handicapped?
handicapés ?
senior citizens?
personnes âgées ?

Where are the changing rooms?
Où se trouvent les vestiaires ?

Do you have lockers?
Est-ce que les armoires peuvent être fermées à clé ?

Is the use of the sauna included in the price?
Est-ce que le sauna est compris dans le prix ?

Does everyone have to wear a bathing cap?
Est-ce qu'il faut mettre un bonnet de bain ?

Is there also a restaurant at the swimming pool?
Y a-t-il un restaurant dans la piscine ?

What is the water temperature today?
Quelle est la température de l'eau aujourd'hui ?

How do you purify the water, with chlorine or ozone?
L'eau est nettoyée avec du chlore ou de l'ozone ?

Do you use salt water or fresh water?
Vous utilisez de l'eau de mer ou de l'eau douce ?

Water Sports

kayak **le kayac**

canoe **le canoë**

motorboat **le canot à moteur**

paddle **la pagaie**

paddle boat **le bateau à aubes**

oar **la rame**

rowboat **la barque à rames**

rubber dinghy **le canot pneumatique**

diving **la plongée**

pedal boat **le pédalo**

waterskiing **le ski nautique**

surfing **le surf**

windsurfing **la planche à voile**

Wind Surfing

sails **la voile**

mast **le mât**

boom **le bôme de surf**

surfboard **la planche à surf**

centerboard **la dérive principale**

auxiliary board **la dérive secondaire**

foot strap **la sangle pour les pieds**

The word for windsurfing in "franglais" is *le surf à voile.*

Diving

I would like to go deep-sea diving.
Je voudrais faire de la plongée sous-marine.

I would like go cave-diving.
Je voudrais faire des excursions spéléologiques.

I have a diving certification.
J'ai un brevet de plongeur.

I would like to get a diving certificate.
Je voudrais passer un brevet de plongeur.

How much does it cost to get a diving certificate?
Combien coûte l'obtention d'un brevet de plongeur ?

How long does it take to get a diving certificate?
Combien de temps faut-il pour obtenir un brevet de plongeur ?

Will this diving certificate be accepted internationally?
Est-ce que le brevet est valable dans le monde entier ?

flippers
les palmes

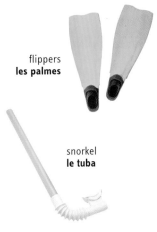

snorkel
le tuba

diving mask/ face mask
les lunettes de plongée

weight belts **la ceinture en plomb**

decometer **le décomètre**

compressed-air bottles **la bouteille à air comprimé**

wetsuit **la combinaison de plongée**

diving clock **la montre de plongée**

depth meter **le bathomètre**

Eau douce (sweet or fresh water) is the opposite of salt water, *eau salée.*

Sailing

I have a class B sailing license.
J'ai le permis nautique classe B.

I would like get a sailing license.
Je voudrais passer un permis nautique.

Do you also organize sailing trips that last several days?
Est-ce qu'il y a aussi des régates de voiles qui durent plusieurs jours ?

What does that cost?
Combien est-ce que ça coûte ?

When can we cast off?
Quand pouvons-nous embarquer ?

Have any other people put down their names?
Est-ce qu'il y a déjà des personnes inscrites ?

I would like to sail in coastal waters.
Je voudrais faire de la voile dans les eaux côtières.

I am interested in sailing in the open sea.
Je voudrais faire de la voile en haute mer.

knot
le nœud

paddle
la pagaie

life preserver
la bouée

life-jacket
le gilet de sauvetage

The life preserver is properly termed *la bouée de sauvetage*.

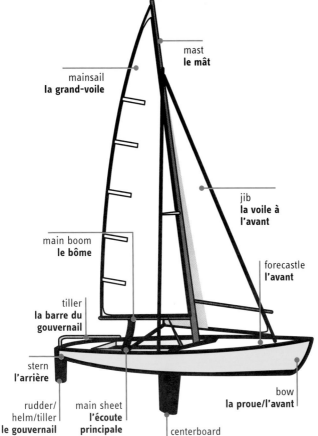

mast
le mât

mainsail
la grand-voile

jib
**la voile à
l'avant**

main boom
le bôme

forecastle
l'avant

tiller
**la barre du
gouvernail**

stern
l'arrière

rudder/
helm/tiller
le gouvernail

main sheet
**l'écoute
principale**

centerboard
la dérive

bow
la proue/l'avant

anchor **l'ancre**
port **à bâbord**
leeward **sous le vent**
lighthouse **le phare**
windward **au vent**
motor **le moteur**
starboard **à tribord**
rigging **le palan**

yawl **le youyou/la yole**
cruiser **le croiseur**
trawler **le cuner**
schooner **le schooner**
yacht **le yacht**

La voile is *the sail*; *le voile* is the *barn owl*.

Fishing

I would like to go fishing.
Je voudrais pêcher.

Do I need a fishing license?
Est-ce qu'il faut avoir un permis de pêche ?

What does the license cost per day/per week?
Combien coûte le permis par jour/par semaine ?

Where can I get a license?
A qui dois-je m'adresser pour obtenir le permis ?

I am interested in deep-sea fishing.
Je voudrais pêcher en haute mer.

What does it cost to take part in a fishing tournament?
Combien faut-il compter pour participer à une sortie de pêche ?

Whom should I contact?
A qui puis-je m'adresser ?

Can we sail to other fishing grounds too?
Est-ce qu'on peut aussi pêcher à d'autres endroits ?

I am particularly interested in catching ...
Je voudrais pêcher surtout ...

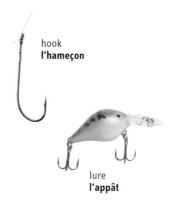

hook
l'hameçon

lure
l'appât

Which types of fish can be caught?
Quels types de poissons peut-on pêcher ?

fishing rod **la canne à pêche**
fishing line **la ligne**
fishing reel **le moulinet**
weights/sinker **le plomb**
float **le flotteur**

→ Also see FISH AND SHELLFISH, p. 117

L'hameçon is the hook—thus the designation *pêche à l'hameçon* for angling. An equally correct and shorter way to refer to angling is *pêche à la ligne*.

Hiking

Do you have a hiking map?
Est-ce que vous avez une carte de randonnée ?

Are the trails well marked?
Est-ce que les parcours sont bien balisés ?

Is the route easy/difficult?
Ce parcours est-il facile ou difficile ?

Is the route suitable for children?
Est-ce que ce parcours est approprié aux enfants ?

Approximately what altitude is that?
A quelle altitude arrive-t-on environ ?

Is there anything special to watch out for on the hike?
A quoi faut-il prêter particulièrement attention durant la randonnée ?

About how long will take me to go to ...?
Combien de temps faut-il pour arriver à ... ?

Is the water drinkable?
Est-ce que l'eau est potable ?

In this area, am I allowed to ...
Dans cette région, est-ce que l'on peut ...

 spend the night in a tent?
 dormir sous une tente ?
 light a fire?
 allumer un feu ?

Do I need any special permission for this area?
Est-ce qu'il me faut une autorisation spéciale pour faire des randonnées dans cette zone ?

Where do I get permission?
Où puis-je demander cette autorisation ?

Is that the right way to ...?
Est-ce que je suis sur le bon chemin pour ... ?

Can you show me the way on the map?
Pouvez-vous m'indiquer le chemin sur la carte ?

I got lost.
Je me suis perdu(e).

How much farther is it to ...?
Combien de kilomètres y a-t-il encore pour arriver à ... ?

Climbing

I am looking for climbing possibilities in the area.
Je cherche des parcours pour grimpeur dans cette région.

Where can I rent the necessary equipment?
Où puis-je louer l'équipement nécessaire ?

Do you have guides?
Est-ce qu'il y a des guides de montagne ?

How much does a guide cost per day?
Combien coûte un guide de montagne par jour ?

Do you have a guide who speaks English?
Est-ce qu'il y a des guides qui parlent anglais ?

A hiker is *un excursioniste*. Many people refer to mountain climbers as *grimpeurs*.

Equipment

compass
la boussole

canteen
la gourde

backpack/knapsack
le sac à dos

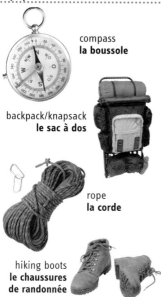

reflective blanket **la couverture en aluminium**

helmet **le casque**

snaphook/clip/carabiner **la carabine**

climbing belt **le baudrier**

climbing boots **les chaussures pour grimpeurs**

emergency kit **le nécessaire de secours**

crampons **les crampons**

flashlight **la lampe de poche**

tent **la tente**

rope
la corde

hiking boots
le chaussures de randonnée

Important Vocabulary

descent **la descente**

ascent **la montée**

brook **le ruisseau**

mountain **la montagne**

mountain hut **le chalet de montagne**

mountain peak **le sommet de la montagne**

bridge **le pont**

field **le champ**

footpath **le sentier**

gradient **le dénivelé**

cave **la caverne/la grotte**

hill **la colline**

canal **le canal**

climbing path **le sentier**

climbing track **le parcours pour grimpeurs**

cliff **le rocher**

nature park **le parc naturel**

sanctuary/reservation **le parc national**

pass **le col**

mountain spring **la source**

degree of difficulty **le degré de difficulté**

lake **le lac**

cable railway **le téléphérique**

one-day hike **la randonnée d'une journée**

valley **la vallée**

pond **l'étang**

footpath **le sentier de randonnée**

waterfall **la cascade**

vineyard **le vignoble**

meadow **le pré**

In Alpes-Maritimes you can combine excellent mountain climbing with a stay by the ocean.

Nature

maple
l'érable

laurel
le laurier

tree
l'arbre

daisy
la marguerite

beech
le hêtre

narcissus
la narcisse

oak
le chêne

carnation
l'œillet

hibiscus
l'hibisque

orchid
l'orchidée

chestnut
le châtaigner

rose
la rose

lily
le lis

sunflower
le tournesol

lime tree
le tilleul

pine cone
les pommes de pin

Les pins-parasols are the stone pines so typical of Provence.

Winter Sports

I would like to go skiing.
Je voudrais skier.

I would like to like to learn to ski.
Je voudrais apprendre à skier.

Do you have off-trail skiing?
Est-ce qu'on peut faire du ski hors-piste ?

I am a beginner.
Je suis débutant.

I am an experienced skier.
Je suis un skieur chevronné.

Can you recommend a ski instructor?
Pouvez-vous me conseiller un moniteur de ski ?

Where can I rent/buy ski equipment?
Où puis-je louer/acheter l'équipement de ski ?

What are the current snow/ski conditions?
Comment est la neige en ce moment?

How difficult are the ski runs?
Quel est le degré de difficuté des pistes ?

downhill skiing **la descente**

binding **la fixation des skis**

cross-country skiing **le ski de fond**

ski lift **le remonte-pente**

ski trail **la piste**

sled **la luge**

ice skates **les patins à glace**

ski **le ski**

ski instructor **le moniteur de ski**

ski pass **le forfait**

ski boot **la chaussure de ski**

ski pole **le bâton de ski**

snowboard **le snowboard**

wax **la cire**

cable railway **le téléphérique**

chair lift **le télésiège**

Spectator Sports

Is there a soccer game this week?
Est-ce qu'il y a un match de football cette semaine ?

Where do I get tickets?
Où puis-je acheter les billets ?

I would like to buy a ticket for the game of ... against ...
Je voudrais acheter un billet pour le match ... contre ...

What is the admission fee?
Combien coûte le billet ?

Which teams are playing?
Quelles sont les équipes qui s'affrontent ?

What is the score?
Où en est le match ?

A tie/draw right now.
Pour l'instant, ils sont à égalité.

Four to one in favor of Olympique Marseille.
Quatre à un pour l'Olympique Marseille.

Marseille won.
Marseille a gagné.

Marseille lost.
Marseille a perdu.

referee
l'arbitre

win
la victoire

loss/defeat
la défaite

Le forfait, the ski pass in this instance, can be all-inclusive in other areas.

What Is There?

ballet **le ballet**

discotheque/disco **la discothèque**

festival **le festival**

film **le film**

folklore festival **la fête folklorique**

jazz concert **le concert de jazz**

cabaret **le cabaret**

concert **le concert**

musical **la comédie musicale**

nightclub **la boîte de nuit**

opera **l'opéra**

operetta **l'opérette**

procession **la procession**

casino **le casino**

theater **le théâtre**

parade **le défilé**

circus **le cirque**

What You Hear or Read

Je regrette, c'est complet.
I'm sorry, we are sold out.

Votre billet, s'il vous plaît.
Your ticket, please.

Voici votre place.
Here is your seat.

le vestiaire
cloakroom

les toilettes
toilets

la sortie
exit

Information

What is playing at the theater tonight?
Quelle pièce joue-t-on ce soir au théâtre ?

Can you recommend a play?
Quelle pièce de théâtre me conseillez-vous ?

What is playing at the cinema today?
Quel film passe-t-on aujourd'hui au cinéma ?

I would like to see a good musical.
Je voudrais voir une belle comédie musicale.

Where is ...
Où se trouve ...
   the cinema/movie theatre?
   le cinéma ?
   the theater?
   le théâtre ?
   the concert hall?
   la salle de concerts ?
   the opera?
   l'opéra ?

When does the performance begin?
A quelle heure commence le spectacle ?

How long is the piece?
Combien de temps dure-t-il ?

When does the show end?
A quelle heure finit-il ?

Where is the cloakroom, please?
Où se trouvent les vestiaires ?

How long is the intermission?
Combien de temps dure l'entracte ?

Is evening attire necessary?
Est-ce qu'il faut une tenue de soirée ?

La toile really denotes the canvas, but the word is also used for *painting*.

Theater and Concerts

What type of play is this?
De quel genre de pièce s'agit-il ?
comedy
la comédie
tragedy
la tragédie
drama
le drame

Who is the playwright?
Qui est l'auteur de cette pièce ?

Who is the producer?
Qui est le metteur en scène de cette pièce ?

Who plays the leading role?
Qui tient le rôle principal ?

Who are ...
Qui sont ...
the actors?
les acteurs ?
the singers?
les chanteurs ?
the dancers?
les danseurs ?

Who is ...
Qui est ...
the director?
le metteur en scène ?
the choreographer?
le chorégraphe ?
the conductor?
le chef d'orchestre ?
the author?
l'auteur ?
the set designer?
le décorateur ?
the orchestra?
l'orchestre ?
the composer?
le compositeur ?

Can I rent binoculars?
Est-ce que je peux louer des jumelles de théâtre ?

Buying Tickets

Do you still have tickets for today?
Est-ce qu'il y a encore des billets pour aujourd'hui ?

Do you also have discounted tickets?
Est-ce qu'il y a des tarifs réduits ?

How much does a seat cost in a ...
Combien coûte une place ...
lower price range?
à bas prix ?
expensive price range?
à prix élevé ?

I would like a seat ...
Je voudrais une place ...
in the orchestra.
de parterre.
in the balcony.
de balcon.
in the middle.
au milieu.
with a good view.
avec une bonne vue.
in the box.
de loges.

I would like to reserve three tickets.
Je voudrais réserver trois places.

Discos and Nightclubs

Where do people go in the evening around here?
Où est-ce qu'on sort le soir ici ?

Is there a discotheque/disco here?
Est-ce qu'il y a une boîte de nuit dans les environs ?

What does one wear?
Comment faut-il s'habiller ?

Are there young/older people there?
Le public est-il jeune ou vieux ?

Would you like to dance?
Voulez-vous danser ?

May I invite you?
Puis-je vous inviter ?

Can I take you home?
Puis-je vous accompagner chez vous ?

Often the *cabaret* sign also designates a nightclub.

Offices and Institutions

Offices and Institutions

bank **la banque**

library **la bibliothèque**

embassy **l'ambassade**

mayor's office **le bureau du maire**

immigration authority **le bureau des immigrés**

fire department **les sapeurs-pompiers**

lost-and-found **le bureau des objets trouvés**

consulate **le consulat**

hospital **l'hôpital**

police **la police**

post office **la poste**

town hall **la mairie**

environmental protection agency **le bureau de la protection de l'environement**

Where can I find the nearest police station?
Pouvez-vous m'indiquer le commissariat de police le plus proche ?

When does the bank open?
A quelle heure ouvre la banque ?

When are you open?
Vous ouvrez à partir de quelle heure ?

Are you also open on Saturdays?
Est-ce que vous êtes ouvert le samedi ?

closed
Fermé

I am looking for ...
Je cherche ...

The Right Address

M Jean Leblanc
50, rue des Belges
92140 Clamart

Art expositions are known as *manifestations*. The schedule of expositions is *le calendrier de manifestations*.

At the Post Office Counter

Where is the nearest post office?
Pouvez-vous m'indiquer le bureau de poste le plus proche ?

What are the working hours?
Quels sont les horaires d'ouverture au public ?

Where is the nearest mailbox?
Pouvez-vous m'indiquer la boîte aux lettres la plus proche ?

What color is it?
De quelle couleur est-elle ?

How much does a letter cost ...
Combien coûte l'envoi d'une lettre ...
　to the United States?
　aux Etats-Unis ?
　to Canada?
　au Canada ?
　to Australia?
　en Australie ?

How long does a letter take to ... ?
Dans combien de temps la lettre arrivera-t-elle en... ?

Please give me a ... cent stamp.
Je voudrais un timbre à ... cent.

Can you help me fill this out?
Pouvez-vous m'aider à le remplir ?

Next day delivery, please.
Distribution demain, s'il vous plaît.

Can I send a fax from here?
Est-ce que je peux envoyer un fax d'ici ?

Can I insure this parcel?
Est-ce que je peux assurer ce colis ?

sender **l'expéditeur**
address **l'adresse**
stamp **le timbre**
printed matter **l'imprimé**
express mail **express**
registered mail **la lettre recommandée**
recipient **le destinataire**
acknowledgment **le reçu**
fax **le fax**
charge **le tarif**
money order **le mandat**
weight **le poids**
airmail **par avion**
COD **contre remboursement**
small parcel **le petit paquet**
parcel **le colis**
postage **l'affranchissement**
remittance **le mandat postal**
postcard **la carte postale**
general delivery **la poste restante**
zip code **le code postal**
counter **le guichet**
telegram **le télégramme**
telex **le télex**
insurance **l'assurance**
customs declaration **la déclaration douanière**

Telegrams

I would like to send a telegram.
Je voudrais envoyer un télégramme

How much does it cost per word?
Combien coûte chaque mot ?

Will the telegram arrive today?
Est-ce que le télégramme arrive dans la journée ?

Picking Up Mail

Is there any mail for me?
Est-ce qu'il y a du courrier pour moi ?

My name is ...
Je m'appelle ...

Your ID, please.
Votre carte d'identité, s'il vous plaît ?

Contre remboursement means *upon payment.*

The Bank

Where is the nearest bank?
Pouvez-vous m'indiquer la banque la plus proche ?

I would like to cash a traveler's check.
Je voudrais encaisser un chèque de voyage.

What is the exchange rate today?
A combien est le change aujourd'hui ?

I would like to withdraw 400 euros with my credit card.
Je voudrais retirer 400 euro avec ma carte de crédit.

I am having problems with your automatic teller. Would you please help me?
Je n'arrive pas à faire fonctionner le distributeur automatique de billets. Pouvez-vous m'aider, s'il vous plaît ?

The automatic teller has taken my credit card.
Le distributeur a englouti ma carte de crédit.

I would like to make a transfer.
Je voudrais envoyer un mandat.

I would like to open an account.
Je voudrais ouvrir un compte.

Can you give me the customer service-number of my credit card company?
Pourriez-vous m'indiquer le numéro de service de mon établissement de crédit ?

My credit card was stolen.
On m'a volé ma carte de crédit.

I would like to have my credit card canceled.
Je voudrais bloquer ma carte de crédit.

In France you can pay using the common credit cards, but Eurochecks are not yet widely accepted. Especially when traveling into the countryside you should always keep a certain amount of cash on hand, since credit cards are not very common.

Before the adoption of the euro, the French currency was the franc. Now the currency denominations are the same as in other European Union countries: coins are 1, 2, 5, 10, 20, and 50 cents, plus 1 and 2 euros; and bills are 5, 10, 20, 50, 100, 200, and 500 euros.

It's a good idea to keep some coins on hand for using taxis and the metro.

cash **comptant**

PIN (personal identification number) **le code confidentiel**

remittance **le mandat**

automatic teller (ATM) **le distributeur automatique de billets**

money exchange **le change (de devises)**

cash register/cashier **la caisse**

change **la monnaie**

credit card **la carte de crédit**

coins **la monnaie/les pièces**

working hours **les horaires d'ouverture**

traveler's check **le chèque de voyage**

counter **le guichet**

check **le chèque**

bills/notes **les billets de banque**

transfer **le virement**

currency **la devise**

exchange rate **le taux de charge**

exchange bureau **le bureau de change**

The word *monnaie* can also be used for *currency*.

Help! Thief!

My car was broken into.
On a forcé la serrure de ma voiture.

Where did it happen?
Où cela s'est-il passé ?

There in the parking lot.
Dans le parking.

When did it happen?
Quand cela s'est-il passé ?

Between 11 a.m. and 12 noon.
Entre onze et douze heures.

What was stolen?
Que vous a-t-on volé ?

All our luggage.
Tous nos bagages.

Your ID, please.
Pouvez-vous me donner votre carte d'identité, s'il vous plaît ?

My ID card was also stolen.
Même ma carte d'identité a été volée.

Commissariat de police is also used for *police station*.

At the Police Station

Help!
Au secours !

Where is the nearest police station?
Pouvez-vous m'indiquer le poste de police le plus proche ?

I would like to make a complaint
Je voudrais porter plainte.

I would like to report an accident.
Je voudrais déclarer un accident.

Does anyone here speak English?
Est-ce que quelqu'un parle anglais ?

I don't understand you.
Je ne vous comprends pas.

I need a lawyer.
J'ai besoin d'un avocat.

I need an interpreter.
J'ai besoin d'un interprète.

Please inform my consulate.
Contactez mon consulat.

Please inform me of my rights.
Pouvez-vous m'expliquer quels sont mes droits ?

I need a report for my insurance.
J'ai besoin d'un certificat pour mon assurance.

I am not responsible.
Je ne suis pas responsable (de l'accident).

What Happened?

I have lost my wallet.
J'ai perdu mon porte-monnaie.

My money has been stolen.
On a volé mon argent.

My car was broken into.
On a forcé la serrure de ma voiture.

I have been cheated.
On m'a trompé/volé.

I have been molested.
On m'a importuné.

I have been robbed.
On m'a volé mon argent/mon sac.

I have been attacked/mugged.
On m'a agressé.

My son is missing.
J'ai perdu mon fils.

I have been raped.
On m'a violée.

Dévaliser can also be used to mean *to rob.*

What Was Stolen?

ID card **la carte d'identité**

car **la voiture**

car documents **les papiers de la voiture**

wallet **le portefeuille**

camera **l'appareil photo**

purse **le porte-monnaie**

luggage **les bagages**

handbag **le sac à main**

credit card **la carte de crédit**

check **le chèque**

watch **la montre**

Lost and Found

Where is the lost and found office?
Pouvez-vous m'indiquer le bureau des objets trouvés ?

I have lost my clock.
J'ai perdu ma montre.

I have lost my handbag.
J'ai perdu mon sac à main.

Has a suitcase been turned in to you?
Est-ce que vous avez trouvé ma valise ?

Would you please get in touch with me?
Pouvez-vous me tenir au courant ?

Here is my address.
Voici mon adresse.

Important Vocabulary

lawyer **l'avocat**

complaint **la plainte**

statement **la déclaration**

right to remain silent **le droit de refuser de témoigner**

swindler/cheat **l'escroc**

thief **le voleur**

theft **le vol**

prison **la prison**

hearing **l'audience**

marriage fraud **le responsable d'escroquerie avec promesse de mariage**

report **le procès-verbal**

trial **le procès**

dope/drugs **la drogue**

judge **le juge**

district attorney **le substitut du procureur**

pickpocket **le pickpocket/voleur à la tire**

mugging **l'agression**

crime **le crime**

rape **le viol**

arrest **l'arrestation**

The word *to rape* has two forms: *violer* and *violenter*.

Illnesses

allergy **l'allergie**

angina **l'angine**

asthma **l'asthme**

rash **l'irruption cutanée**

lump/swelling **la bosse/l'enflure**

bite **la morsure**

boil **le furoncle**

stomachache **le mal de ventre**

flatulence **l'aérophagie**

inflammation of the bladder **la cystite**

appendicitis **l'appendicite**

hemorrhage **l'hématome**

high blood pressure **l'hypertension**

bleeding **l'hémorragie/le saignement**

burn **la brûlure**

bronchitis **la bronchite**

diabetes **le diabète**

diphteria **la diphtérie**

diarrhea **la diarrhée**

inflammation **l'inflammation**

cold **le rhume**

fever **la fièvre**

concussion **le traumatisme crânien**

jaundice **la jaunisse**

ulcer **l'ulcère**

flu **la grippe**

sore throat **le mal de gorge**

heart problems **le mal au cœur**

heart attack **la crise cardiaque/l'infarctus**

hay fever **le rhume des foins**

lumbago **le lumbago/le tour de rein**

cough **la toux**

infection **l'infection**

insect bite **la piqûre d'insecte**

whooping cough **la coqueluche**

fracture **la fracture des os**

headache **le mal de tête**

circulatory disorder **les troubles de la circulation**

paralysis **la paralysie**

pneumonia **la pneumonie**

stomachache **le mal d'estomac**

tonsillitis **l'infection des amygdales**

measles **la rougeole**

migraine **la migraine**

mumps **les oreillons**

nosebleed **l'hémorragie nasale/le soignement de nez**

smallpox **la variole**

bruise **la contusion**

rheumatism **le rhumatisme**

German measles **la rubéole**

backache **le mal de dos**

salmonella **les salmonelles**

gash **la coupure**

head cold **le rhume**

chills **les frissons**

swelling **l'enflure**

stitch in the side **le point de côté**

heartburn **la brûlure d'estomac**

sunburn **le coup de soleil**

sunstroke **l'insolation**

tetanus **le tétanos**

nausea **la nausée**

burn **la brûlure**

poisoning **l'empoisonnement**

injury **la blessure**

sprain **l'entorse**

constipation **la constipation**

viral illness **la maladie virale**

chickenpox **la varicelle**

wound **la blessure**

strain **l'élongation/la déchirure**

A cold is also referred to more commonly as *un refroidissement* or *un coup de froid*.

What's the Matter?

I have cut myself.
Je me suis coupé(e).

I have been bitten.
J'ai été mordu(e).

I have something in my eye.
J'ai quelque chose dans l'œil.

My child has fallen down.
Mon enfant est tombé.

My ankle is swollen.
J'ai une cheville enflée.

I have vomited.
J'ai vomi.

At the Gynecologist's

Est-ce que vous êtes enceinte ?
Are you pregnant?

Est-ce que vous prenez la pilule ?
Are you taking the pill?/Are you on the pill?

Quelle est la date de vos dernières règles ?
When was your last period?

I am having my period.
J'ai mes règles.

I have not had a period for two months.
Je n'ai pas eu mes règles depuis deux mois.

I think I am pregnant.
Je crois que je suis enceinte.

I am pregnant.
Je suis enceinte.

I have menstrual pain.
J'ai des douleurs pendant les règles.

I take the pill/I'm on the pill.
Je prends la pilule.

swab **le frottis**

abortion **l'avortement**

inflammation of the bladder
l'inflammation de la vessie

breast **le sein**

ovary **l'ovaire**

miscarriage **la fausse couche**

uterus **l'utérus**

condom **le préservatif**

cramp **la crampe**

vaginitis **la vaginite**

pregnancy **la grossesse**

intra-uterine device **le stérilet**

vagina **le vagin**

Une visite is a visit, including to a doctor.

At the Dentist's

Is there a dentist here?
Est-ce qu'il y a un dentiste dans les environs ?

I need an appointment urgently.
J'ai besoin d'un rendez-vous urgent.

I have toothache.
J'ai mal aux dents.

A filling has fallen out.
J'ai perdu un plomb.

I have a broken tooth.
J'ai une dent cassée.

My denture has broken.
Mon dentier est cassé.

I would like a local anaesthetic.
Je voudrais une anesthésie.

Vous pouvez vous rincer la bouche.
Rinse please.

Je dois plomber la dent.
I will fill your tooth.

Pour l'instant, le plomb est provisoire.
I'm only treating it temporarily.

Voulez-vous une anesthésie ?
Would you like a shot?

Il faut arracher la dent.
I have to remove/ pull the tooth.

abscess **l'abcès**
(local) anaesthetic **l'anesthésie**
inflammation **l'inflammation**
denture **le dentier**
dental surgeon **le mécanicien-dentiste**
crown **la couronne**
nerve **le nerf**

filling **le plomb**
wisdom tooth **la dent de sagesse**
root canal work **le traitement des racines**
(dental) bridge **le bridge**
gum **la gencive**
toothache **le mal de dents**
braces **l'appareil pour les dents**
root (of the tooth) **la racine**

A toothbrush is *une brosse à dents*; toothpaste is *le dentifrice*.

In the Hospital

Does anybody speak English here?
Est-ce que quelqu'un parle anglais ?

Please speak more slowly.
Pouvez-vous parler plus lentement, s'il vous plaît ?

I would like to be flown home.
Je voudrais être rapatrié(e).

I have repatriation insurance.
J'ai une assurance pour le rapatriement.

What do I have?
Qu'est-ce que j'ai ?

Do I have to have an operation?
Est-ce que je dois être opéré(e) ?

How long do I have to stay in the hospital?
Combien de temps dois-je rester à l'hôpital ?

Can you please give me a pain killer?
Pouvez-vous me donner un analgésique ?

Please inform my family.
Pouvez-vous informer ma famille, s'il vous plaît ?

bed **le lit**
bedpan **l'urinoir/le pistolet**
blood transfusion **la transfusion de sang**
surgeon **le chirurgien**
call-button **la sonnette**
male nurse **l'infirmier**
nurse **l'infirmière**
anaesthesia **l'anesthésie**
operation **l'opération**
wheelchair **la chaise roulante**
injection **la piqûre**

A shot can be called either *une injection* or *une seringue*.

Business Travel

At the Reception Desk

I have made an appointment with Mister Leblanc.
J'ai rendez-vous avec M. Leblanc.

M. Leblanc is expecting me.
M. Leblanc m'attend.

Would you please tell him I'm here.
Pouvez-vous m'annoncer, s'il vous plaît ?

Here is my card.
Voici ma carte de visite.

I am sorry, I am somewhat late.
Excusez-moi, je suis un peu en retard.

At the Conference Table

...sends his regards to you.
... vous passe le bonjour.

Our company would be pleased to offer you the following.
Notre société voudrait vous faire cette offre.

Is that your final offer?
C'est votre dernière offre ?

I'm sorry, that's our limit.
Je regrette, nous ne pouvons pas faire davantage.

I think there is a misunderstanding.
Je crois qu'il y a un malentendu.

That is an interesting suggestion.
C'est une proposition intéressante.

Can you explain that in more detail?
Pouvez-vous me l'expliquer plus en détail ?

What exactly are you thinking of?
Que voulez-vous dire précisément ?

Let's summarize once again.
Essayons de résumer.

Let me put it like this.
Laissez-moi résumer avec mes mots.

Would you excuse me a moment?
Pouvez-vous m'excuser un instant ?

I must discuss this with my company first.
Je dois d'abord parler avec ma société.

We will think it over.
On va y réfléchir.

We will check that.
Nous le contrôlerons.

Can I phone you?
Est-ce que je peux téléphoner ?

Could we make another appointment for tomorrow?
Pouvons-nous fixer un autre rendez-vous pour demain ?

We will stay in phone contact.
On se contactera par téléphone.

Thank you for the constructive discussion.
Je vous remercie pour cette conversation fructueuse.

I am very pleased with our negotiations.
Je suis très satisfait(e) de ces négociations.

To our successful cooperation.
A une coopération réussie.

A business meal, *un repas d'affaires*, is the best way to strengthen business contacts.

Important Vocabulary

conclusion/finalization **la conclusion d'un contrat**

shares **les actions**

offer **l'offre**

investment **la participation**

import limitations/restrictions **les restrictions à l'importation**

purchase price **le prix d'achat**

euro **l'euro**

European Union **l'Union Européenne**

freight charges **les frais de transport**

guarantee **la garantie**

business partners **le partenaire (commercial)**

business meeting **le rendez-vous d'affaire**

law **la loi**

profit **les bénéfices**

liability **la responsabilité**

trade agreements **l'accord (commercial)**

profit margin **la marge (commerciale)**

manufacturer **le fabricant**

fees **les honoraires**

imports **les importations**

colleague **le collègue**

conditions **les conditions**

conference **la conférence**

cooperation **la coopération**

expenses/costs **les frais**

retail/selling price **le prix de vente**

supplier **le fournisseur**

licensing fees **la taxe de licence**

marketing **le marketing**

sales tax **la TVA (taxe sur la valeur ajoutée)**

co-worker/employee **l'employé(e)**

price **le prix**

minutes (of a meeting) **le protocole**

commission **la commission**

discount/rebate **l'escompte**

invoice **la facture**

taxes **l'impôt**

price per piece **le prix à l'unité**

agenda **l'ordre du jour**

percentages/royalties **la part de bénéfices**

transportation costs **les frais de transport**

takeover **la prise en charge**

negotiation **la négociation**

loss **la perte**

insurance **l'assurance**

representative/agent **le représentant**

business card **la carte de visite**

chairman **le supérieur**

customs regulations **les dispositions douanières**

The signing of a contract can be translated as *l'accord* or *la passation (d'un contrat).*

Corporate Structure

Corp. (Corporation)
la société à responsabilité limitée (S.R.L)

Inc. (incorporated)
la société par actions (S.P.A.)

board of trustees
le conseil de surveillance

chairman of the board
le président du conseil de surveillance

advisory board
le comité consultatif

board of directors
le conseil d'administration

authorized officer
le fondé de pouvoir

advertising/marketing manager
le directeur du bureau de la publicité

sales manager
le directeur des ventes

secretary
le/la secrétaire

assistant
l'assistant(e)

chief executive officer (CEO), president
le président du conseil d'administration

board member
le membre du conseil d'administration

general manager
le directeur exécutif

executive vice president
le directeur central

divison manager
le chef de service

department manager
le chef de secteur

general manager
le fondé de pouvoir (muni d'une procuration générale)

The business manager is *le gérant. Il dirige les affaires = He runs the business.*

Contracts

appendix/enclosure **la pièce jointe**

order **la commande**

deposit **la caution**

proprietary reservation **la réserve de propriété**

place of fulfillment of contract **le lieu d'exécution**

deadline **le terme/le délai**

guarantee **la garantie**

court of jurisdiction **le tribunal compétent**

business conditions **les conditions commerciales**

liability **la responsabilité**

purchase contract **le contrat d'achat**

delivery terms **les conditions de livraison**

time of delivery **le délai de livraison**

paragraph **le paragraphe**

appointment **la date/l'échéance**

signature **la signature**

agreement **l'accord**

contract **le contrat**

penalty **la pénalité**

right of preemption **le droit de préemption**

payment terms **les conditions de paiement**

Trade Fairs

I am looking for the stall of the company ...
Je cherche le stand de la sociéte ...

We deal in ...
Nous commerçons avec ...

We produce ...
Nous produisons ...

Here is my card.
Voici ma carte de visite.

Can I give you a brochure?
Puis-je vous laisser un dépliant ?

Can I show it to you briefly?
Est-ce que je peux vous le démontrer brièvement ?

Can you send me an offer?
Pouvez-vous m'envoyer une offre ?

Do you have a catalog?
Avez-vous un catalogue ?

Can I arrange a meeting?
Est-ce que je peux avoir un rendez-vous ?

exit **la sortie**

exhibitor **l'exposant**

ID card **la carte d'identité**

entrance **l'entrée**

invitation **l'invitation**

technical visitors **les visiteurs professionnels**

aisle **le couloir**

hall **le hall**

catalog **le catalogue**

brand **la marque**

name badge **la plaquette**

press conference **la conférence de presse**

brochure **le dépliant**

stall/stand **le stand**

floor **l'étage**

trademark **la marque commerciale**

The general provisions of the contract, the so-called fine print, are *les conditions générales du contrat*.

English – French

A

a little un peu de
a, an une, un
abbey abbaye (f)
abortion avortement (m)
abscess abcès (m)
accident accident (m)
acknowledgment reçu (m)
acquaintance connaissance (f)
actor acteur (m)
actress actrice (f)
ad annonce (f)
adapter adaptateur (m)
address adresse (f)
adhesive tape ruban adhésif (m)
administration administration (f)
aerobics aérobic (m)
afterward après
again de nouveau
agent courtier (m)
agreement accord (m)
air air (m)
air conditioning air climatisé (m)
air mattress matelas pneumatique (m)
air pump pompe (f)
airmail par avion
airport aéroport (m)
aisle couloir (m)
aisle seat place près du couloir (f)
alarm clock réveil (m)
all tout, toute, tous, toutes
Allen wrench clé à six pans creux (f)
allergy allergie (f)
alley ruelle (f)
almond amandes (f)
altar autel (m)
alter modifier
although même si
aluminum foil papier aluminium (m)
alumna ancienne étudiante (f)
amazing incroyable
ambulance ambulance (f)
amusing amusant
anchor ancre (f)
anchovies anchois (m)
and et
anesthesia anesthésie (f)

anesthetic anesthésie (f)
angina angine (f)
anglerfish lotte de mer (f)
angry contrarié
ankle cheville (f)
annoyed stressé
anorak anorak (m)
answering machine répondeur automatique (m)
antique store antiquité (f)
antiques antiquités (f)
apartment appartement (m)
appendicitis appendicite (f)
appendix appendice (m), pièce jointe (f)
apple pomme (f)
apple juice jus de pomme (m)
apple pie tarte aux pommes (f)
appointment rendez-vous (m), échéance (f)
apricot abricot (m)
April avril (m)
apron tablier (m)
archaeology archéologie (f)
architect architecte (m)
architecture architecture (f)
area code indicatif (m)
arm bras (m)
armchair fauteuil (m)
army armée (f)
arrest arrestation (f)
arrival entrée (f)
arrival time heure d'arrivée (f)
art art (m)
art gallery galerie d'art (f)
artery artère (f)
artichokes artichauts (m)
artificial leather similicuir (m)
artist artiste (m)
arts and crafts arts décoratifs (m)
as quand
ascent montée (f)
ashtray cendrier (m)
ask demander
asparagus asperges (f)
asthma asthme (m)

at chez
at night la nuit
at noon à midi
athletics athlétisme (m)
August août (m)
aunt tante (f)
Austria Autriche (f)
author auteur (m), écrivain (m)
authorized officer fondé de pouvoir (m)
automatic teller (ATM) distributeur automatique de billets (m)
automatic ticket vending machine distributeur automatique de billets (m)
autumn automne (m)
avocado avocat (m)
awesome incroyable

B

baby cream crème pour bébés (f)
baby food nourriture pour nouveau-né (f)
backache mal de dos (m)
backfire allumage défectueux (m)
backpack sac à dos (m)
backyard jardin de derrière (m)
bacon lard fumé (m)
bad mauvais
badge badge (m)
badminton badminton (m)
badminton rackets badminton (m)
baggage bagage (m)
baggage carts chariot porte-bagages (m)
baggage claim remise des bagages (f)
baggage deposit compartiment pour bagages (m)
baked cuit au four
baked goods biscuits (m)
baker boulanger (m)
bakery boulangerie (f)
balance équilibre (m)
balcony balcon (m)
ball ballon (m)
ballet ballet (m)
balloon ballon (m)
ballpoint pen stylo-bille (m)

balsamic vinegar vinaigre balsamique (m)
banana banane (f)
bandage bandage (m)
band-aid pansement (m)
bank banque (f)
barbecue grillade (f)
barley orge (m)
barrette barrette (f)
baseball base-ball (m)
basil basilique (m)
basketball basket (m)
bath salle de bains (f)
bath slippers chaussures de bain (m)
bath sponge éponge (f)
bath towel serviette de bain (f)
bathing cap bonnet de bain (m)
bathrobe peignoir (m)
bathtub baignoire (f)
batiste batiste (f)
battery batterie (f)
bayleaves feuilles de laurier (f)
beach plage (f)
beach cabin cabine (f)
beach towel drap de plage (m)
beans haricots (m)
beard barbe (f)
beautiful beau, belle
because parce que
bed lit (m)
bed sheet drap (m)
bedpan pistolet (m)
bedroom chambre (f)
bed-warmer bouillotte (f)
beech hêtre (m)
beef bœuf (m)
beef broth bouillon de bœuf (m)
beer bière (f)
before devant
beginner débutant (m)
believe croire
bell cloche (f)
bell pepper peperoni (m)
bellboy groom (m)
belt ceinture (f)
berth couchette (f)
beverage boisson (f)
bicycle pump pompe de la bicyclette (f)
bicycle racing course de bicyclettes (f)
bicycle store magasin pour bicyclettes (m)
bikini bikini (m)
bill addition (f)

billboard panneau d'affichage (m)
billfold portefeuille (m)
billiards billard (m)
billion milliard (m)
binoculars jumelles (f)
biologist biologiste (m)
birthplace maison natale (f)
bite morsure (f)
black noir
black bread pain noir (m)
black salsify scorsonère (m)
black tea thé noir (m)
black-and-white noir et blanc
blackberries mûres (f)
bladder vessie (f)
blanket couverture (f)
blazer blazer (m)
bleeding saignement (m)
blinker feux clignotants (m)
blood sang (m)
blood transfusion transfusion de sang (f)
blood type groupe sanguin (m)
blouse chemisier (m)
blow-dry sécher avec le sèche-cheveux
blue bleu
blue fish poisson bleu (m)
blueberries myrtilles (f)
boar sanglier (m)
board of trustees conseil de surveillance (m)
boarding pass ticket d'embarquement (m)
boat barque (f)
boat rental location de bateaux (f)
body lotion lait pour le corps (m)
boil furoncle (m)
boiled bouilli
bones os (m)
bookkeeper comptable (m)
bookseller libraire (m)
bookstore librairie (f)
bootlegger bootlegger (m)
boots bottes (f)
botanical gardens jardin botanique (m)
botany botanique (f)
bottle biberon (m)
bottle opener décapsuleur (m)
bow proue (f)

bowl bol (m)
bowling quilles (f)
bowtie nœud papillon (m)
boxing boxe (f)
bra soutien-gorge (m)
bracelet bracelet (m)
braces appareil pour les dents (m)
brain cerveau (m), cervelle (f)
braised étouffée
brake freiner
brake cable câble des freins (m)
brake fluid liquide du frein (m)
brake light feux de stop (m)
brake lining garniture de frein (f)
brakes frein (m)
brand marque (f)
Brazil nuts noix du Parà (f)
bread pain (m)
breaded pané
breakdown panne (f)
breakdown assistance assistance mécanique (f)
breakfast petit déjeuner (m)
breast poitrine (f)
bridge pont (m)
briefcase serviette (f)
brilliant génial
broccoli brocoli (m)
brochure dépliant (m)
bronchial tubes bronches (f)
bronchitis bronchite (f)
brooch broche (f)
brook ruisseau (m)
broom balais (m)
brother frère (m)
browned passé à la poêle
bruise contusion (f)
brussel sprouts chou de Bruxelles (m)
buck mâle (m)
bucket seau (m)
building édifice (m)
bumper pare-chocs (m)
bungalow bungalow (m)
burn brûlure (f)
bush-beans flageolet (m)
business card carte de visite (f)
business meeting rendez-vous d'affaire (m)
business partners partenaire (commercial) (m)
businessman entrepreneur (m), commerçant (m)

busy signal tonalité occupée (f)
butane gas gaz butane (m)
butcher boucher (m)
butter beurre (m)
button bouton (m)
buy acheter

C

cab driver chauffeur de taxi (m)
cabaret cabaret (m)
cabbage chou blanc (m), chou (m)
cabin cabine (f)
cable câble (m)
cable railway téléphérique (m)
cactus-fruit fruit du cactus (m)
cake gâteau (m)
calendar calendrier (m)
calf mollet (m), veau (m)
call-button sonnette (f)
cambric batiste (f)
camera appareil photo (m)
camera bag étui de l'appareil photo (m)
camper camping-car (m)
campsite camping (m)
can pouvoir, boîte (f)
can opener ouvre-boîtes (m)
canal canal (m)
cancer cancer (m)
candies douceurs (f)
candle bougie (f)
candlestick chandelier (m)
candy friandises (f)
canned food conserves (f)
canoe canoë (m)
canvas toile (f)
canyon canyon (m)
cap bonnet (f)
cap with visor casquette (f)
capers câpre (f)
capon chapon (m)
cappuccino café crème (m)
captain capitaine (m)
car voiture (f)
car documents papiers de la voiture (m)
car ferry ferry-boat (m)
car mechanic mécanicien (m)
car number numéro du wagon (m)
car racing course automobil (f)
carambola carambolier

caraway seed cumin (m)
carburetor carburateur (m)
card telephone téléphone à carte (m)
carnation œillet (m)
carp carpe (f)
carpenter menuisier (m), charpentier (m)
carrots carottes (f)
cash payment paiement comptant (m)
cash register caisse (f)
cashier caisse (f)
casino casino (m)
cassette player balladeur (m)
cassette recorder magnétophone (m)
castle château (m)
cat chat (m)
catalog catalogue (m)
catfish silure (m)
cathedral cathédrale (f)
Catholic catholique
cauliflower chou-fleur (m)
cave caverne (f)
CD player lecteur laser (m), lecteur CD (m)
CD-ROM drive lecteur de CD-ROM (m)
CD-writer graveur de CD-ROM (m)
celery céleri (m)
cell phone portable (m)
cemetery cimetière (m)
center nave nef centrale (f)
center part raie au milieu (f)
centimeter centimètre (m)
central heating chauffage central (m)
ceramics poterie (f), faïence (f)
chain chaîne (f)
chain guard carter de chaîne (m)
chair chaise (f)
chair lift télésiège (m)
chairman supérieur (m)
chalk craie (f)
chambermaid personnel de service (m)
change monnaie (f)
chapel chapelle (f)
charcoal charbon de bois (m)
charcoal pencils crayons de charbon (m)
charge tarif (m)
cheap bon marché

cheat escroc (m), tromper
check chèque (m)
checkered à carreaux
checkroom dépôt de bagages (m)
cheese fromage (m)
chemist chimiste (m)
chemistry chimie (f)
cherry cerise (f)
chervil cerfeuil (m)
chess échecs (m)
chestnut chataigne (f)
chick poussin (m)
chicken poulet (m), coquelet (m)
chicken broth bouillon de poulet (m)
chickenpox varicelle (f)
chickpeas pois chiche (m)
chicory chicorée (f)
child care encadrement pour les enfants (m)
children enfants (m)
children's book livre pour enfants (m)
children's playground aire de jeu (f)
children's shoes chaussures pour enfants (f)
child's bed lit pour enfants (m)
chili chili (m)
chills frissons (m)
chimney cheminée (f)
chimney sweep ramoneur (m)
chine (of beef) échine (f)
chive ciboulette (f)
chocolate chocolat (m)
choir chœur (m)
choir-loft galerie (f)
Christian chrétien (m)
Christianity christianisme (m)
Christmas Noël (m)
church église (f)
church service messe (f)
cigarette holder fume-cigarette (m)
cigarettes cigarettes (f)
cigarillos petits cigares (m)
cigars cigares (m)
cinema cinéma (m)
cinnamon cannelle (f)
circulatory disorder troubles de la circulation (m)
circus cirque (m)
citizens' initiative comité municipal (m)

civil servant fonctionnaire (m)
clam palourde (f)
cleaning blanchisserie (f)
cleaning rag chiffon (m)
clearing éclaircie (f)
cliff rocher (m)
climbing belt baudrier (m)
climbing boots chaussures pour grimpeurs (m), chaussures de montage (f)
climbing path sentier (m)
clip agrafe (f)
cloakroom vestiaire (m)
cloister cloître (m)
closed fermé
closet vestiaire (m)
clothes brush brosse pour vêtements (f)
clothes dryer séchoir à linge (m)
clothes racks séchoir (m)
clothesline corde pour étendre le linge (f)
clothespins pinces à linge (f)
clothing store commerce d'habillement (m)
clouds nuages (m)
cloudy nuageux
clove clou de girofle (m)
clutch embrayage (m)
coal heating chauffage au charbon (m)
coalition coalition (f)
coast côte (f)
coat manteau (m)
cocoa cacao (m)
coconut noix de coco (f)
COD contre remboursement
codfish morue (f)
coffee café (m)
coffee grinder moulin à café (m)
coffee machine cafetière (f)
coffee with ice cream café liégeois (m)
coins monnaie (f)
cold froid, rhume (m)
collar col (m)
collarbone clavicule (f)
colleague collègue (m)
collect call appel en PCV (m)
college université (f)
color faire une couleur
color rinse reflet (m)
colored coloré

colored laundry vêtements délicats (m)
colored pen crayon de couleur (m)
comb peigne (m)
come venir
comedy comédie (f)
commission commission (f)
commuter train train suburbain (m)
compartment compartiment (m)
compass boussole (f)
complaint plainte (f)
compressed-air bottles bouteille à air comprimé (f)
computer expert expert EDP (m)
computer store commerce d'ordinateurs (m)
concealer crayon (m)
concert concert (m)
concert hall salles des concerts (f)
concussion traumatisme crânien (m)
condom préservatif (m)
condominium copropriété (f)
conductor guichetier (m)
conference conférence (f)
congressman membre du congrès (m)
connecting flight vol de correspondance (m)
constipation constipation (f)
constitution constitution (f)
construction worker employé du bâtiment (m)
consulate consulat (m)
contact lenses lentilles (f)
contract contrat (m)
convention congrès (m)
cook cuisinier (m)
cookbook livre de cuisine (m)
cookies petits fours (m)
cooking course cours de cuisine (m)
coolant eau de refroidissement (f)
cooler seau à champagne (m), glacière (f)
cooperation coopération (f)
copper cuivre (m)
corduroy velours (m)
cork bouchon (m)

corkscrew tire-bouchon (m)
corn maïs (m)
cosmetics store institut de beauté (f)
costs frais (m)
cotton coton (m)
cough toux (f)
cough drops pastilles contre le mal de gorge (f)
cough syrup sirop contre la toux (m)
counter guichet (m)
country road route départementale (f)
county comté (f)
course cours (m)
cousin cousin, cousine (m, f)
cover couverture (f)
cow vache (f)
crab crabe (m), écrevisse (f), crevette (f)
crab cocktail cocktail de crevettes (m)
cracker pain de seigle croustillant (m)
craftsperson artisan (m)
cramp crampe (f)
crampons crampons (m)
cranberries myrtilles rouges (f)
crawfish langouste (f)
crayon crayons couleur (m)
cream crème Chantilly (f)
creamer pot à crème (m)
creamery fromager (m)
credit card carte de crédit (f)
crepe crêpé (m)
cress cresson (m)
crew équipage (m)
crime crime (m)
croissant croissant (m)
croquettes croquettes (f)
cross croix (f)
cross-country skiing ski de fond (m)
crossroad croisement (m)
crossroads carrefour (m)
crosswalk passage piéton (m)
crown couronne (f)
cruise croisière (f)
crypt crypte (f)
cucumber concombre (m)
cufflinks boutons de manchette (m)
cuffs poignées (f)
culture culture (f)

cup tasse (f)
curd fromage blanc (m)
curler bigoudi (m)
curls boucles (f)
currants groseilles rouges (f)
currency devise (f)
current courant (m)
curtain rideau (m)
customer service service clients (m)
customs douane (f)
customs check contrôle douanier (m)
customs declaration déclaration douanière (f)
customs regulations réglementations douanières (f)
cute mignon
cutlery couverts (m)
cutlet côtelette (f)
cycling cyclisme (m)
cylinder head culasse de cylindres (f)

D........................
daily quotidien
dairy products produits laitiers (m)
daisy marguerite (f)
dam barrage (m)
dance danse (f)
dandruff pellicules (f)
dark foncé
darling chérie, chéri (f/m)
darts fléchettes (f)
date date (f)
date of arrival jour d'arrivée (m)
date of departure jour de départ (m)
dates dattes (f)
daughter fille (f)
daughter-in-law belle-fille (f)
dawn aube (f)
day jour (m)
day after tomorrow après demain
day before yesterday avant hier
day ticket billet journalier (m)
deadline terme (m)
deceive tromper
December décembre (m)
deck pont (m)
deck chair chaise sur le pont (f), chaise longue (f)
decorator décorateur (m)

deep profond
deep-fried frit
deep-fried cutlet escalope (f)
deer chevreuil (m)
defeat défaite (f)
degree of difficulty degré de difficulté (m)
delay retard (m)
delicatessen traiteur (m)
delivery terms conditions de livraison (f)
democracy démocratie (f)
denomination religion (f)
dental bridge bridge (m)
dental floss fil dentaire (m)
dental surgeon mécanicien-dentiste (m)
dental technician mécanicien-dentiste (m)
dentist dentiste (m)
denture dentier (m)
deodorant déodorant (m)
department rayon (m)
department store grand magasin (m)
departure sortie (f), départ (m)
departure time heure de décollage (f)
deposit caution (f)
depressed déprimé
depth meter bathomètre (m)
descent descente (f)
desert désert (m)
desk bureau (m)
dessert dessert (m)
detergent détergent (m)
diabetes diabète (m)
diagonally striped à raies transversales
dial tone tonalité libre (f)
diamond diamant (m)
diapers couches (f)
diarrhea diarrhée (f)
dictionary dictionnaire (m)
diesel Diesel (m)
dill aneth (m)
dining car wagon-restaurant (m)
dinner dîner (m)
diphteria diphtérie (f)
direct dialing numéro direct (m)
discotheque discothèque (f)
dish assiette (f)
dishes vaisselle (f)
dishrack égouttoir à vaisselle (m)

dishwasher lave-vaisselle (m)
dishwashing liquid liquide vaisselle (m)
disinfectant désinfectant (m)
disposable needle seringue jetable (f)
distance meter télémètre (m)
distributor distributeur (m)
district attorney substitut du procureur (m)
diving plongée (f)
diving clock montre de plongée (f)
diving goggles lunettes de plongée (f)
diving license brevet de plongeur (m)
do faire
dock quai (m)
doctor docteur (m)
doctor's assistant secrétaire médicale (f)
dog chien (m)
dome coupole (f)
donkey âne (m)
door porte (f)
door handle poignée de la portière (f)
double bed lit à deux places (m)
double cabin double cabine (f)
double room chambre pour deux personnes (f)
double-decker autobus à deux étages (m)
downhill skiing descente (f)
downtown centre ville (m)
dozen douzaine (f)
drain filtre d'évacuation (m)
drama drame (m)
dreadful épouvantable
dress robe (f)
drill perceuse (f)
drink boire
drinking water eau potable (f)
driver conducteur (m)
drizzle pluie fine (f)
drug drogue (f)
druggist droguiste (m)
drugstore pharmacie (f)
drum brake frein à tambour (m)
dry sec

dry cleaning pressing (m)
dry goods articles de mercerie (m)
dry-cleaning lavage à sec (m)
dryer sèche-linge (m)
duck canard (m)
dumb-bell haltère (m)
dune dune (f)
during the day durant la journée
dustpan balayette (f)
dutiable passible du droit de douane
duty-free exempt du droit de douane
DVD player lecteur DVD (m)
dynamo dynamo (f)

E
each chacun, chacune
ear oreille (f)
ear drops gouttes pour les oreilles (f)
ear of grain épi (m)
ear, nose, and throat specialist oto-rhino(-laryngologiste) (m)
earlier autrefois
early tôt
earrings boucles d'oreille (f)
easel chevalet (m)
Easter Pâques
eat manger
economy économie (f)
eel anguille (f)
egg dishes plats à base d'œufs (m)
eggplant aubergine (f)
elastic gomina (f), élastique (m)
elbows coude (m)
elderberries sureau (m)
elections élections (f)
electric blanket couverture chauffante (f)
electric heating chauffage électrique (m)
electric range four électrique (m)
electrical appliances store commerce d'électroménagers (m)
electrical connection branchement électrique (m)
electrical cord câble d'alimentation (m)
electrician électricien (m)
electricity électricité (f)

elevator ascenseur (m)
embassy ambassade (f)
emergency appel d'urgence (m)
emergency brake frein de secours (m)
emergency exit sortie de secours (f)
emergency flashers feux de détresse (m)
employee employé (m)
empty vide
enclosure pièce jointe (f)
engineer ingénieur (m)
English anglais (m)
enough assez
entrance entrée (f)
envelope enveloppe (f)
eraser gomme (f)
essays essais (m)
escalator escalier roulant (m)
espresso express (m)
event spectacle (m)
excavations fouilles (f)
excellent excellent
excess baggage bagage en excédent (m)
exchange change (f)
exchange bureau bureau de change (m)
exchange rate taux de charge (m)
exhaust échappement (m)
exhibition exposition (f)
exhibitor exposant (m)
exit sortie (f)
expenses frais (m)
expensive cher, chère
export exportation (f)
express mail express (m)
express train train direct (m)
extension cord rallonge (f)
external à usage externe
extra costs frais supplémentaires (m)
eye œil (m)
eyebrow sourcil (m)
eyebrow pencil mascara (m)
eyelid paupière (f)
eye-shadow fard à paupières (m)

F
fabric store magasin de tissus (m)
face visage (m)
face cloths gant de toilette (m)
factory usine (f)

fall tomber
fall in love tomber amoureux
fallopian tubes trompe de fallope (f)
family ticket billet pour famille (m)
fantastic fantastique
far loin
farm ferme (f)
farmer agriculteur (m)
far-sighted presbyte
fashion mode (f)
fast rapide
father père (m)
father-in-law beau-père (m)
faucet robinet (m)
fax fax (m)
February février (m)
feel sentir
fees honoraires (m)
felt feutre (m)
felt-tip pen feutre (m)
fender aile (f)
fennel fenouil (m)
ferry ferry-boat (m)
festival festival (m)
fever fièvre (f)
few peu
fiancé fiancé (m)
fiancée fiancée (f)
field champ (m)
figs figues (f)
figure skating patinage artistique (m)
fillet steak bifteck dans le filet (m)
filling plomb (m)
film film (m)
finance finance (f)
find trouver
finger doigt (m)
fins palmes (f)
fire feu (m)
fire department sapeurs-pompiers (m)
first premier
fish poisson (m)
fish store poissonnerie (f)
fishing pêche (f)
fishing license permis de pêche (m)
fishing line ligne (f)
fishing rod canne à pêche (f)
fixative fixateur (m)
flannel flanelle (f)
flashbulb flash (m)
flasher feux clignotants (m)
flashlight lampe de poche (f)

flat noodles les taglitesses (f)
flatulence aérophagie (f)
flavor parfum (m)
flea market marché aux puces (m)
flight vol (m)
flight number numéro du vol (m)
flight schedule horaire du vol (m)
float flotteur (m)
flood inondation (f)
floor étage (m)
florist fleuriste (m)
flounder sole (f), flet (m)
flour farine (f)
flu grippe (f)
fly swatter attrape-mouches (m)
fog brouillard (m)
folding chair chaise pliante (f)
folding table table pliante (f)
folk festival fête folklorique (f)
font fonts baptismaux (m)
foot pied (m)
footpath sentier (m)
for pour
forefinger auriculaire (m)
foreigner étranger (m)
forget oublier
fork fourchette (f)
format format (m)
fortress forteresse (f)
fountain fontaine (f)
fountain pen stylo-plume (m)
fracture fracture des os (f)
freight charges frais de transport (m)
freighter navire marchand (m)
french fries frites (f)
fresh cheese fromage frais (m)
fresh produce stand fruits et légumes
Friday vendredi (m)
fried egg œufs à la poêle (m)
fried potatoes pommes de terre sautées (f)
friend ami, amie (m/f)
frieze frise (f)
front axle essieu avant (m)
front wheel fork fourche roue avant (f)
frost gel (m)

fruit fruits (m)
fruit juice jus de fruits (m)
fruit stand fruits et légumes
fruit tea thé aux fruits (m)
fruity fruité
frustrated frustré
frying pan poêle (f)
fuel guage témoin du carburant (m)
fuel injector pump injecteur (m)
full plein/satisfait
full board pension complète (f)
full-bodied onctueux
funnel entonnoir (m)
furniture meubles (m)
furrier magasin de fourrures (m)

G..........................
gall bladder vésicule biliaire (f)
gallery galerie (f)
garage garage (m)
garbage ordures (f)
garbage can poubelle (f)
garden jardin (m)
gardener jardinier (m)
garlic ail (m)
gas essence (f)
gas can bidon d'essence (m)
gas cylinder bouteille de gaz (f)
gas pedal accélérateur (m)
gas range poêle à gaz (m)
gas station station service (f)
gas stove fourneau à gaz (m)
gash coupure (f)
gaskets garniture (f)
gate porte d'embarquement (f)
gear roue dentée (f)
gear lever levier de vitesse (m)
gear shift dérailleur (m)
general delivery poste restante (f)
general practitioner généraliste (m)
gentle wash programme délicat (m)
geology géologie (f)
German measles rubéole (f)
Germany Allemagne (f)
get recevoir

gift cadeau (m)
ginger gingembre (m)
give donner
glass verre (m)
glass painting peinture sur verre (f)
glasses case étui (pour lunettes) (m)
glazed glacé
glazier vitrier (m)
glossy brillant
glove compartment boîte à gants (f)
gloves gants (m)
glue colle (f)
go aller
goat chèvre (f)
goat's milk cheese fromage de chèvre (m)
gold or (m)
golden bream dorade (f)
golden perch rascasse du Nord (f)
golf golf (m)
golf bag sac de golf (m)
golf ball balle de golf (f)
golf clubs club de golf (m)
good bon, bonne
Good Friday Vendredi saint (m)
goose oie (f)
gooseberry groseille à maquereau (f)
gorgeous splendide
Gothic gothique (m)
goulash ragoût (m)
government gouvernement (m)
gradient dénivelé (m)
grain blé (m)
gram gramme (m)
grandfather grand-père (m)
grandmother grand-mère (f)
grandson petit-fils (m)
grape raisin (m)
grape juice jus de raisin (m)
grapefruit pamplemousse (f)
graphics card carte graphique (f)
grave tombe (f)
gray gris
grayling ombre (m)
great remarquable
green vert
green beans haricots verts (m)
green pepper poivron vert (m)

green salad salade verte (f)
greeting formule de salutations (f)
grill barbecue (m)
grilled grillé
grilled chicken poulet rôti (m)
grocery store magasin d'alimentation (m)
ground haché
group card billet de groupe (m)
guarantee garantie (f)
guidebook guide touristique (m)
guinea fowl pintade (f)
gum gencive (f)
gymnastics gymnastique (f)
gynecologist gynécologue (m)

H
haddock églefin (m)
hail grêle (f)
hair cheveux (m)
hair dye teinture pour cheveux (f)
hairbrush brosse à cheveux (f)
hairdresser coiffeur (m)
hairdryer sèche-cheveux (m)
hairpins épingle à cheveux (f)
hairsetting lotion fixateur (m)
hairspray laque (f)
half demi, moitié
half board demi-pension (f)
halibut flétan (m)
hall hall (m)
ham jambon (m)
hammer marteau (m)
hammock hamac (m)
hand main (f), aiguille (f)
hand baggage bagage à main (m)
hand brake frein à main (m)
hand cream crème pour les mains (f)
hand towel serviette (f)
handbag sac à main (m)
handball handball (m)
hand-broom balayette (f)
handicrafts artisanat (m)
handlebars guidon (m)
hanger portemanteau (m)
hang-gliding parapente (m)

harbor port (m)
harbor tour tour du port (m)
hard disk disque dur (m)
hard-boiled egg œuf dur (m)
hardware quincaillerie (f)
hare lièvre (m)
harvester moissonneuse-batteuse (f)
hash browns pommes de terre sautées (f)
hat chapeau (m)
have avoir
hay foin (m)
hay fever rhume des foins (m)
hazelnut noisette (f)
hazy maussade
head tête (f)
head cold rhume (m)
head of department chef de service (m)
headache mal de tête (m)
headlight feu avant (m), phare (m)
headlight flasher clignotant (m)
headphones casque (m)
healer médecin en médecines douces (m)
health-food store produits diététiques (m)
hear entendre
hearing audience (f)
heart cœur (m)
heart attack infarctus (m)
heart problems mal au cœur (m)
heartburn brûlure d'estomac (f)
heat chaleur (f)
heater radiateur (m)
heating chauffage (m)
heel talon (m)
hello bonjour
helmet casque (m)
help aide (f), aider
hemorrhage hémorragie (m)
herbal tea tisane (f)
here ici
herring hareng (m)
hibiscus hibiscus (m)
high haut
high blood pressure hypertension (f)
high grade steel acier spécial (m)
high pressure haute pression (f)

high tide marée haute (f)
highchair chaise haute (f)
high-contrast très contrasté
highway autoroute (f)
hike faire des randonnées
hiking boots chaussures de marche (f)
hill colline (f)
hillbilly plouc (m)
hip hanche (f)
history histoire (f)
homemaker homme au foyer (m)
honey miel (m)
hood capot (m)
hooker prostituée (f)
horn klaxon (m)
horse cheval (m)
horse racing course de chevaux (f)
horseback riding équitation (f)
horseradish raifort (m)
hose tuyau (m)
hospital hôpital (m)
hot chaud
hot water eau chaude (f)
hot water heater chauffe-eau (m)
hot-air balloon montgolfière (f)
hotel hôtel (m)
hotelier hôtelier (m)
hot-water wash lessive lavable à 90 degrés (f)
hour heure (f)
hourly toutes les heures
housecoat robe de chambre (f)
household merchandise store magasin d'articles ménagers (m)
housewife femme au foyer (f)
how long combien de temps
how much combien
hub moyeu (m)
humidity humidité (f)
hunger faim (f)
hurricane ouragan (m)
husband mari (m)
hydrofoil hydroptère (m)

I
ice cream glace (f)
ice cream cone cornet (m)
ice cube glaçon (m)
ice hockey hockey sur glace (m)

ice skates patins à glace (m)
ID card carte d'identité (f)
if si
ignition allumage (m)
illustrated book volume illustré (m)
immersion heater thermoplongeur (m)
immigration immigration (f)
immigration authority bureau des immigrés (m)
import importation (f)
impressive impressionnant
in dans
in season pleine saison (f)
in the afternoon dans l'après-midi
in the evening le soir
in the morning au matin (m)
industry industrie (f)
infection infection (f)
inflammation inflammation (f)
inflammation of the bladder inflammation de la vessie (f)
information informations (f)
injection piqûre (f)
injure blesser
injury blessure (f)
ink encre (f)
inkjet printer imprimante jet d'encre (f)
inline skates patins en ligne (m)
inner tube tuyau (m)
insect bite piqûre d'insecte (f)
insect repellent insectifuge (m)
inside dedans
inside cabin cabine interne (f)
insulated bag sac thermique (m)
insurance assurance (f)
intermission entracte (m)
internal use à usage interne
interpreter interprète (m)
intestine intestin (m)
intra-uterine device stérilet (m)
introduce présenter
investment participation (f)
invitation invitation (f)

invoice facture (f)
iron fer à repasser (m)
ironing board planche à repasser (f)

J
jack cric (m)
jacket veste (f)
jacknife canif (m)
jam confiture (f)
January janvier (m)
jaundice jaunisse (f)
jaw mâchoire (f)
jazz jazz (m)
jellyfish méduse (f)
jetty passerelle (f)
Jew juif (m)
jeweler bijoutier (m)
jogging jogging (m)
joint articulation (f)
journalist journaliste (m)
judge juge (m)
judo judo (m)
July juillet (m)
jumper cables chargeur de câble à batterie (m)
June juin (m)

K
karate karaté (m)
kayak kayac (m)
kerosene lamp lampe à pétrole (f)
key clé (f)
keyboard clavier (m)
kid cabri (m)
kidneys reins (m)
kilo kilo (m)
kilometer kilomètre (m)
kingdom monarchie (f)
kitchen cuisine (f)
kitchen sponge éponge (f)
kitchenette cuisinette (f)
kite cerf-volant (m)
kiwi fruit kiwi (m)
kleenex mouchoirs en papier (m)
knee genou (m)
knife couteau (m)
knot nœud (m)
knotted bouclé
know savoir

L
labels étiquette (f)
ladder échelle (f)
lake lac (m)
lamb agneau (m)
lamp lampe (f)
landing atterrissage (m)
landlord locataire (m)

landscape panorama (m)
language course cours de langue étrangère (m)
larded entrelardé
large grand(e)
laser printer imprimante laser (f)
last stop terminus (m)
late tard
later plus tard
laundromat laverie automatique (f)
laundry basket panier à linge (m)
laundry detergent (powder) lessive en poudre (f)
laurel laurier (m)
law droit (m), loi (f)
lawyer licencié en droit (m), avocat (m)
laxative laxatif (m)
leafy celery céleri (m)
leather cuir (m)
leather coat manteau en cuir (m)
leather goods maroquinerie (f)
leather jacket veste en cuir (f)
leather soles semelle en cuir (f)
leek poireau (m)
leeward sous le vent
left à gauche
leg jarret (m), jambe (f)
lemon citron (m)
lemon squeezer presse-citron (m)
lens objectif (m)
lens shade pare-soleil (m)
lentils lentilles (f)
let laissez
letter lettre (f)
letterhead en-tête (m)
lettuce laitue (f)
liability responsabilité (f)
library bibliothèque (f)
licensing fees taxe de licence (f)
life guard maître nageur (m)
life jacket gilet de secours (m)
life preserver bouée de secours (f)
lifeboat bateau de sauvetage (m)
light clair, doux
light meter posemètre (m)
light switch interrupteur (m)

lightbulb ampoule (f)
lighter briquet (m)
lighthouse phare (m)
lightning éclair (m)
like plaire, comme
lily lis (m)
lime limette (f)
lime tree tilleul (m)
linen lin (m)
lip lèvre (f)
lipstick rouge à lèvres (m)
liqueur liqueur (f)
liquor store vins et liqueurs
listen écouter
liter litre (m)
literature littérature (f)
little peu
liver foie (m)
living room salle de séjour (f)
loafer flemmard (m)
lobster homard (m)
local call communication urbaine (f)
lock serrure (f)
locker petite armoire (f)
locking system fusible (m)
locksmith serrurier (m)
locomotive locomotive (f)
loin longe (f)
loin steak bifteck de longe (m)
long long
long-distance call communication extra urbaine (f)
look for chercher
loose desserré
loose-leaf notebook classeur (m)
loss perte (f)
lost-and-found office bureau des objets trouvés (m)
low basse pression (f)
low cholesterol pauvre en cholestérol
low season hors saison
low tide marée basse (f)
low-calorie pauvre en calories
low-contrast peu contrasté
lower leg jambe (en bas du genou) (f)
low-fat pas trop gras
luggage bagage (m)
lumbago lumbago (m)
lump bosse (f)
lunch déjeuner (m)
lung poumon (m)
lure appât (m)

M........................
macaroni macaronis (m)
mackerel maquereau (m)
magazine magazine (m)
magnet aimant (m)
magnifying glass loupe (f)
mailbox boîte aux lettres (f)
main entrance portail (m)
mainland continent (m)
male nurse infirmier (m)
management expert économiste (m)
manager manager (m), directeur (m)
mango mangue (f)
manufacturer fabriquant (m)
many beaucoup de
map carte (f)
map of the city plan de la ville (m)
maple érable (m)
March mars (m)
margarine margarine (f)
marjoram marjolaine (f)
market marché (m)
marketing marketing (m)
married marié
mascara rimmel (m)
mashed potatoes purée (f)
mason maçon (m)
master chef (m)
matches allumettes (f)
material matériel (m)
matte opaque
mattress matelas (m)
maximum (values) valeurs maximum (f)
May mai (m)
mayonnaise mayonnaise (f)
mayor's office bureau du maire (m)
meadow pré (m)
measles rougeole (f)
measuring tape mètre (m)
meat viande (f)
meat knife couteau à viande (m)
meat loaf rouleau de viande de hachée (f)
mechanic mécanicien (m)
medication médicament (m)
medicine médecine (f)
medieval médiéval
medium moyen(ne)
medlar nèfle (f)
meet connaître
meeting place point de rencontre (m)

melon melon (m)
menu menu (m)
merchant commerçant (m)
meter mètre (m)
microfiber microfibre (f)
microwave four à micro-ondes (m)
Middle Ages moyen âge (m)
middle finger majeur (m)
midnight minuit
midwife sage-femme (f)
migraine migraine (f)
milk lait (m)
milk jug bouilloire (f)
millimeter millimètre (m)
mineral water eau minérale (f)
mini-bar mini-bar (m)
minimum (values) valeurs minimum (f)
mint menthe (f)
minute minute (f)
mirabelle mirabelle (f)
mirror miroir (m)
miscarriage fausse couche (f)
mixed salad salade composée (f)
mocha moka (f)
modem modem (m)
moderately warm tempéré
Monday lundi (m)
money argent (m)
money exchange change (de devises) (m)
money order mandat (m)
month mois (m)
monument monument (m)
mooring embarcadère (m)
more plus
mosquito net voile anti-moustiques (m)
motel motel (m)
mother mère (f)
mother-in-law belle-mère (f)
motor moteur (m)
motorboat bateau à moteur (m)
mottled mélangé
mountain montagne (f)
mountain climbing alpinisme (m)
mountain hut chalet de montagne (m)
mountain peak sommet de la montagne (m)
mountain spring source (f)
mountaineering alpinisme (m)

mouth bouche (f)
mouthwash collutoire (m)
movie film (m)
much beaucoup
mudguard garde-boue (m)
mug pot (m)
mugging agression (f)
mulberries baies du mûrier (f)
mullet rouget (m)
mumps oreillons (m)
mural peinture murale (f)
muscle muscle (m)
museum musée (m)
mushrooms champignons (m)
music musique (f)
musical comédie musicale (f)
musician musicien (m)
Muslim musulman
mussel moule (f), coquillage (m)
must devoir
mustache moustaches (f)
mustard moutarde (f)
mutton mouton (m)
mystery novel roman policier (m)

N
nail clou/ongle (m)
nail file lime à ongles (f)
nail polish vernis à ongles (m)
nail polish remover dissolvant (m)
nail scissors ciseaux à ongles (m)
name badge plaquette (f)
nape of the neck nuque (f)
napkin serviette de table (f)
narcissus narcisse (f)
narrow étroit
national highway route nationale (f)
nature park parc naturel (m)
nausea nausée (f)
nave nef (f)
neck cou (m)
necklace collier (m)
negotiation négociation (f)
nephew neveu (m)
nerve nerf (m)
network cable câble réseau (m)
network card carte réseau (f)
new nouveau
New Year's Day nouvel an (m)

New Year's eve Saint-Sylvestre (f)
news nouvelles (f)
newsagent kiosque à journaux (m)
newspaper journal (m)
newsstand kiosque (m)
niece nièce (f)
night table table de chevet (f)
nightclub boîte de nuit (f)
nightshirt chemise de nuit (f)
nipple tétine (f)
no non
non-smoking section non-fumeur (m)
non-swimmer non-nageur (m)
noodle soup potage avec des pâtes (m)
noodles pâtes (f)
nose nez (m)
nosebleed saignement de nez (m)
notary notaire (m)
notebook cahier (m)
notepad bloc-notes (m)
nothing rien
notions mercerie (f)
November novembre (m)
now maintenant
nurse infirmière (f)
nut écrou/noix (m/f)
nutmeg noix de muscat (f)
nuts noix (f)

O
oak chêne (m)
oars pagaie (f)
oat avoine (f)
oatmeal bouillie d'avoine (f)
occupied occupé
ocean océan (m)
ocean view vue sur la mer (f)
October octobre (m)
off season hors saison
offer offre (f)
office hours horaire de visite (m)
office supplies papeterie (f)
official fonctionnaire (m)
oil huile (f)
oil filter filtre à l'huile (m)
oil paints couleurs à l'huile (f)
oil pastels bâton de craie (m)
ointment for burns pommade contre les brûlures (f)

okra gombo
old vieux, vieil, vieille
old city vieille ville (f)
olive oil huile d'olive (f)
omelet omelette (f)
on sur
one-week ticket billet hebdomadaire (m)
onions oignons (m)
only seulement
open hours horaires d'ouverture (m)
opera opéra (m)
operation opération (f)
operetta opérette (f)
opinion opinion (f)
optician opticien (m)
or ou
orange orange (f)
orange juice jus d'orange (m)
orchid orchidée (f)
order commander
oregano origan (m)
organic food produits biologiques (m)
ornithology ornithologie (f)
other d'autres
out (of) de
outfit costume (m)
outside dehors
outside cabin cabine externe (f)
outstanding excellent
oysters huîtres (f)
ozone ozone (m)

P
pacifier tétine (f)
padlock cadenas (m)
pail seau (m)
pain douleurs (f)
painkillers cachet anti-douleur (m)
paintbrush pinceau (m)
painter peintre en bâtiment (m)
painting peinture (f), tableau (m)
painting course cours de peinture (m)
pair une paire de
pajamas pyjama (m)
palette palette (f)
pancake crêpe (f)
panhandler mendiant (m)
panties culotte (f)
pants pantalon (m)
papaya papaye (f)
paper papier (m)

paper clips agrafes (f)
paper napkins serviettes en papier (f)
paragraph paragraphe (m)
paralysis paralysie (f)
parasol parasol (m)
parcel colis (m)
park parc (m)
parking fee prix du parking (m)
parking garage garage (m)
parking place parking (m)
parliament parlement (m)
parsley persil (m)
partridge perdrix (f)
pass col (m)
passenger passager (m)
passion-fruit fruits de la passion (m)
passport passeport (m)
pastels teintes pastel (f)
pastries pâtisseries (f)
pastry shop pâtisserie (f)
patterned avec des motifs
pawnbroker mont-de-piété (m)
pay phone téléphone à pièces (m)
payment terms conditions de paiement (f)
peach pêche (f)
peanut cacahouète (f)
pearl perle (f)
pearl necklace colier en perles (m)
pears poire (f)
peas petits pois (m)
pebble beach plage de galets (f)
pecan nut noix de pecan (f)
pedal pédale (f)
pedal boat pédalo (m)
pedestrian zone zone piétonne (f)
pediatrician pédiatre (m)
pencil crayon (m)
pencil sharpener cutter (m)
pendant pendentif (m)
Pentecost Pentecôte (f)
pepper poivre (m)
perch perche (f)
perfume parfum (m)
perfumery parfumerie (f)
perm permanente (f)
persimmon kaki (m)
pharmacy pharmacie (f)
pheasant faisan (m)
philosophy philosophie (f)
phone call appel téléphonique (m)

phone card carte téléphonique (f)
photo store photographe (m)
photographer photographe (m)
physics physique (f)
pickpocket pickpocket (m)
picture book livre illustré (m)
pie tarte aux fruits (f)
pig cochon (m)
pigeon pigeon (m)
pike brochet (m)
pike-perch sandre (m)
pilgrim pèlerin (m)
pillow oreiller (m)
PIN code confidentiel (m)
pin épingle (f)
pincers tenailles (f)
pine cone pommes de pin (f)
pine nut pignon (m)
pineapple ananas (m)
ping-pong ball balle de ping-pong (f)
ping-pong rackets raquette de ping-pong (f)
pink rose
pinkie auriculaire (m)
pipe pipe (f)
pipe accessories nécessaire pour pipe (m)
pipe cleaner cure-pipe (m)
pipe filters filtre pour pipe (m)
pistachios pistaches (f)
piston piston (m)
place place (f)
plane ticket billet d'avion (m)
planetarium planétarium (m)
plastic bags sachet en plastique (m)
plastic wrap sachet pour aliments (m)
platform quai (m)
platinum platine (m)
playing cards cartes à jouer (f)
please s'il vous plaît
pliers pinces (f)
plug bouchon (m), fiche (f)
plum prune (f)
plumber plombier (m)
pneumonia pneumonie (f)
poached eggs œufs pochés (m)
pocket calculator calculette (f)

pocket watch montre de poche (f)
poisoning empoisonnement (m)
police police (f)
police station commissariat de police (m)
policeman policier (m)
political asylum asile politique (m)
politics politique (f)
polka-dotted pointillé
pollution pollution (f)
pomegranate grenade (f)
pond étang (m)
poplin popeline (f)
port à bâbord
porter portier (m), porteur (m)
post office poste (f)
post office box (P.O. Box) boîte postale (f)
postage affranchissement (m)
postcard carte postale (f)
pot casserole (f), marmite (f)
potatoes pommes de terre (f)
poultry volaille (f)
pound demi-kilo (m)
powder poudre (f)
powder (snow) neige poudreuse (f)
powder room toilette pour dames (f)
power courant (m)
prawn crevettes (f)
preferably préférablement
pregnancy grossesse (f)
pregnancy test test de grossesse (m)
pregnant enceinte
pre-season hors saison
president président (m)
press presse (f)
press conference conférence de presse (f)
pretty beau
previously avant
price prix (f)
priest prêtre (m)
printed matter imprimé (f)
prison prison (f)
private beach plage privée (f)
private guest house habitant (m)
procession procession (f)
processor processeur (m)
production production (f)

professor professeur (m)
profit bénéfices (m)
programmer programmateur (m)
prom bal d'étudiants (m)
propane gaz propane (m)
Protestant protestant (m)
psychiatrist psychiatre (m)
psychologist psychologue (m)
psychology psychologie (f)
public school école publique (f)
public service service public (m)
puddle flaque (f)
pulpit chaire (f)
pumpkin citrouille (f)
purchase contract contrat d'achat (m)
purchase price prix d'achat (m)
purple mauve
purse porte-monnaie (m)
putty knife spatule (f)

Q
quail caille (f)
quarter quart (m)
quarterback quarterback (m)
quiet tranquille
quince coing (m)

R
rabbit lapin (m)
racing bike bicyclette de course (f)
radiator radiateur (m)
radio radio (f)
radish radis (m)
railroad chemin de fer (m)
railway station gare (f)
rain pluie (f), pleuvoir
raincoat imperméable (m)
raisins raisins secs (m)
RAM mémoire de travail (f)
rambutan ramboutan (f)
rape viol (m)
rape (v) violer
rash irruption cutanée (f)
raspberries framboises (f)
raw cru
ray rayon (m)
razor rasoir (m)
razor blades lames de rasoir (f)
read lire
rear partie arrière (f)
rear axle essieu arrière (m)

rear windshield lunette arrière (f)
rearview mirror rétroviseur (m)
rebate escompte (m)
receipt reçu (m)
receiver combiné (m)
reception réception (f)
reception desk enregistrement (m)
recipient destinataire (m)
recommend conseiller
record player tourne-disques (m)
record store magasin de disques (m)
red rouge
red beans haricots rouges (m)
red beets navet rouge (m)
red cabbage chou rouge (m)
red perch sébaste (m)
red wine vin rouge (m)
redneck péquenaud (m)
reduction réduction (f)
referee arbitre (m)
reflector réflecteur (m)
refrigerator frigidaire (m)
regatta régate (f)
regional régional
registered mail lettre recommandée (f)
regular essence normale (f)
relief relief (m)
religion religion (f)
remittance mandat postal (m)
remote control télécommande (f)
rent prêter, loyer
rental fee tarif de location (m)
repair réparer
repair kit kit de réparation des pneus (m)
repeat répéter
report protocole (m)
representative député (m), représentant (m)
reservation réservation (f)
reserve réserver
restaurant restaurant (m)
restroom toilettes (f)
retail commerce au détail (m)
retraining reclassement professionnel (f)
return flight vol de retour (m)
rheumatism rhumatisme (m)

rhubarb rhubarbe (f)
rib côte (f)
rice riz (m)
ride faire de la bicyclette
right droite, à droite
right to remain silent droit de refuser de témoigner (m)
rim jante (f)
ring bague (f)
ring finger annulaire (m)
rinse rincer
river fleuve (m)
riverboat trip excursion sur le fleuve (f)
roast rôti (m)
roast beef rosbif (m)
roasted rôti
rob dévaliser
rocky shoreline côte rocheuse (f)
roe œufs de poisson (m)
roll petit pain (m)
rolling pin rouleau à pâtisserie (m)
romanesque roman (m)
romantic romantique
roofer couvreur (m)
room chambre (f)
room number numéro de chambre (m)
room service service en chambre (m)
rooster coq (m)
root (of the tooth) racine (f)
root canal work traitement des racines (m)
rope corde (f)
rose rose (f)
rosemary romarin (m)
rosette rosace (f)
rouge fard (m)
round steak jambe (f)
round trip tour (m)
round-trip ticket billet aller retour (m)
rowboat barque à rames (f)
rowing/oar aviron (m)
rubber boots bottes en caoutchouc (f)
rubber dinghy canot pneumatique (m)
rubber raft aéroglisseur (m)
rubber soles semelle en caoutchouc (f)
rubberneck curieux (m)
rudder gouvernail (m)
rugby rugby (m)

ruins ruines (f)
ruler mètre (m), règle (f)
rump steak côte de bœuf (f)
rutabaga navet (m)
rye seigle (m)

S
saccharin saccharine (f)
sacristy sacristie (f)
saddle selle (f)
saddle (of lamb) dos (m)
saddlebags sac porte-outils (m)
safe coffre-fort (m)
safety pin épingle de nourrice (f)
saffron safran (m)
sage sauge (f)
sail voile (f)
sailing faire de la voile
sailing boat bateau à voile (m)
sailing licence permis nautique (m)
sailor marin (m)
salad salade (f)
salesperson vendeur (m)
salmon saumon (m)
salmonella salmonelles (f)
salt sel (m)
salt cod morue (f)
salutation titre (m)
same pareil
sanctuary réserve naturelle (f)
sand sable (m)
sand pail seau (m)
sandals sandales (f)
sandy beach plage de sable (f)
sanitary napkins serviettes hygiéniques (f)
sarcophagus sarcophage (m)
sardines sardines (f)
satin satin (m)
Saturday samedi (m)
sauerkraut choucroute (f)
sauna sauna (m)
sausage saucisse (f)
savoy cabbage chou frisé (m)
saw scie (f)
say dire
scales balance (f)
scallion petits oignons (m)
scallop vénéricarde (m), coquille Saint-Jacques (f), coquille (f)
scanner scanneur (m)

scarf écharpe (f)
schedule horaire (m)
schnapps eau de vie (f)
sciatica sciatique (f)
scientist scientifique (m)
scissors ciseaux (m)
scrambled eggs œufs brouillés (m)
screen écran (m)
screwdriver tournevis (m)
screws vis (f)
scrub brush brosse (f)
sculpture sculpture (f)
sea mer (f)
sea snail escargot de mer (m)
sea-bream daurade (f)
seahorse hippocampe (m)
sea-pike merluche (f)
seasickness mal de mer (m)
season ticket abonnement (m)
seat siège (m)
seat belt ceinture de sécurité (f)
seaweed algues (f)
second seconde (f), deuxième
secondhand store magasin de vêtements d'occasion (m)
security check contrôle de sécurité (m)
sedative sédatif (m)
see voir
self-timer câble du dispositif à retardement (m)
sell vendre
semolina semoule (f)
sender expéditeur (m)
senior citizen retraité (m)
September septembre (m)
sequoia séquoia (m)
sewing kit nécessaire de couture (m)
sewing needle aiguille (f)
shadows ombre (f)
shampoo shampooing (m)
shares actions (f)
shark requin (m)
shatter casser
shaving brush blaireau (m)
shaving cream mousse à raser (f)
sheep mouton (m)
sheep's milk cheese fromage de brebis (m)
sheet ice verglas (m)
shellfish fruits de mer (m)

sheriff shérif (m)
shiny brillant
shirt chemise (f)
shit merde
shock absorber pare-chocs (m)
shoe brush brosse pour chaussures (f)
shoe polish cirage (m)
shoe store magasin de chaussures (m)
shoelaces lacets (m)
shoemaker cordonnier (m)
shoes chaussures (f)
shopping bag sac (m)
shopping basket panier (m)
shopping cart chariot (m)
shopping center grande surface (f)
shore excursion excursion à terre (f)
short court
short circuit court-circuit (m)
short novel contes (m)
shorts short (m)
short-sighted myope
shoulder épaule (f)
shoulder bag sac en bandoulière (m)
shovel pelle (f)
shower douche (f)
showers ondée (f)
shutters volet (m)
shuttle navette (f)
shuttlecock volant (m)
sick malade
side aisle nef latérale (f)
side dishes garnitures (f)
sideburns pattes (f)
side part raie (f)
sideview mirrors rétroviseur extérieur (m)
sidewalk trottoir (m)
signature signature (f)
silk soie (f)
silver argent (m)
silverware couverts (m)
single célibataire
single bed lit à une place (m)
single cabin cabine individuelle (f)
sinker plomb (m)
sister sœur (f)
size pointure (f)
skate raie (f)
skateboard skate-board (m)
sketch pad bloc à dessin (m)

ski ski (m)
ski boots chaussure de ski (f)
ski instructor moniteur de ski (m)
ski lift remonte-pente (m)
ski pass forfait (m)
ski pole bâton de ski (m)
ski trail piste (f)
skiing skier
skilled worker travailleur spécialisé (m)
skin peau (f)
skirt jupe (f)
sky diving parachutisme (m)
skyscraper gratte-ciel (m)
sled luge (f)
sleeper wagon avec couchettes (m)
sleeping bag sac de couchage (m)
sleeping car wagon-lit (m)
sleeping pills somnifères (m)
sleet neige fondue (f)
sleeves manches (f)
slide frames petit cadre pour diapositives (m)
slip jupon (m)
slippers pantoufles (f)
slot machine machine à sous (f)
slow lent
small petit(e)
small parcel petit paquet (m)
smallpox variole (f)
smell sentir
smelt éperlan (m)
smoke fumer
smoked fumé
smoked salmon saumon fumé (m)
smoking section fumeur (m)
snaphook carabine (f)
snorkel tuba (m)
snow neiger, neige
snow chains chaînes à neige (f)
snowboard snowboard (m)
soap savon (m)
soccer football (m)
soccer ball ballon de foot (m)
socket prise de courant (f)
socks chaussettes (f)
soft drink limonade (f)
soft-boiled egg œuf à la coque (m)
sole semelle (f), sole (f)

some certain
son fils (m)
son-in-law gendre (m)
sore throat mal de gorge (m)
sorry pardon
sound card carte audio (f)
soup soupe (f)
sour cream crème fraiche (f)
souvenir shop magasin de souvenirs (m)
soy sauce sauce de soja (f)
spaghetti spaghettis (m)
spare parts pièces de rechange (f)
spare ribs côte (f)
spare wheel roue de secours (f)
spark plug bougie (f)
speak parler
speaker haut-parleur (m)
speedometer compteur de vitesse (m)
spices épices (f)
spider crab araignée de mer (f)
spinach épinards (m)
spinal column épine dorsale (f)
spin-dry essorage (m)
spin-dry (v) essorer
spin-dryer essoreuse (f)
spirits cognac (m)
splendid magnifique
spoke rayon (m)
spoon petite cuillère (f)
sport sport (m)
sporting goods store magasin d'articles de sport (m)
sprain entorse (f)
spring printemps (m)
square kilometer kilomètre carré (m)
square meter mètre carré (m)
squash squash (m)
squid calamar (m)
stadium stade (m)
stag cerf (m)
stain remover détachant (m)
stairways marches (f)
stamp timbre (m)
starboard à tribord
starfish étoile de mer (f)
starter démarreur (m)
statement déclaration (f)
stationery papier à lettres (m), articles de papeterie (m)
statue statue (f)

steak bifteck (m)
steal voler
steamed cuit à la vapeur
steamer navire à vapeur (m)
steeple clocher (m)
steering direction (f)
steering wheel volant (m)
stereo system chaîne Hi-Fi (f)
stew tailladé
still encore
stirred battu
stitch in the side point de côté (m)
stockings chaussettes (f)
stomach ventre (m), estomac (m)
stomachache mal de ventre (m), mal d'estomac (m)
stop arrêt (m)
stopover escale (f), séjour (m)
stopwatch chronomètre (m)
storm tempête (f)
straight ahead tout droit
strain déchirure (f)
strands mèche (f)
strange étrange
straw paille (f)
strawberries fraises (f)
street route (f)
street number numéro de la rue (m)
streetcar tramway (m)
string ficelle (f)
string beans haricots grimpeurs (m)
strong fort
student écolier (m), étudiant (m)
stuffed farci
subway métro (m)
suckling pig cochon de lait (m)
suction pump pompe d'aspiration (f)
suede daim (m)
sugar sucre (m)
suit complet (m)
suitcase valise (f)
suite suite (f)
summer été (m)
sun soleil (m)
sun glasses lunettes de soleil (f)
sunblock crème solaire (f)
sunburn coup de soleil (m)

Sunday dimanche (m)
sunflower tournesol (m)
sunflower oil huile de tournesol (f)
sunflower seeds graines de tournesol (f)
sunroof toit ouvrant (m)
sunset coucher du soleil (m)
sunstroke insolation (f)
super essence Super (f)
supermarket supermarché (m)
supplier fournisseur (m)
surcharge supplément (m)
surf ressac (m)
surfboard planche à surf (f)
surfing surf (m)
surgeon chirurgien (m)
suspenders bretelles (f)
swab frottis (m)
swamp marais (m)
sweater pull (m)
sweet sucré
sweet potatoes patates douces (f)
sweetbread ris (m)
swell houle (f)
swelling enflure (f), bosse (f)
swimmers nageur (m)
swimming pool piscine (f)
swimming ring bouée (f)
swimming trunks slip de bain (m)
swindler escroc (m)
swiss chard bette (f)
switchboard centrale (f)
Switzerland Suisse (f)
swollen enflé
swordfish espadon (m)
synagogue synagogue (f)
synthetic fiber fibre synthétique (f)
syringes seringue (f)
syrup sirop (m)

T............................
table table (f)
table tennis ping-pong (m)
tablecloth nappe (f)
tablets for headache cachets contre le mal de tête (m)
tablets for poor circulation médicament pour la circulation du sang (m)
tachometer compte-tours (m)
tail queue (f)

taillight feux de recul (m)
tailor couturier (m)
take prendre
takeoff décollage (m)
tamarind tamarin (m)
tampons tampons (m)
tangerine mandarine (f)
tangy piquant
tank réservoir (m)
tarragon estragon (m)
taste goûter
tax advisor conseiller fiscal (m)
taxes impôts (m)
tea thé (m)
teacher enseignant (m)
teaspoon cuillère à café (f)
technical book livre spécialisé (m)
telegram télégramme (m)
telephone téléphone (m)
telephone book annuaire (m)
telephone booth cabine téléphonique (f)
telephone line ligne (f)
telephone number numéro de téléphone (m)
telephoto lens téléobjectif (m)
television, TV télévision (f)
telex télex (m)
tell raconter
temple temple (m)
tendon tendon (m)
tennis tennis (m)
tennis ball balle de tennis (f)
tennis racket raquette de tennis (f)
tent tente (f)
tent peg piquet de tente (m)
tent pole mât de tente (m)
terrace terrasse (f)
terrific merveilleux
terrycloth tissu-éponge (m)
tetanus tétanos (m)
thank you merci
that cela
that one celui-là
thaw dégel (m)
theater théâtre (m)
theft vol (m)
then puis
there là
therefore en conséquence
thermometer thermomètre (m)
thermos bouteille thermos (f)

thief voleur (m)
thighs cuisse (f)
thimble dé à coudre (m)
think penser
thirst soif (f)
this one celui-ci
thread fil (m)
through à travers
thumb pouce (m)
thumbtacks petits clous/punaise (m/f)
thunder tonnerre (m)
thunderstorm orage (m)
Thursday jeudi (m)
thyme thym (m)
ticket billet (m)
ticket counter guichet (m)
ticket inspector contrôleur (m)
tie cravate (f)
tie pin épingle à cravate (f)
tights collant (m)
time of delivery délai de livraison (m)
timetable horaire (m)
tiny green peas petits pois doux (m)
tip pourboire (m)
tired fatigué
tires pneu (m)
tissues kleenex (m)
toast toast (m)
toaster grille-pain (m)
tobacco tabac (m)
tobacco store bureau de tabac (m)
today aujourd'hui
toe orteil (m)
toilet paper papier-toilette (m)
tomato juice jus de tomate (m)
tomatoes tomates (f)
tomorrow demain
ton tonne (f)
tongue langue (f)
tonsil amygdale (f)
tonsillitis infection des amygdales (f)
too much trop
tool outil (m)
tooth dent (f)
toothache mal de dents (m)
toothbrush brosse à dents (f)
toothpaste dentifrice (m)
tornado tornade (f)
tow remorquer
tower tour (f)

towing cable câble de remorque (m)
towing service service de remorquage (m)
town hall mairie (f)
toy jouet (m)
toy store magasin de jouets (m)
track quai (m)
track and field athlétisme (m)
track shoes chaussures d'athlétisme (f)
tractor tracteur (m)
trade fair messe (f)
trademark marque commerciale (f)
traffic light feu (m)
tragedy tragédie (f)
trailer caravane (f)
trainee apprenti (m)
tranquilizer sédatif (m)
transept nef transversale (f)
transfer virement (m), changer
transit voyage (m)
transmission boîte de vitesse (f)
transportation costs frais de transport (m)
trash bags sac-poubelle (m)
travel agency agence de voyage (f)
traveler's check chèque de voyage (m)
traveling bag sac de voyage (m)
traveling bed lit de camp (m)
tree arbre (m)
trial procès (m)
trillion billion (m)
tripe tripes (f)
tripod trépied (m)
trout truite (f)
trunk coffre (m)
try on essayer
t-shirt tee-shirt (m)
Tuesday mardi (m)
tuna thon (m)
turbot turbot (m)
turkey dindon (m)
turn signals feux clignotants (m)
turnips navet (m)
tuxedo smoking (m)
tweezers pince à épiler (f)
twine ficelle (f)
typhoon typhon (m)

U

ugly laid
ulcer ulcère (m)
umbrella parapluie (m)
uncanny mystérieux
uncle oncle (m)
unconscious perdre connaissance
underpants caleçon (m)
undershirt maillot de corps (m)
understand comprendre
underwear lingerie (f)
unit unité (f)
university université (f)
unleaded sans plomb
urologist urologue (m)
uterus utérus (m)

V

vacation apartment appartement (pour les vacances) (m)
vacation house maison de vacances (f)
vacation spot résidence hôtel (f)
vacuum cleaner aspirateur (m)
vagina vagin (m)
vaginitis vaginite (f)
valley vallée (f)
valuables objets de valeur (m)
valve soupape (f)
vanilla vanille (f)
v-belt courroie trapézoïdale (f)
VCR magnétoscope (m)
vegetable soup soupe de légumes (f)
vegetables légumes (m)
vein veine (f)
velvet velours (m)
ventilator ventilateur (m)
vertically striped à raies longitudinales
very très
veterinarian vétérinaire (m)
video cassette cassette vidéo (f)
vinegar vinaigre (m)
vineyard vignoble (m)
vintage vendanges (f)
viral illness maladie virale (f)
vision tension de l'œil (f)
volcano volcan (m)
volleyball volley-ball (m)
voltage tension électrique (f)
vote vote (m)

W

waffles gaufrette (f)
waistcoat gilet (m)
waiter garçon (m)
waiting room salle d'attente (f)
wall clock horloge (f)
wallet portefeuille (m)
walnut noix (f)
wardrobe vestiaire (m)
warm chaud
warning-triangle triangle (m)
wash basin lavabo (m)
washing machine machine à laver (f)
washroom lavabos (m)
wastepaper basket corbeille (f)
watchmaker horloger (m)
water eau (f)
water bottle gourde (f)
water connection branchement de l'eau (m)
water jug bidon d'eau (m)
water polo ballon de plage (m)
water pump pompe à eau (f)
watercolor crayons pastels (m)
watercolor paper papier pour peinture à l'eau (m)
watercolors peinture à l'eau (f), aquarelles (m)
watercress cresson (m)
waterfall cascade (f)
watering can arrosoir (m)
watermelon pastèque (f)
waterproof étanche
waterskiing ski nautique (m)
water-wings brassard (m)
wave vague (f)
wax cire (f)
weak faible
Wednesday mercredi (m)
weekend week-end (m)
weight poids (m)
weight belts ceinture en plomb (f)
wetland région marécageuse (f)
wetsuit combinaison de plongée (f)
what comment
wheat blé (m)
wheel roue (f)
wheelchair chaise roulante (f)
when quand

where où
whipped cream crème Chantilly (f)
whisk fouet (m)
white blanc
white beans haricots blancs (m)
white bread baguette (f)
white wine vin blanc (m)
Whitsun Pentecôte (f)
who qui
whole wheat bread pain complet (m)
whooping cough coqueluche (f)
why pourquoi
wide large
wife épouse (f)
wig perruque (f)
wild duck canard sauvage (m)
win victoire (f)
wind vent (m)
windbreaker anorak (m)
window pane vitre (f)
window seat place à côté de la fenêtre (f)
windows fenêtre (f)
windshield pare-brise (m)
windshield wiper essuie-glace (m)

windsurfing planche à voile (f)
windward au vent
wine vin (m)
wine list carte des vins (f)
wine store vins et liqueurs (f)
winter hiver (m)
wisdom tooth dent de sagesse (f)
with avec
without sans
wolf perch bar (m)
wooden spoon cuillère en bois (f)
wool laine (f)
work travailler
worker travailleur (f)
worsted tissu peigné (m)
wound blessure (f)
wrapping paper papier cadeau (m)
wrench clé plate (f)
wrestling catch (m)
wrinkle-free ne pas repasser
wrist poignet (m)
wristband bracelet (m)
wristwatch montre-bracelet (f)
write écrire
wrong faux

X
X-ray rayon x (m)

Y
yacht yacht (m)
year année (f)
yellow jaune
yellow pages pages jaunes (f)
yes oui
yesterday hier
yogurt yaourt (m)
young jeune
young fattened hen poulet d'engrais (m)
youth hostel auberge de jeunesse (f)

Z
zip code code postal (m)
zipper fermeture éclair (f)
zoo zoo (m)
zoology zoologie (f)
zucchini courgette (f)
zwieback biscotte (f)

French – English

A

à bâbord port
à carreaux checkered
à droite right
à gauche left
à midi at noon
à raies longitudinales vertically striped
à raies transversales diagonally striped
à travers through
à tribord starboard
à usage externe external
à usage interne internal use
abbaye (f) abbey
abcès (m) abscess
abonnement (m) season ticket
abricot (m) apricot
accélérateur (m) gas pedal
accident (m) accident
accord (m) agreement
acheter buy
acier spécial (m) high grade steel
acteur (m) actor
actions (f) shares
actrice (f) actress
adaptateur (m) adapter
addition (f) bill
administration (f) administration
adresse (f) address
aérobic (m) aerobics
aéroglisseur (m) rubber raft
aérophagie (f) flatulence
aéroport (m) airport
affranchissement (m) postage
agence de voyage (f) travel agency
agneau (m) lamb
agrafe (f) clip
agrafes (f) paper clips
agression (f) mugging
agriculteur (m) farmer
aide (f) help
aider help
aiguille (f) sewing needle, hands
ail (m) garlic
aile (f) fender
aimant (m) magnet
air (m) air
air climatisé (m) air conditioning

aire de jeu (f) children's playground
algues (f) seaweed
Allemagne (f) Germany
aller go
allergie (f) allergy
allumage (m) ignition
allumage défectueux (m) backfire
allumettes (f) matches
alpinisme (m) mountaineering, mountain climbing
amandes (f) almond
ambassade (f) embassy
ambulance (f) ambulance
ami, amie (m/f) friend
ampoule (f) lightbulb
amusant amusing
amygdale (f) tonsil
ananas (m) pineapple
anchois (m) anchovies
ancienne étudiante (f) alumna
ancre (f) anchor
âne (m) donkey
anesthésie (f) anesthetic, anesthesia
aneth (m) dill
angine (f) angina
anglais (m) English
anguille (f) eel
année (f) year
annonce (f) ad
annuaire (m) telephone book
anorak (m) anorak, windbreaker
antiquité (f) antique store
antiquités (f) antiques
août (m) August
appareil photo (m) camera
appareil pour les dents (m) braces
appartement (m) apartment
appartement (pour les vacances) (m) vacation apartment
appât (m) lure
appel d'urgence (m) emergency
appel en PCV (m) collect call
appel téléphonique (m) phone call
appendice (m) appendix

appendicite (f) appendicitis
apprenti (m) trainee
après afterward
après demain day after tomorrow
aquarelles (f) watercolors
araignée de mer (f) spider crab
arbitre (m) referee
arbre (m) tree
archéologie (f) archaeology
architecte (m) architect
architecture (f) architecture
argent (m) silver, money
armée (f) army
arrestation (f) arrest
arrêt (m) stop
arrosoir (m) watering can
art (m) art
artère (f) artery
artichauts (m) artichokes
articles de mercerie (m) dry goods
articles de papeterie (m) stationery
articulation (f) joint
artisan (m) craftsperson
artisanat (m) handicrafts
artiste (m) artist
arts décoratifs (m) arts and crafts
ascenseur (m) elevator
asile politique (m) political asylum
asperges (f) asparagus
aspirateur (m) vacuum cleaner
assez enough
assiette (f) dish
assistance mécanique (f) breakdown assistance
assurance (f) insurance
asthme (m) asthma
athlétisme (m) athletics, track and field
atterrissage (m) landing
attrape-mouches (m) fly swatter
au matin (m) in the morning
au vent windward
aube (f) dawn
auberge de jeunesse (f) youth hostel

aubergine (f) eggplant
audience (f) hearing
aujourd'hui today
auriculaire (m) index finger
autel (m) altar
auteur (m) author
autobus à deux étages (m) double-decker
automne (m) autumn
autoroute (f) highway
autrefois earlier
Autriche (f) Austria
avant previously
avant hier day before yesterday
avec with
avec des motifs patterned
aviron (m) rowing/oar
avocat (m) avocado, lawyer
avoine (f) oat
avoir have
avortement (m) abortion
avril (m) April

B . . . .
badge (m) badge
badminton (m) badminton, badminton rackets
bagage (m) baggage, luggage
bagage à main (m) hand baggage
bagage en excédent (m) excess baggage
bague (f) ring
baguette (f) white bread
baies du mûrier (f) mulberries
baignoire (f) bathtub
bal d'étudiants (m) prom
balais (m) broom
balance (f) scales
balayette (f) hand-broom, dustpan
balcon (m) balcony
balladeur (m) cassette player
balle de golf (f) golf ball
balle de ping-pong (f) ping-pong ball
balle de tennis (f) tennis ball
ballet (m) ballet
ballon (m) balloon, ball
ballon de foot (m) soccer ball
ballon de plage (m) beach ball

banane (f) banana
bandage (m) bandage
banque (f) bank
bar (m) wolf perch
barbe (f) beard
barbecue (m) grill
barque (f) boat
barque à rames (f) rowboat
barrage (m) dam
barrette (f) barrette
base-ball (m) baseball
basilique (m) basil
basket (m) basketball
basse pression (f) low
bateau à moteur (m) motorboat
bateau à voile (m) sailing boat
bateau de sauvetage (m) lifeboat
bathomètre (m) depth meter
batiste (f) cambric, batiste
bâton de craie (m) oil pastels
bâton de ski (m) ski pole
batterie (f) battery
battu stirred
baudrier (m) climbing belt
beau pretty
beau, belle beautiful
beaucoup much
beaucoup de many
beau-père (m) father-in-law
belle-fille (f) daughter-in-law
belle-mère (f) mother-in-law
bénéfices (m) profit
bette (f) swiss chard
beurre (m) butter
biberon (m) bottle
bibliothèque (f) library
bicyclette de course (f) racing bike
bidon d'eau (m) water jug
bidon d'essence (m) gas can
bière (f) beer
bifteck (m) steak
bifteck dans le filet (m) fillet steak
bifteck de longe (m) loin steak
bigoudi (m) curler
bijoutier (m) jeweler
bikini (m) bikini
billard (m) billiards
billet (m) ticket

billet aller retour (m) round-trip ticket
billet d'avion (m) plane ticket
billet de groupe (m) group card
billet hebdomadaire (m) one-week ticket
billet journalier (m) day ticket
billet pour famille (m) family ticket
billion (m) trillion
biologiste (m) biologist
biscotte (f) zwieback
biscuits (m) baked goods
blaireau (m) shaving brush
blanc white
blanchisserie (f) cleaning
blazer (m) blazer
blé (m) grain, wheat
blesser injure
blessure (f) injury, wound
bleu blue
bloc à dessin (m) sketch pad
bloc-notes (m) notepad
bœuf (m) beef
boire drink
boisson (f) beverage
boîte (f) can
boîte à gants (f) glove compartment
boîte aux lettres (f) mailbox
boîte de nuit (f) nightclub
boîte de vitesse (f) transmission
boîte postale (f) post office box (P.O. Box)
bol (m) bowl
bon marché cheap
bon, bonne good
bonjour hello
bonnet (m) cap
bonnet de bain (m) bathing cap
bootlegger (m) bootlegger
bosse (f) lump, swelling
botanique (f) botany
bottes (f) boots
bottes en caoutchouc (f) rubber boots
bouche (f) mouth
boucher (m) butcher
bouchon (m) cork, plug
bouclé knotted
boucles (f) curls
boucles d'oreille (f) earrings

bouée (f) swimming ring
bouée de secours (f) life preserver
bougie (f) spark plug, candle
bouilli boiled
bouillie d'avoine (f) oatmeal
bouilloire (f) milk jug
bouillon de bœuf (m) beef broth
bouillon de poulet (m) chicken broth
bouillotte (f) bed-warmer
boulanger (m) baker
boulangerie (f) bakery
boussole (f) compass
bouteille à air comprimé (f) compressed-air bottles
bouteille de gaz (f) gas cylinder
bouteille thermos (f) thermos
bouton (m) button
boutons de manchette (m) cufflinks
boxe (f) boxing
bracelet (m) wristband, bracelet
branchement de l'eau (m) water connection
branchement électrique (m) electrical connection
bras (m) arm
brassard (m) water-wings
bretelles (f) suspenders
brevet de plongeur (m) diving license
bridge (m) dental bridge
brillant glossy, shiny
briquet (m) lighter
broche (f) brooch
brochet (m) pike
brocoli (m) broccoli
bronches (f) bronchial tubes
bronchite (f) bronchitis
brosse (f) scrub brush
brosse à cheveux (f) hairbrush
brosse à dents (f) toothbrush
brosse pour chaussures (f) shoe brush
brosse pour vêtements (f) clothes brush
brouillard (m) fog
brûlure (f) burn
brûlure d'estomac (f) heartburn

bungalow (m) bungalow
bureau (m) desk
bureau de change (m) exchange bureau
bureau de tabac (m) tobacco store
bureau des immigrés (m) immigration authority
bureau des objets trouvés (m) lost-and-found office
bureau du maire (m) mayor's office

C

cabaret (m) cabaret
cabine (f) cabin, beach cabin
cabine externe (f) outside cabin
cabine individuelle (f) single cabin
cabine interne (f) inside cabin
cabine téléphonique (f) telephone booth
câble (m) cable
câble d'alimentation (m) electrical cord
câble de remorque (m) towing cable
câble des freins (m) brake cable
câble du dispositif à retardement (m) self-timer
câble réseau (m) network cable
cabri (m) kid
cacahouète (f) peanut
cacao (m) cocoa
cachet anti-douleur (m) painkillers
cachets contre le mal de tête (m) tablets for headache
cadeau (m) gift
cadenas (m) padlock
café (m) coffee
café crème (m) cappuccino
café liégeois (m) coffee with ice cream
cafetière (f) coffee machine
cahier (m) notebook
caille (f) quail
caisse (f) cash register, cashier
calamar (m) squid
calculette (f) pocket calculator
caleçon (m) underpants
calendrier (m) calendar

camping (m) campsite
camping-car (m) camper
canal (m) canal
canard (m) duck
canard sauvage (m) wild duck
cancer (m) cancer
canif (m) jacknife
canne à pêche (f) fishing rod
cannelle (f) cinnamon
canoë (m) canoe
canot pneumatique (m) rubber dinghy
canyon (m) canyon
capitaine (m) captain
capot (m) hood
câpre (f) capers
carabine (f) snaphook
carambolier carambola
caravane (f) trailer
carburateur (m) carburetor
carottes (f) carrots
carpe (f) carp
carrefour (m) crossroads
carte (f) map
carte audio (f) sound card
carte de crédit (f) credit card
carte de visite (f) business card
carte des vins (f) wine list
carte d'identité (f) ID card
carte graphique (f) graphics card
carte postale (f) postcard
carte réseau (f) network card
carte téléphonique (f) phone card
carter de chaîne (m) chain guard
cartes à jouer (f) playing cards
cascade (f) waterfall
casino (m) casino
casque (m) headphones, helmet
casquette (f) cap with visor
casser shatter
casserole (f) pot
cassette vidéo (f) video cassette
catalogue (m) catalog
catch (m) wrestling
cathédrale (f) cathedral
catholique Catholic
caution (f) deposit
caverne (f) cave

ceinture (f) belt
ceinture de sécurité (f) seat belt
ceinture en plomb (f) weight belts
cela that
céleri (m) leafy celery, celery
célibataire single
celui-ci this one
celui-là that one
cendrier (m) ashtray
centimètre (m) centimeter
centrale (f) switchboard
centre ville (m) downtown
cerf (m) stag
cerfeuil (m) chervil
cerf-volant (m) kite
cerise (f) cherry
certain some
cerveau (m) brain
cervelle (f) brain
chacun, chacune each
chaîne (f) chain
chaîne Hi-Fi (f) stereo system
chaînes à neige (f) snow chains
chaire (f) pulpit
chaise (f) chair
chaise haute (f) highchair
chaise longue (f) deck chair
chaise pliante (f) folding chair
chaise roulante (f) wheelchair
chaise sur le pont (f) deck chair
chalet de montage (m) mountain hut
chaleur (f) heat
chambre (f) room, bedroom
chambre pour deux personnes (f) double room
champ (m) field
champignons (m) mushrooms
chandelier (m) candlestick
change (f) exchange
change (de devises) (m) money exchange
changer transfer
chapeau (m) hat
chapelle (f) chapel
chapon (m) capon
charbon de bois (m) charcoal
chargeur de câble à batterie (m) jumper cables

chariot (m) shopping cart
chariot porte-bagages (m) baggage carts
charpentier (m) carpenter
chat (m) cat
chataigne (f) chestnut
château (m) castle
chaud warm, hot
chauffage (m) heating
chauffage au charbon (m) coal heating
chauffage central (m) central heating
chauffage électrique (m) electric heating
chauffe-eau (m) hot water heater
chauffeur de taxi (m) cab driver
chaussettes (f) stockings, socks
chaussure de ski (f) ski boots
chaussures (f) shoes
chaussures d'athlétisme (f) track shoes
chaussures de bain (m) bath slippers
chaussures de marche (f) hiking boots
chaussures de montage (f) climbing boots
chaussures pour enfants (f) children's shoes
chaussures pour grimpeurs (m) climbing boots
chef (m) master
chef de service (m) head of department
chemin de fer (m) railroad
cheminée (f) chimney
chemise (f) shirt
chemise de nuit (f) nightshirt
chemisier (m) blouse
chêne (m) oak
chèque (m) check
chèque de voyage (m) traveler's check
cher, chère expensive
chercher look for
chérie, chéri (f/m) darling
cheval (m) horse
chevalet (m) easel
cheveux (m) hair
cheville (f) ankle
chèvre (f) goat
chevreuil (m) deer
chez at
chicorée (f) chicory

chien (m) dog
chiffon (m) cleaning rag
chili (m) chili
chimie (f) chemistry
chimiste (m) chemist
chirurgien (m) surgeon
chocolat (m) chocolate
chœur (m) choir
chou (m) cabbage
chou blanc (m) cabbage
chou de Bruxelles (m) brussel sprouts
chou frisé (m) savoy cabbage
chou rouge (m) red cabbage
choucroute (f) sauerkraut
chou-fleur (m) cauliflower
chrétien (m) Christian
christianisme (m) Christianity
chronomètre (m) stopwatch
ciboulette (f) chive
cigares (m) cigars
cigarettes (f) cigarettes
cimetière (m) cemetery
cinéma (m) cinema
cirage (m) shoe polish
cire (f) wax
cirque (m) circus
ciseaux (m) scissors
ciseaux à ongles (m) nail scissors
citron (m) lemon
citrouille (f) pumpkin
clair light
classeur (m) loose-leaf notebook
clavicule (f) collarbone
clavier (m) keyboard
clé (f) key
clé à six pans creux (f) Allen wrench
clé plate (f) wrench
clignotant (m) headlight flasher
cloche (f) bell
clocher (m) steeple
cloître (m) cloister
clou de girofle (m) clove
clou/ongle (m) nail
club de golf (m) golf clubs
coalition (f) coalition
cochon (m) pig
cochon de lait (m) suckling pig
cocktail de crevettes (m) crab cocktail
code confidentiel (m) PIN
code postal (m) zip code

cœur (m) heart
coffre (m) trunk
coffre-fort (m) safe
cognac (m) spirits
coiffeur (m) hairdresser
coing (m) quince
col (m) collar, pass
colier en perles (m) pearl necklace
colis (m) parcel
collant (m) tights
colle (f) glue
collègue (m) colleague
collier (m) necklace
colline (f) hill
collutoire (m) mouthwash
coloré colored
combien how much
combien de temps how long
combinaison de plongée (f) wetsuit
combiné (m) receiver
comédie (f) comedy
comédie musicale (f) musical
comité municipal (m) citizens' initiative
commander order
comme like
comment what
commerçant (m) businessman, merchant
commerce au détail (m) retail
commerce d'électroménagers (m) electrical appliances store
commerce d'habillement (m) clothing store
commerce d'ordinateurs (m) computer store
commissariat de police (m) police station
commission (f) commission
communication extra urbaine (f) long-distance call
communication urbaine (f) local call
compartiment (m) compartment
compartiment pour bagages (m) baggage deposit
complet (m) suit
comprendre understand
comptable (m) bookkeeper
compte-tours (m) tachometer

compteur de vitesse (m) speedometer
comté (m) county
concert (m) concert
concombre (m) cucumber
conditions de livraison (f) delivery terms
conditions de paiement (f) payment terms
conducteur (m) driver
conférence (f) conference
conférence de presse (f) press conference
confiture (f) jam
congrès (m) convention
connaissance (f) acquaintance
connaître meet
conseil de surveillance (m) board of trustees
conseiller recommend
conseiller fiscal (m) tax advisor
conserves (f) canned food
constipation (f) constipation
constitution (f) constitution
consulat (m) consulate
contes (m) short novel
continent (m) mainland
contrarié angry
contrat (m) contract
contrat d'achat (m) purchase contract
contre remboursement COD
contrôle de sécurité (m) security check
contrôle douanier (m) customs check
contrôleur (m) ticket inspector
contusion (f) bruise
coopération (f) cooperation
copropriété (f) condominium
coq (m) rooster
coquelet (m) chicken
coqueluche (f) whooping cough
coquillage (m) mussel
coquille (f) scallop
coquille Saint-Jacques (f) scallop
corbeille (f) wastepaper basket
corde (f) rope
corde pour étendre le linge (f) clothesline
cordonnier (m) shoemaker

cornet (m) ice cream cone
costume (m) outfit
côte (f) rib, coast, spare ribs
côte de bœuf (f) rump steak
côte rocheuse (f) rocky shoreline
côtelette (f) cutlet
coton (m) cotton
cou (m) neck
coucher du soleil (m) sunset
couches (f) diapers
couchette (f) berth
coude (m) elbows
couleurs à l'huile (f) oil paints
couloir (m) aisle
coup de soleil (m) sunburn
coupole (f) dome
coupure (f) gash
courant (m) current, power
courgette (f) zucchini
couronne (f) crown
courroie trapézoïdale (f) v-belt
cours (m) course
cours de cuisine (m) cooking course
cours de langue étrangère (m) language course
cours de peinture (m) painting course
course automobil (f) car racing
course de bicyclettes (f) bicycle racing
course de chevaux (f) horse racing
court short
court-circuit (m) short circuit
courtier (m) agent
cousin, cousine (m, f) cousin
couteau (m) knife
couteau à viande (m) meat knife
couturier (m) tailor
couverts (m) cutlery, silverware
couverture (f) blanket, cover
couverture chauffante (f) electric blanket
couvreur (m) roofer
crabe (m) crab
craie (m) chalk

crampe (f) cramp
crampons (m) crampons
cravate (f) tie
crayon (m) pencil, concealer
crayon de couleur (m) colored pen
crayons couleur (m) crayon
crayons de charbon (m) charcoal pencils
crème Chantilly (f) cream, whipped cream
crème fraiche (f) sour cream
crème pour bébés (f) baby cream
crème pour les mains (f) hand cream
crème solaire (f) sunblock
crêpe (f) pancake
crêpé (m) crepe
cresson (m) cress, watercress
crevette (f) crab
crevettes (f) prawn
cric (m) jack
crime (m) crime
croire believe
croisement (m) crossroad
croisière (f) cruise
croissant (m) croissant
croix (f) cross
croquettes (f) croquettes
cru raw
crypte (f) crypt
cuillère à café (f) teaspoon
cuillère en bois (f) wooden spoon
cuir (m) leather
cuisine (f) kitchen
cuisinette (f) kitchenette
cuisinier (m) cook
cuisse (f) thighs
cuit à la vapeur steamed
cuit au four baked
cuivre (m) copper
culasse de cylindres (f) cylinder head
culotte (f) panties
culture (f) culture
cumin (m) caraway seed
cure-pipe (m) pipe cleaner
curieux (m) rubberneck
cutter (m) pencil sharpener
cyclisme (m) cycling

D................................
d'autres other
daim (m) suede
dans in

dans l'après-midi in the afternoon
danse (f) dance
date (f) date
dattes (f) dates
daurade (f) sea-bream
de out (of)
dé à coudre (m) thimble
de nouveau again
débutant (m) beginner
décapsuleur (m) bottle opener
décembre (m) December
déchirure (f) strain
déclaration (f) statement
déclaration douanière (f) customs declaration
décollage (m) takeoff
décorateur (m) decorator
dedans inside
défaite (f) defeat
dégel (m) thaw
degré de difficulté (m) degree of difficulty
dehors outside
déjeuner (m) lunch
délai de livraison (m) time of delivery
demain tomorrow
demander ask
démarreur (m) starter
demi half
demi-kilo (m) pound
demi-pension (f) half board
démocratie (f) democracy
dénivelé (m) gradient
dent (f) tooth
dent de sagesse (f) wisdom tooth
dentier (m) denture
dentifrice (m) toothpaste
dentiste (m) dentist
déodorant (m) deodorant
départ (m) departure
dépliant (m) brochure
dépôt de bagages (m) checkroom
déprimé depressed
député (m) representative
dérailleur (m) gear shift
descente (f) descent, downhill skiing
désert (m) desert
désinfectant (m) disinfectant
desserré loose
dessert (m) dessert
destinataire (m) recipient
détachant (m) stain remover
détergent (m) detergent
deuxième second

dévaliser rob
devant before
devise (f) currency
devoir must
diabète (m) diabetes
diamant (m) diamond
diarrhée (f) diarrhea
dictionnaire (m) dictionary
Diesel (m) diesel
dimanche (m) Sunday
dindon (m) turkey
dîner (m) dinner
diphtérie (f) diphteria
dire say
directeur (m) manager
direction (f) steering
discothèque (f) discotheque
disque dur (m) hard disk
dissolvant (m) nail polish remover
distributeur (m) distributor
distributeur automatique de billets (m) automatic ticket vending machine, automatic teller (ATM)
docteur (m) doctor
doigt (m) finger
donner give
dorade (f) golden bream
dos (m) saddle (of lamb)
douane (f) customs
double cabine (f) double cabin
douceurs (f) candies
douche (f) shower
douleurs (f) pain
doux light
douzaine (f) dozen
drame (m) drama
drap (m) bed sheet
drap de plage (m) beach towel
drogue (f) drug
droguiste (m) druggist
droit (m) law
droit de refuser de témoigner (m) right to remain silent
droite right
dune (f) dune
durant la journée during the day
dynamo (f) dynamo

E................................
eau (f) water
eau chaude (f) hot water
eau de refroidissement (f) coolant
eau de vie (f) schnapps

eau minérale (f) mineral water
eau potable (f) drinking water
échappement (m) exhaust
écharpe (f) scarf
échéance (f) appointment
échecs (m) chess
échelle (f) ladder
échine (f) chine (of beef)
éclair (m) lightning
éclaircie (f) clearing
école publique (f) public school
écolier (m) student
économie (f) economy
économiste (m) management expert
écouter listen
écran (m) screen
écrevisse (f) crab
écrire write
écrivain (m) author
écrou/noix (m/f) nut
édifice (m) building
églefin (m) haddock
église (f) church
égouttoir à vaisselle (m) dishrack
élastique (m) elastic
élections (f) elections
électricien (m) electrician
électricité (f) electricity
embarcadère (m) mooring
embrayage (m) clutch
employé (m) employee
employé du bâtiment (m) construction worker
empoisonnement (m) poisoning
en conséquence therefore
encadrement pour les enfants (m) child care
enceinte pregnant
encore still
encre (f) ink
enfants (m) children
enflé swollen
enflure (f) swelling
enregistrement (m) reception desk
enseignant (m) teacher
entendre hear
en-tête (m) letterhead
entonnoir (m) funnel
entorse (f) sprain
entracte (m) intermission
entrée (f) arrival, entrance
entrelardé larded
entrepreneur (m) businessman

enveloppe (f) envelope
épaule (f) shoulder
éperlan (m) smelt
épi (m) ear of grain
épices (f) spices
épinards (m) spinach
épine dorsale (f) spinal column
épingle (f) pin
épingle à cheveux (f) hairpins
épingle à cravate (f) tie pin
épingle de nourrice (f) safety pin
éponge (f) kitchen sponge, bath sponge
épouse (f) wife
épouvantable dreadful
équilibre (m) balance
équipage (m) crew
équitation (f) horseback riding
érable (m) maple
escale (f) stopover
escalier roulant (m) escalator
escalope (f) deep-fried cutlet
escargot de mer (m) sea snail
escompte (m) rebate
escroc (m) swindler, cheat
espadon (m) swordfish
essais (m) essays
essayer try on
essence (f) gas
essence normale (f) regular
essence Super (f) super
essieu arrière (m) rear axle
essieu avant (m) front axle
essorage (m) spin-dry
essorer spin-dry (v)
essoreuse (f) spin-dryer
essuie-glace (m) windshield wiper
estomac (m) stomach
estragon (m) tarragon
et and
étage (m) floor
étanche waterproof
étang (m) pond
été (m) summer
étiquette (f) labels
étoile de mer (f) starfish
étouffée braised
étrange strange
étranger (m) foreigner
étroit narrow

étudiant (m) student
étui (pour lunettes) (m) glasses case
étui de l'appareil photo (m) camera bag
excellent excellent, outstanding
excursion à terre (f) shore excursion
excursion sur le fleuve (f) riverboat trip
exempt du droit de douane duty-free
expéditeur (m) sender
expert EDP (m) computer expert
exportation (f) export
exposant (m) exhibitor
exposition (f) exhibition
express (m) espresso, express mail

F . . . .
fabriquant (m) manufacturer
facture (f) invoice
faible weak
faïence (f) ceramics
faim (f) hunger
faire do
faire de la bicyclette ride
faire de la voile sailing
faire des randonnées hike
faire une couleur color
faisan (m) pheasant
fantastique fantastic
farci stuffed
fard (m) rouge
fard à paupières (m) eyeshadow
farine (f) flour
fatigué tired
fausse couche (f) miscarriage
fauteuil (m) armchair
faux wrong
fax (m) fax
femme au foyer (f) housewife
fenêtre (f) windows
fenouil (m) fennel
fer à repasser (m) iron
ferme (f) farm
fermé closed
fermeture éclair (f) zipper
ferry-boat (m) ferry, car ferry
festival (m) festival
fête folklorique (f) folk festival
feu (m) traffic light, fire

feu avant (m) headlight
feuilles de laurier (f) bayleaves
feutre (m) felt, felt-tip pen
feux clignotants (m) turn signals, flasher, blinker
feux de détresse (m) emergency flashers
feux de recul (m) back-up lights
feux de stop (m) brake light
février (m) February
fiancé (m) fiancé
fiancée (f) fiancée
fibre synthétique (f) synthetic fiber
ficelle (f) string, twine
fiche (f) plug
fièvre (f) fever
figues (f) figs
fil (m) thread
fil dentaire (m) dental floss
fille (f) daughter
film (m) movie, film
fils (m) son
filtre à l'huile (m) oil filter
filtre d'évacuation (m) drain
filtre pour pipe (m) pipe filters
finance (f) finance
fixateur (m) hairsetting lotion, fixative
flageolet (m) bush-beans
flanelle (f) flannel
flaque (f) puddle
flash (m) flashbulb
fléchettes (f) darts
flemmard (m) loafer
flet (m) flounder
flétan (m) halibut
fleuriste (m) florist
fleuve (m) river
flotteur (m) float
foie (m) liver
foin (m) hay
foncé dark
fonctionnaire (m) official, civil servant
fondé de pouvoir (m) authorized officer
fontaine (f) fountain
fonts baptismaux (m) font
football (m) soccer
forfait (m) ski pass
format (m) format
formule de salutations (f) greeting
fort strong
forteresse (f) fortress

fouet (m) whisk
fouilles (f) excavations
four à micro-ondes (m) microwave
four électrique (m) electric range
fourche roue avant (f) front wheel fork
fourchette (f) fork
fourneau à gaz (m) gas stove
fournisseur (m) supplier
fracture des os (f) fracture
frais (m) expenses, costs
frais de transport (m) transportation costs, freight charges
frais supplémentaires (m) extra costs
fraises (f) strawberries
framboises (f) raspberries
frein (m) brakes
frein à main (m) hand brake
frein à tambour (m) drum brake
frein de secours (m) emergency brake
freiner brake
frère (m) brother
friandises (f) candy
frigidaire (m) refrigerator
frise (f) frieze
frissons (m) chills
frit deep-fried
frites (f) french fries
froid cold
fromage (m) cheese
fromage blanc (m) curd
fromage de brebis (m) sheep's milk cheese
fromage de chèvre (m) goat's milk cheese
fromage frais (m) fresh cheese
fromager (m) creamery
frottis (m) swab
fruit du cactus (m) cactus-fruit
fruité fruity
fruits (m) fruit
fruits de la passion (m) passion-fruit
fruits de mer (m) shellfish
fruits et légumes fruit stand, fresh produce stand
frustré frustrated
fumé smoked
fume-cigarette (m) cigarette holder

fumer smoke
fumeur (m) smoking section
furoncle (m) boil
fusible (m) locking system

G
galerie (f) gallery, choirloft
galerie d'art (f) art gallery
gant de toilette (m) face cloths
gants (m) gloves
garage (m) garage, parking garage
garantie (f) guarantee
garçon (m) waiter
garde-boue (m) mudguard
gare (f) railway station
garniture (f) gaskets
garniture de frein (f) brake lining
garnitures (f) side dishes
gâteau (m) cake
gaufrette (f) waffles
gaz butane (m) butane gas
gaz propane (m) propane
gel (m) frost
gencive (f) gum
gendre (m) son-in-law
généraliste (m) general practitioner
génial brilliant
genou (m) knee
géologie (f) geology
gilet (m) waistcoat
gilet de secours (m) life jacket
gingembre (m) ginger
glace (f) ice cream
glacé glazed
glacière (f) cooler
glaçon (m) ice cube
golf (m) golf
gombo okra
gomina (f) elastic
gomme (f) eraser
gothique (m) Gothic
gourde (f) water bottle
goûter taste
gouttes pour les oreilles (f) ear drops
gouvernail (m) rudder
gouvernement (m) government
graines de tournesol (f) sunflower seeds
gramme (m) gram
grand magasin (m) department store
grand(e) large

grande surface (f) shopping center
grand-mère (f) grandmother
grand-père (m) grandfather
gratte-ciel (m) skyscraper
graveur de CD-ROM (m) CD-writer
grêle (f) hail
grenade (f) pomegranate
grillade (f) barbecue
grillé grilled
grille-pain (m) toaster
grippe (f) flu
gris gray
groom (m) bellboy
groseille à maquereau (f) gooseberry
groseilles rouges (f) currants
grossesse (f) pregnancy
groupe sanguin (m) blood type
guichet (m) counter, ticket counter
guichetier (m) conductor
guide touristique (m) guidebook
guidon (m) handlebars
gymnastique (f) gymnastics
gynécologue (m) gynecologist

H ....
habitant (m) private guest house
haché ground
hall (m) hall
haltère (m) dumb-bell
hamac (m) hammock
hanche (f) hip
handball (m) handball
hareng (m) herring
haricots (m) beans
haricots blancs (m) white beans
haricots grimpeurs (m) string beans
haricots rouges (m) red beans
haricots verts (m) green beans
haut high
haute pression (f) high pressure
haut-parleur (m) speaker
hémorragie (m) hemorrhage
hêtre (m) beech

heure (f) hour
heure d'arrivée (f) arrival time
heure de décollage (f) departure time
hibiscus (m) hibiscus
hier yesterday
hippocampe (m) seahorse
histoire (f) history
hiver (m) winter
hockey sur glace (m) ice hockey
homard (m) lobster
homme au foyer (m) homemaker
honoraires (m) fees
hôpital (m) hospital
horaire (m) schedule, timetable
horaire de visite (m) office hours
horaire du vol (m) flight schedule
horaires d'ouverture (m) open hours
horloge (f) wall clock
horloger (m) watchmaker
hors saison off season, pre-season, low season
hôtel (m) hotel
hôtelier (m) hotelier
houle (f) swell
huile (f) oil
huile de tournesol (f) sunflower oil
huile d'olive (f) olive oil
huîtres (f) oysters
humidité (f) humidity
hydroptère (m) hydrofoil
hypertension (f) high blood pressure

I ....
ici here
immigration (f) immigration
imperméable (m) raincoat
importation (f) import
impôts (m) taxes
impressionnant impressive
imprimante jet d'encre (f) inkjet printer
imprimante laser (f) laser printer
imprimé (f) printed matter
incroyable awesome, amazing
index (m) index finger
indicatif (m) area code
industrie (f) industry
infarctus (m) heart attack

infection (f) infection
infection des amygdales (f) tonsillitis
infirmier (m) male nurse
infirmière (f) nurse
inflammation (f) inflammation
inflammation de la vessie (f) inflammation of the bladder
informations (f) information
ingénieur (m) engineer
injecteur (m) fuel injector pump
inondation (f) flood
insectifuge (m) insect repellent
insolation (f) sunstroke
institut de beauté (m) cosmetics store
interprète (m) interpreter
interrupteur (m) light switch
intestin (m) intestine
invitation (f) invitation
irruption cutanée (f) rash

J ....
jambe (f) round steak, leg
jambe (en bas du genou) (f) lower leg
jambon (m) ham
jante (f) rim
janvier (m) January
jardin (m) garden
jardin botanique (m) botanical gardens
jardin de derrière (m) backyard
jardinier (m) gardener
jarret (m) leg
jaune yellow
jaunisse (f) jaundice
jazz (m) jazz
jeudi (m) Thursday
jeune young
jogging (m) jogging
jouet (m) toy
jour (m) day
jour d'arrivée (m) date of arrival
jour de départ (m) date of departure
journal (m) newspaper
journaliste (m) journalist
judo (m) judo
juge (m) judge
juif (m) Jew
juillet (m) July
juin (m) June

jumelles (f) binoculars
jupe (f) skirt
jupon (m) slip
jus de fruits (m) fruit juice
jus de pomme (m) apple juice
jus de raisin (m) grape juice
jus de tomate (m) tomato juice
jus d'orange (m) orange juice

K
kaki (m) persimmon
karaté (m) karate
kayac (m) kayak
kilo (m) kilo
kilomètre (m) kilometer
kilomètre carré (m) square kilometer
kiosque (m) newsstand
kiosque à journaux (m) newsagent
kit de réparation des pneus (m) repair kit
kiwi (m) kiwi fruit
klaxon (m) horn
kleenex tissues

L
là there
la nuit at night
lac (m) lake
lacets (m) shoelaces
laid ugly
laine (f) wool
laissez let
lait (m) milk
lait pour le corps (m) body lotion
laitue (f) lettuce
lames de rasoir (f) razor blades
lampe (f) lamp
lampe à pétrole (f) kerosene lamp
lampe de poche (f) flashlight
langouste (f) crawfish
langue (f) tongue
lapin (m) rabbit
laque (f) hairspray
lard fumé (m) bacon
large wide
laurier (m) laurel
lavabo (m) wash basin
lavabos (m) washroom
lavage à sec (m) dry-cleaning
laverie automatique (f) laundromat

lave-vaisselle (m) dish-washer
laxatif (m) laxative
le soir in the evening
lecteur CD (m) CD player
lecteur de CD-ROM (m) CD-ROM drive
lecteur DVD (m) DVD player
lecteur laser (m) CD player
légumes (m) vegetables
lent slow
lentilles (f) contact lenses, lentils
les taglitesses (f) flat noodles
lessive en poudre (f) laundry detergent (powder)
lessive lavable à 90 degrés (f) hot-water wash
lettre (f) letter
lettre recommandée (f) registered mail
levier de vitesse (m) gear lever
lèvre (f) lip
libraire (m) bookseller
librairie (f) bookstore
licencié en droit (m) lawyer
lièvre (m) hare
ligne (f) fishing line, telephone line
lime à ongles (f) nail file
limette (f) lime
limonade (f) soft drink
lin (m) linen
lingerie (f) underwear
liqueur (f) liqueur
liquide du frein (m) brake fluid
liquide vaisselle (m) dishwashing liquid
lire read
lis (m) lily
lit (m) bed
lit à deux places (m) double bed
lit à une place (m) single bed
lit de camp (m) traveling bed
lit pour enfants (m) child's bed
litre (m) liter
littérature (f) literature
livre de cuisine (m) cook-book
livre illustré (m) picture book
livre pour enfants (m) children's book

livre spécialisé (m) technical book
locataire (m) landlord
location de bateaux (f) boat rental
locomotive (f) locomotive
loi (f) law
loin far
long long
longe (f) loin
lotte de mer (f) anglerfish
loupe (f) magnifying glass
loyer (m) rent
luge (f) sled
lumbago (m) lumbago
lundi (m) Monday
lunette arrière (f) rear windshield
lunettes de plongée (f) diving goggles
lunettes de soleil (f) sun glasses

M
macaronis (m) macaroni
machine à laver (f) washing machine
machine à sous (f) slot machine
mâchoire (f) jaw
maçon (m) mason
magasin d'alimentation (m) grocery store
magasin d'articles de sport (m) sporting goods store
magasin d'articles ménagers (m) household merchandise store
magasin de chaussures (m) shoe store
magasin de disques (m) record store
magasin de fourrures (m) furrier
magasin de jouets (m) toy store
magasin de souvenirs (m) souvenir shop
magasin de tissus (m) fabric store
magasin de vêtements d'occasion (m) second-hand store
magasin pour bicyclettes (m) bicycle store
magazine (m) magazine
magnétophone (m) cassette recorder
magnétoscope (m) VCR
magnifique splendid

mai (m) May
maillot de corps (m) undershirt
main (f) hand
maintenant now
mairie (f) town hall
maïs (m) corn
maison de vacances (f) vacation house
maison natale (f) birthplace
maître nageur (m) life guard
majeur (m) middle finger
mal au cœur (m) heart problems
mal de dents (m) toothache
mal de dos (m) backache
mal de gorge (m) sore throat
mal de mer (m) seasickness
mal de tête (m) headache
mal de ventre (m) stomachache
mal d'estomac (m) stomachache
malade sick
maladie virale (f) viral illness
mâle (m) buck
manager (m) manager
manches (f) sleeves
mandarine (f) tangerine
mandat (m) money order
mandat postal (m) remittance
manger eat
mangue (f) mango
manteau (m) coat
manteau en cuir (m) leather coat
maquereau (m) mackerel
marais (m) swamp
marché (m) market
marché aux puces (m) flea market
marches (f) stairways
mardi (m) Tuesday
marée basse (f) low tide
marée haute (f) high tide
margarine (f) margarine
marguerite (f) daisy
mari (m) husband
marié married
marin (m) sailor
marjolaine (f) marjoram
marketing (m) marketing
marmite (f) pot
maroquinerie (f) leather goods

marque (f) brand
marque commerciale (f) trademark
mars (m) March
marteau (m) hammer
mascara (f) eyebrow pencil
mât de tente (m) tent pole
matelas (m) mattress
matelas pneumatique (m) air mattress
matériel (m) material
maussade hazy
mauvais bad
mauve purple
mayonnaise (f) mayonnaise
mécanicien (m) car mechanic, mechanic
mécanicien-dentiste (m) dental technician, dental surgeon
mèche (f) strands
médecin en médecines douces (m) healer
médecine (f) medicine
médicament (m) medication
médicament pour la circulation du sang (m) tablets for poor circulation
médiéval medieval
méduse (f) jellyfish
mélangé mottled
melon (m) melon
membre du congrès (m) congressman
même si although
mémoire de travail (f) RAM
mendiant (m) panhandler
menthe (f) mint
menu (m) menu
menuisier (m) carpenter
mer (f) sea
mercerie (f) notions
merci thank you
mercredi (m) Wednesday
merde shit
mère (f) mother
merluche (m) sea-pike
merveilleux terrific
messe (f) church service, trade fair
mètre (m) measuring tape, meter, ruler
mètre carré (m) square meter
métro (m) subway
meubles (m) furniture

microfibre (f) microfiber
miel (m) honey
mignon cute
migraine (f) migraine
milliard (m) billion
millimètre (m) millimeter
mini-bar (m) mini-bar
minuit midnight
minute (f) minute
mirabelle (f) mirabelle
miroir (m) mirror
mode (f) fashion
modem (m) modem
modifier alter
mois (m) month
moissonneuse-batteuse (f) harvester
moitié (f) half
moka (m) mocha
mollet (m) calf
monarchie (f) kingdom
moniteur de ski (m) ski instructor
monnaie (f) coins, change
montagne (f) mountain
mont-de-piété (m) pawnbroker
montée (f) ascent
montgolfière (f) hot-air balloon
montre de plongée (f) diving clock
montre de poche (f) pocket watch
montre-bracelet (f) wristwatch
monument (m) monument
morsure (f) bite
morue (f) salt cod, codfish
motel (m) motel
moteur (m) motor
mouchoirs en papier (m) kleenex
moule (f) mussel
moulin à café (m) coffee grinder
mousse à raser (f) shaving cream
moustaches (f) mustache
moutarde (f) mustard
mouton (m) mutton, sheep
moyen âge (m) Middle Ages
moyen(ne) medium
moyeu (m) hub
mûres (f) blackberries
muscle (m) muscle
musée (m) museum
musicien (m) musician
musique (f) music
musulman Muslim

myope short-sighted
myrtilles (f) blueberries
myrtilles rouges (f) cranberries
mystérieux uncanny

N

nageur (m) swimmers
nappe (f) tablecloth
narcisse (f) narcissus
nausée (f) nausea
navet (m) rutabaga, turnips
navet rouge (m) red beets
navette (f) shuttle
navire à vapeur (m) steamer
navire marchand (m) freighter
ne pas repasser wrinkle-free
nécessaire de couture (m) sewing kit
nécessaire pour pipe (m) pipe accessories
nef (f) nave
nef centrale (f) center nave
nef latérale (f) side aisle
nef transversale (f) transept
nèfle (m) medlar
négociation (f) negotiation
neige (f) snow
neige fondue (f) sleet
neige poudreuse (f) powder (snow)
neiger snow
nerf (m) nerve
neveu (m) nephew
nez (m) nose
nièce (f) niece
Noël (m) Christmas
nœud (m) knot
nœud papillon (m) bowtie
noir black
noir et blanc black-and-white
noisette (f) hazelnut
noix (f) nuts, walnut
noix de coco (f) coconut
noix de muscat (f) nutmeg
noix de pecan (f) pecan nut
noix du Parà (f) Brazil nuts
non no
non-fumeur (m) non-smoking section
non-nageur (m) non-swimmer
notaire (m) notary
nourriture pour nouveau-

né (f) baby food
nouveau new
nouvel an (m) New Year's day
nouvelles (f) news
novembre (m) November
nuages (m) clouds
nuageux cloudy
numéro de chambre (m) room number
numéro de la rue (m) street number
numéro de téléphone (m) telephone number
numéro direct (m) direct dialing
numéro du vol (m) flight number
numéro du wagon (m) car number
nuque (f) nape of the neck

O

objectif (m) lens
objets de valeur (m) valuables
occupé occupied
océan (m) ocean
octobre (m) October
œil (m) eye
œillet (m) carnation
œuf à la coque (m) soft-boiled egg
œuf dur (m) hard-boiled egg
œufs à la poêle (m) fried egg
œufs brouillés (m) scrambled eggs
œufs de poisson (m) roe
œufs pochés (m) poached eggs
offre (f) offer
oie (f) goose
oignons (m) onions
ombre (f) shadows, grayling
omelette (f) omelet
oncle (m) uncle
onctueux full-bodied
ondée (f) showers
opaque matte
opéra (m) opera
opération (f) operation
opérette (f) operetta
opinion (f) opinion
opticien (m) optician
or (m) gold
orage (m) thunderstorm
orange (f) orange
orchidée (f) orchid

ordures (f) garbage
oreille (f) ear
oreiller (m) pillow
oreillons (m) mumps
orge (m) barley
origan (m) oregano
ornithologie (f) ornithology
orteil (m) toe
os (m) bones
oto-rhino(-laryngologiste) (m) ear, nose, and throat specialist
ou or
où where
oublier forget
oui yes
ouragan (m) hurricane
outil (m) tool
ouvre-boîtes (m) can opener
ovaire (m) ovary
ozone (m) ozone

P

pagaie (f) oars
pages jaunes (f) yellow pages
paiement comptant (m) cash payment
paille (f) straw
pain (m) bread
pain complet (m) whole wheat bread
pain de seigle croustillant (m) cracker
pain noir (m) black bread
palette (f) palette
palmes (f) fins
palourde (f) clam
pamplemousse (f) grapefruit
pané breaded
panier (m) shopping basket
panier à linge (m) laundry basket
panne (f) breakdown
panneau d'affichage (m) billboard
panorama (m) landscape
pansement (m) band-aid
pantalon (m) pants
pantoufles (f) slippers
papaye (f) papaya
papeterie (f) office supplies
papier (m) paper
papier à lettres (m) stationery
papier aluminium (m) aluminum foil

papier cadeau (m) wrapping paper
papier pour peinture à l'eau (m) watercolor paper
papiers de la voiture (m) car documents
papier-toilette (m) toilet paper
Pâques Easter
par avion airmail
parachutisme (m) sky diving
paragraphe (m) paragraph
paralysie (f) paralysis
parapente (m) hang-gliding
parapluie (m) umbrella
parasol (m) parasol
parc (m) park
parc naturel (m) nature park
parce que because
pardon sorry
pare-brise (m) windshield
pare-chocs (m) shock absorber, bumper
pareil same
pare-soleil (m) lens shade
parfum (m) perfume, flavor
parfumerie (f) perfumery
parking (m) parking place
parlement (m) parliament
parler speak
partenaire (commercial) (m) business partners
participation (f) investment
partie arrière (f) rear
pas trop gras low-fat
passage piéton (m) crosswalk
passager (m) passenger
passé à la poêle browned
passeport (m) passport
passerelle (f) jetty
passible du droit de douane dutiable
pastels (m) watercolor crayons
pastèque (f) watermelon
pastilles contre le mal de gorge (f) cough drops
patates douces (f) sweet potatoes
pâtes (f) noodles
patinage artistique (m) figure skating
patins à glace (m) ice skates
patins en ligne (m) inline skates

pâtisserie (f) pastry shop
pâtisseries (f) pastries
pattes (f) sideburns
paupière (f) eyelid
pauvre en calories low-calorie
pauvre en cholestérol low cholesterol
peau (f) skin
pêche (f) peach, fishing
pédale (f) pedal
pédalo (m) pedal boat
pédiatre (m) pediatrician
peigne (m) comb
peignoir (m) bathrobe
peintre en bâtiment (m) painter
peinture (f) painting
peinture à l'eau (f) watercolors
peinture murale (f) mural
peinture sur verre (f) glass painting
pèlerin (m) pilgrim
pelle (f) shovel
pellicules (f) dandruff
pendentif (m) pendant
penser think
pension complète (f) full board
Pentecôte (f) Whitsun, Pentecost
peperoni (m) bell pepper
péquenaud (m) redneck
perceuse (f) drill
perche (f) perch
perdre connaissance unconscious
perdrix (f) partridge
père (m) father
perle (f) pearl
permanente (f) perm
permis de pêche (m) fishing license
permis nautique (m) sailing licence
perruque (f) wig
persil (m) parsley
personnel de service (m) chambermaid
perte (f) loss
petit cadre pour diapositives (m) slide frames
petit déjeuner (m) breakfast
petit pain (m) roll
petit paquet (m) small parcel
petit(e) small
petite armoire (f) locker
petite cuillère (f) spoon

petit-fils (m) grandson
petits cigares (m) cigarillos
petits clous/punaise (m/f) thumbtacks
petits fours (m) cookies
petits oignons (m) scallion
petits pois (m) peas
petits pois doux (m) tiny green peas
peu few, little
peu contrasté low-contrast
phare (m) headlight, lighthouse
pharmacie (f) pharmacy, drugstore
philosophie (f) philosophy
photographe (m) photo store, photographer
physique (f) physics
pickpocket (m) pickpocket
pièce jointe (f) enclosure, appendix
pièces de rechange (f) spare parts
pied (m) foot
pigeon (m) pigeon
pignon (m) pine nut
pince à épiler (f) tweezers
pinceau (m) paintbrush
pinces (f) pliers
pinces à linge (f) clothespins
ping-pong (m) table tennis
pintade (f) guinea fowl
pipe (f) pipe
piquant tangy
piquet de tente (m) tent peg
piqûre (f) injection
piqûre d'insecte (f) insect bite
piscine (f) swimming pool
pistaches (f) pistachios
piste (f) ski trail
pistolet (m) bedpan
piston (m) piston
place (f) place
place à côté de la fenêtre (f) window seat
place près du couloir (f) aisle seat
plage (f) beach
plage de galets (f) pebble beach
plage de sable (f) sandy beach
plage privée (f) private beach
plainte (f) complaint

plaire like
plan de la ville (m) map of the city
planche à repasser (f) ironing board
planche à surf (f) surfboard
planche à voile (f) windsurfing
planétarium (m) planetarium
plaquette (f) name badge
platine (f) platinum
plats à base d'œufs (m) egg dishes
plein/satisfait full
pleine saison (f) in season
pleuvoir rain
plomb (m) filling, sinker
plombier (m) plumber
plongée (f) diving
plouc (m) hillbilly
pluie (f) rain
pluie fine (f) drizzle
plus more
plus tard later
pneu (m) tires
pneumonie (f) pneumonia
poêle (f) frying pan
poêle à gaz (m) gas range
poids (m) weight
poignée de la portière (f) door handle
poignées (f) cuffs
poignet (m) wrist
point de côté (m) stitch in the side
point de rencontre (m) meeting place
pointillé polka-dotted
pointure (f) size
poire (f) pears
poireau (m) leek
pois chiche (m) chickpeas
poisson (m) fish
poisson bleu (m) blue fish
poissonnerie (f) fish store
poitrine (f) breast
poivre (m) pepper
poivron vert (m) green pepper
police (f) police
policier (m) policeman
politique (f) politics
pollution (f) pollution
pommade contre les brûlures (f) ointment for burns
pomme (f) apple
pommes de pin (f) pine cone

pommes de terre (f) potatoes
pommes de terre sautées (f) hash browns, fried potatoes
pompe (f) air pump
pompe à eau (f) water pump
pompe d'aspiration (f) suction pump
pompe de la bicyclette (f) bicycle pump
pont (m) bridge, deck
popeline (f) poplin
port (m) harbor
portable (m) cell phone
portail (m) main entrance
porte (f) door
porte d'embarquement (f) gate
portefeuille (m) wallet, billfold
portemanteau (f) hanger
porte-monnaie (m) purse
porteur (m) porter
portier (m) porter
posemètre (m) light meter
poste (f) post office
poste restante (f) general delivery
pot (m) mug
pot à crème (m) creamer
potage avec des pâtes (m) noodle soup
poterie (f) ceramics
poubelle (f) garbage can
pouce (m) thumb
poudre (f) powder
poulet (m) chicken
poulet d'engrais (m) young fattened hen
poulet rôti (m) grilled chicken
poumon (m) lung
pour for
pourboire (m) tip
pourquoi why
poussin (m) chick
pouvoir can
pré (m) meadow
préférablement preferably
premier first
prendre take
presbyte far-sighted
présenter introduce
préservatif (m) condom
président (m) president
presse (f) press
presse-citron (m) lemon squeezer
pressing (m) dry cleaning

prêter rent
prêtre (m) priest
printemps (m) spring
prise de courant (f) socket
prison (f) prison
prix (m) price
prix d'achat (m) purchase price
prix du parking (m) parking fee
procès (m) trial
processeur (m) processor
procession (f) procession
production (f) production
produits biologiques (m) organic food
produits diététiques (m) health-food store
produits laitiers (m) dairy products
professeur (m) professor
profond deep
programmateur (m) programmer
programme délicat (m) gentle wash
prostituée (f) hooker
protestant (m) Protestant
protocole (m) report
proue (f) bow
prune (f) plum
psychiatre (m) psychiatrist
psychologie (f) psychology
psychologue (m) psychologist
puis then
pull (m) sweater
purée (f) mashed potatoes
pyjama (m) pajamas

Q . . . .
quai (m) dock, platform, track
quand when, as
quart (m) quarter
quarterback (m) quarterback
queue (f) tail
qui who
quilles (f) bowling
quincaillerie (f) hardware
quotidien daily

R . . . .
race (f) skate
racine (f) root (of the tooth)
raconter tell
radiateur (m) heater, radiator
radio (f) radio
radis (m) radish

ragoût (m) goulash
raie au milieu (f) center part
raie sur le côté (f) side part
raifort (m) horseradish
raisin (m) grape
raisins secs (m) raisins
rallonge (f) extension cord
rambutan (f) rambutan
ramoneur (m) chimney sweep
rapide fast
raquette de ping-pong (f) ping-pong rackets
raquette de tennis (f) tennis racket
rascasse du Nord (f) golden perch
rasoir (m) razor
rayon (m) ray, department, spoke
rayon x (m) X-ray
réception (f) reception
recevoir get
reclassement professionnel (f) retraining
reçu (m) acknowledgment, receipt
réduction (f) reduction
réflecteur (m) reflector
reflet (m) color rinse
régate (f) regatta
région marécageuse (f) wetland
régional regional
règle (f) ruler
réglementations douanières (f) customs regulations
reins (m) kidneys
relief (m) relief
religion (f) religion, denomination
remarquable great
remise des bagages (f) baggage claim
remonte-pente (m) ski lift
remorquer tow
rendez-vous (m) appointment
rendez-vous d'affaire (m) business meeting
réparer repair
répéter repeat
répondeur automatique (m) answering machine
représentant (m) representative
requin (m) shark
réservation (f) reservation
réserve naturelle (f) sanctuary

réserver reserve
réservoir (m) tank
résidence hôtel (f) vacation spot
responsabilité (f) liability
ressac (m) surf
restaurant (m) restaurant
retard (m) delay
retraité (m) senior citizen
rétroviseur (m) rearview mirror
rétroviseur extérieur (m) sideview mirrors
réveil (m) alarm clock
rhubarbe (f) rhubarb
rhumatisme (m) rheumatism
rhume (m) head cold, cold
rhume des foins (m) hay fever
rideau (m) curtain
rien nothing
rimmel (m) mascara
rincer rinse
ris (m) sweetbread
riz (m) rice
robe (f) dress
robe de chambre (f) housecoat
robinet (m) faucet
rocher (m) cliff
roman (m) romanesque
roman policier (m) mystery novel
romantique romantic
romarin (m) rosemary
rosace (f) rosette
rosbif (m) roast beef
rose (f) rose, pink
rôti roasted, roast
roue (f) wheel
roue de secours (f) spare wheel
roue dentée (f) gear
rouge red
rouge à lèvres (m) lipstick
rougeole (f) measles
rouget (m) mullet
rouleau à pâtisserie (m) rolling pin
rouleau de viande hachée (m) meat loaf
route (f) street
route départementale (f) country road
route nationale (f) national highway
ruban adhésif (m) adhesive tape
rubéole (f) German measles
ruelle (f) alley

rugby (m) rugby
ruines (f) ruins
ruisseau (m) brook

S..........................
sable (m) sand
sac (m) shopping bag
sac à dos (m) backpack
sac à main (m) handbag
sac de couchage (m) sleeping bag
sac de golf (m) golf bag
sac de voyage (m) traveling bag
sac en bandoulière (m) shoulder bag
sac porte-outils (m) saddlebags
sac thermique (m) insulated bag
saccharine (f) saccharin
sachet en plastique (m) plastic bags
sachet pour aliments (m) plastic wrap
sac-poubelle (m) trash bags
sacristie (f) sacristy
safran (m) saffron
sage-femme (f) midwife
saignement (m) bleeding
saignement de nez (m) nosebleed
Saint-Sylvestre (f) New Year's eve
salade (f) salad
salade composée (f) mixed salad
salade verte (f) green salad
salle d'attente (f) waiting room
salle de bains (f) bath
salle de séjour (f) living room
salles des concerts (f) concert hall
salmonelles (f) salmonella
samedi (m) Saturday
sandales (f) sandals
sandre (m) pike-perch
sang (m) blood
sanglier (m) boar
sans without
sans plomb unleaded
sapeurs-pompiers (m) fire department
sarcophage (m) sarcophagus
sardines (f) sardines
satin (m) satin

sauce de soja (f) soy sauce
saucisse (f) sausage
sauge (f) sage
saumon (m) salmon
saumon fumé (m) smoked salmon
sauna (m) sauna
savoir know
savon (m) soap
scanneur (m) scanner
sciatique (f) sciatica
scie (f) saw
scientifique (m) scientist
scorsonère (m) black salsify
sculpture (f) sculpture
seau (m) bucket, sand pail, pail
seau à champagne (m) cooler
sébaste (m) red perch
sec dry
sèche-cheveux (m) hairdryer
sèche-linge (m) dryer
sécher avec le sèche-cheveux blow-dry
séchoir (m) clothes racks
séchoir à linge (m) clothes dryer
seconde (f) second
secrétaire médicale (f) doctor's assistant
sédatif (m) tranquilizer, sedative
seigle (m) rye
séjour (m) stopover
sel (m) salt
selle (f) saddle
semelle (f) sole
semelle en caoutchouc (f) rubber soles
semelle en cuir (f) leather soles
semoule (f) semolina
sentier (m) footpath, climbing path
sentir feel, smell
septembre (m) September
séquoia (m) sequoia
seringue (f) syringes
seringue jetable (f) disposable needle
serrure (f) lock
serrurier (m) locksmith
service clients (m) customer service
service de remorquage (m) towing service
service en chambre (m) room service

service public (m) public service
serviette (f) briefcase, hand towel
serviette de bain (f) bath towel
serviette de table (f) napkin
serviettes en papier (f) paper napkins
serviettes hygiéniques (f) sanitary napkins
seulement only
shampooing (m) shampoo
shérif (m) sheriff
short (m) shorts
si if
siège (m) seat
signature (f) signature
silure (m) catfish
s'il vous plaît please
similicuir (m) artificial leather
sirop (m) syrup
sirop contre la toux (m) cough syrup
skate-board (m) skateboard
ski (m) ski
ski de fond (m) cross-country skiing
ski nautique (m) waterskiing
skier skiing
slip de bain (m) swimming trunks
smoking (m) tuxedo
snowboard (m) snowboard
sœur (f) sister
soie (f) silk
soif (f) thirst
sole (f) sole
soleil (m) sun
sommet de la montagne (m) mountain peak
somnifères (m) sleeping pills
sonnette (f) call-button
sortie (f) exit, departure
sortie de secours (f) emergency exit
soupape (f) valve
soupe de légumes (f) vegetable soup
soupes (f) soup
source (f) mountain spring
sourcil (m) eyebrow
sous le vent leeward
soutien-gorge (m) bra
spaghettis (m) spaghetti

spatule (f) putty knife
spectacle (m) event
splendide gorgeous
sport (m) sport
squash (m) squash
stade (m) stadium
station service (f) gas station
statue (f) statue
stérilet (m) intra-uterine device
stressé annoyed
stylo-bille (m) ballpoint pen
stylo-plume (m) fountain pen
substitut du procureur (m) district attorney
sucre (m) sugar
sucré sweet
Suisse (f) Switzerland
suite (f) suite
supérieur (m) chairman
supermarché (m) supermarket
supplément (m) surcharge
sur on
sureau (m) elderberries
surf (m) surfing
synagogue (f) synagogue

T..............................
tabac (m) tobacco
table (f) table
table de chevet (f) night table
table pliante (f) folding table
tableau (m) painting
tablier (m) apron
tailladé stew
talon (m) heel
tamarin (m) tamarind
tampons (m) tampons
tante (f) aunt
tard late
tarif (m) charge
tarif de location (m) rental fee
tarte aux fruits (f) pie
tarte aux pommes (f) apple pie
tasse (f) cup
taux de charge (m) exchange rate
taxe de licence (f) licensing fees
tee-shirt (m) t-shirt
teintes pastel (f) pastels
teinture pour cheveux (f) hair dye

télécommande (f) remote control
télégramme (m) telegram
télémètre (m) distance meter
téléobjectif (m) telephoto lens
téléphérique (m) cable railway
téléphone (m) telephone
téléphone à carte (m) card telephone
téléphone à pièces (m) pay phone
télésiège (m) chair lift
télévision (f) television, TV
télex (m) telex
témoin du carburant (m) fuel guage
tempéré moderately warm
tempête (f) storm
temple (m) temple
tenailles (f) pincers
tendon (m) tendon
tennis (m) tennis
tension de l'œil (f) vision
tension électrique (f) voltage
tente (f) tent
terme (m) deadline
terminus (m) last stop
terrasse (f) terrace
test de grossesse (m) pregnancy test
tétanos (m) tetanus
tête (f) head
tétine (f) nipple, pacifier
thé (m) tea
thé aux fruits (m) fruit tea
thé noir (m) black tea
théâtre (m) theater
thermomètre (m) thermometer
thermoplongeur (m) immersion heater
thon (m) tuna
thym (m) thyme
ticket d'embarquement (m) boarding pass
tilleul (m) lime tree
timbre (m) stamp
tire-bouchon (m) corkscrew
tisane (f) herbal tea
tissu peigné (m) worsted
tissu-éponge (m) terrycloth
titre (m) salutation
toast (m) toast
toile (f) canvas
toilette pour dames (f) powder room

toilettes (f) restroom
toit ouvrant (m) sunroof
tomates (f) tomatoes
tombe (f) grave
tomber fall
tomber amoureux fall in love
tonalité libre (f) dial tone
tonalité occupée (f) busy signal
tonne (f) ton
tonnerre (m) thunder
tornade (f) tornado
tôt early
tour (f) tower, round trip
tour du port (m) harbor tour
tourne-disques (m) record player
tournesol (m) sunflower
tournevis (m) screwdriver
tout droit straight ahead
tout, toute, tous, toutes all
toutes les heures hourly
toux (f) cough
tracteur (m) tractor
tragédie (f) tragedy
train direct (m) express train
train suburbain (m) commuter train
traitement des racines (m) root canal work
traiteur (m) delicatessen
tramway (m) streetcar
tranquille quiet
transfusion de sang (f) blood transfusion
traumatisme crânien (m) concussion
travailler work
travailleur (m) worker
travailleur spécialisé (m) skilled worker
trépied (m) tripod
très very
très contrasté high-contrast
triangle (m) warning-triangle
tripes (f) tripe
tromper deceive, cheat
trop too much
trottoir (m) sidewalk
troubles de la circulation (m) circulatory disorder
trouver find
truite (f) trout
tuba (m) snorkel
turbot (m) turbot
tuyau (m) inner tube, hose

typhon (m) typhoon

U.
ulcère (m) ulcer
un peu de a little
une paire de pair
une, un a, an
unité (f) unit
université (f) college, university
urologue (m) urologist
usine (f) factory
utérus (m) uterus

V.
vache (f) cow
vagin (m) vagina
vaginite (f) vaginitis
vague (f) wave
vaisselle (f) dishes
valeurs maximum (f) maximum (values)
valeurs minimum (f) minimum (values)
valise (f) suitcase
vallée (f) valley
vanille (f) vanilla
varicelle (f) chickenpox
variole (f) smallpox
veau (m) calf
veine (f) vein
velours (m) corduroy, velvet
vendanges (f) vintage
vendeur (m) salesperson
vendre sell
vendredi (m) Friday
Vendredi saint (m) Good Friday
vénéricarde (m) scallop
venir come
vent (m) wind
ventilateur (m) ventilator
ventre (m) stomach
verglas (m) sheet ice
vernis à ongles (m) nail polish
verre (m) glass
vert green
vésicule biliaire (f) gall bladder
vessie (f) bladder
veste (f) jacket
veste en cuir (f) leather jacket
vestiaire (m) cloakroom, wardrobe, closet
vêtements délicats (m) colored laundry
vétérinaire (m) veterinarian
viande (f) meat

victoire (f) win
vide empty
vieille ville (f) old city
vieux, vieil, vieille old
vignoble (m) vineyard
vin (m) wine
vin blanc (m) white wine
vin rouge (m) red wine
vinaigre (m) vinegar
vinaigre balsamique (m) balsamic vinegar
vins et liqueurs wine store, liquor store
viol (m) rape
violer rape (v)
virement (m) transfer
vis (f) screws
visage (m) face
vitre (f) window pane
vitrier (m) glazier
voile (f) sail

voile anti-moustiques (m) mosquito net
voir see
voiture (f) car
vol (m) theft, flight
vol de correspondance (m) connecting flight
vol de retour (m) return flight
volaille (f) poultry
volant (m) steering wheel, shuttlecock
volcan (m) volcano
voler steal
volet (m) shutters
voleur (m) thief
volley-ball (m) volleyball
volume illustré (m) illustrated book
vote (m) vote
voyage (m) transit
vue sur la mer (f) ocean view

W

wagon avec couchettes (m) sleeper
wagon-lit (m) sleeping car
wagon-restaurant (m) dining car
week-end (m) weekend

Y

yacht (m) yacht
yaourt (m) yogurt

Z

zone piétonne (f) pedestrian zone
zoo (m) zoo
zoologie (f) zoology

© Copyright 2001 by Koval Verlag GmbH, Weilerbachstrasse 44, D-74423 Unterfischach, Germany
First edition for the United States and Canada published in 2003 by Barron's Educational Series, Inc.

All inquiries should be addressed to:
Barron's Educational Series, Inc.
250 Wireless Boulevard
Hauppauge, New York 11788
http://www.barronseduc.com

International Standard Book Number 0-7641-2281-9
Library of Congress Catalog Card Number 2002101236

Printed in China
9 8 7 6 5 4